**In QUEST
of TOLSTOY**

Studies in Russian and Slavic Literatures, Cultures and History

Series Editor: Lazar Fleishman

ACADEMIC
STUDIES
PRESS

In QUEST of TOLSTOY

Hugh McLean

Boston
2010

Copyright © 2010 Academic Studies Press
All rights reserved

Book design by Yuri Alexandrov

ISBN 978-1-936235-08-7 (paperback)

Published by Academic Studies Press in 2010
28 Montfern Avenue
Brighton, MA 02135, USA
press@academicstudiespress.com
www.academicstudiespress.com

Contents

Preface vii

I. Tolstoy the Artist

"Buried as a Writer and as a Man": The Puzzle of *Family Happiness* . . . 3
The Case of the Missing Mothers, or When Does a Beginning Begin? . . 21
Truth in Dying 30
Which English *Anna*? 53
Love in *Resurrection*: Eros or Agape? 71
Could the Master Err? A Note on "God Sees the Truth but Waits" 87
Gary R. Jahn. Was the Master Well Served? Further Comment
 on "God Sees the Truth but Waits" 95

II. Tolstoy the Thinker

A Woman's Place . . . The Young Tolstoy and the "Woman Question"   105
Tolstoy and Jesus 117
Rousseau's God and Tolstoy's God 143
Claws on the Behind: Tolstoy and Darwin 159
A Clash of Utopias: Tolstoy and Gorky 181

III. Tolstoy beyond Tolstoy

Hemingway and Tolstoy. A Pugilistic Encounter 197
Foxes into Hedgehogs. Berlin and Tolstoy 214

Works Cited 227
Index of Tolstoy's Works 237
Index of Names 239

Preface

Lev Tolstoy has fascinated me ever since my early youth, long before I knew any Russian or had any idea of a professional career that would engage me with him as a teacher and scholar. I was captivated by him, both the incomparable artist who created fictional worlds that seem to us as close and as real as our own lives, and the fearlessly independent thinker who from his splendid isolation at Yasnaya Polyana issued a powerful challenge to the religious, moral, and socio-political systems of the entire world. In later years I came to teach courses on Tolstoy and found that his effect on students was often as great as it had been on me. I was eventually impelled to study Tolstoy as a scholar, trying to isolate and investigate Tolstoy problems that seemed to require research and thought.

The essays assembled here have all been written within the last twenty years, between 1989 and 2007. Regardless of their date of composition, they have been grouped here in three sections on other grounds. The first deals with Tolstoy the artist. It includes essays on all three great novels as well as some of the short stories. The second section treats Tolstoy the thinker, with articles exploring his ideas on God, on Jesus, on the moral reform of the world, on what was then known as the "woman question," and finally on evolution. The final section I have called "Tolstoy beyond Tolstoy." There I deal with Tolstoy's effect on such diverse figures as Ernest Hemingway and Isaiah Berlin.

I am especially gratified to be able to include in this volume the discussion I carried on on the pages of *Tolstoy Studies Journal* with Gary R. Jahn concerning "God Sees the Truth but Waits." Professor Jahn has kindly agreed to allow his side of the dispute to be reprinted along with mine in this volume.

Besides individuals thanked for helpful comments and criticisms of particular articles, I must express here my gratitude to my much esteemed colleague Lazar Fleishman of Stanford University, who provided impetus and encouragement to the project of collecting these essays in a book.

I am also grateful to the various publishers who have permitted republication of texts to which they hold copyright. They are as follows:

Gareth Perkins, of Berkeley Slavic Specialties, for "The Case of the Missing Mothers," from *For SK: In Celebration of the Life and Career of Simon Karlinsky*, ed. Michael S. Flier and Robert P. Hughes (1994); "A Woman's Place . . . The Young Tolstoy and the 'Woman Question'," from *Word, Music, History: A Festschrift for Caryl Emerson*, ed. Lazar Fleishman, Gabriella Safran and Michael Wachtel = *Stanford Slavic Studies*, 29 (2005); "Buried as a Writer and as a Man: The Puzzle of 'Family Happiness'," in *A Century's Perspective: Essays on Russian Literature in Honor of Olga Raevsky Hughes and Robert P. Hughes*, ed. Lazar Fleishman and Hugh McLean = *Stanford Slavic Studies*, 32 (2006).

Michael Denner, editor of *Tolstoy Studies Journal*, for the following essays: "Rousseau's God and Tolstoy's" (1997); "Hemingway and Tolstoy: A Pugilistic Encounter" (1999); "Which English *Anna*?" (2001); "A Clash of Utopias, Tolstoy and Gorky" (2002); "Could the Master Err? A Note on 'God Sees the Truth but Waits'," along with Gary R. Jahn, "Was the Master Well Served? Further Comments on 'God Sees the Truth but Waits" (2004); and "Claws on the Behind: Tolstoy and Darwin" (2007).

University of California Press, for "Truth in Dying," from *In the Shade of the Giant: Essays on Tolstoy*, ed. Hugh McLean (1989); and for "Tolstoy and Jesus," from *Christianity and the Eastern Slavs*, vol. 2, ed. Robert P. Hughes and Irina Paperno = *California Slavic Studies*, XVII (1994).

Cambridge University Press, for "*Resurrection*," from *The Cambridge Companion to Tolstoy*, ed. Donna Tussing Orwin (2002).

Rowman & Littlefield, for "Foxes into Hedgehogs: Berlin and Tolstoy," in *The Cultural Gradient: The Transmission of Ideas in Europe, 1789–1991*, ed. Catherine Evtuhov and Stephen Kotkin (2003).

Hugh McLean

I

TOLSTOY the ARTIST

"Buried as a Writer and as a Man"
The Puzzle of *Family Happiness*

Tolstoy finished writing *Family Happiness* in the spring of 1859. On April 9 he wrote in his diary, the first entry since February 19, "Worked, finished Anna. But not good."[1] Earlier, however, he had been quite enthusiastic about this offspring. The diary entry for February 19 reads, "All this time I worked on the novel and accomplished much, although not on paper. I changed everything. It is a poem. I am very pleased with what is in my head."[2] Tolstoy's friend Vasily Botkin also testifies to the author's early affection for *Family Happiness*, an emotion Botkin did not then share.[3] In March Tolstoy took the story with him to Petersburg and there read it aloud at least twice, once in Botkin's circle of friends and later in the salon of his relative and close confidante, Countess Aleksandra Andreevna Tolstaya. The Botkin group apparently thought the story "rather unsuccessful,"[4] but the loyal "granny" (*babushka*) (Countess Tolstaya), as Tolstoy fondly called her, found it "charming," "full of the highest comedy."[5]

---

[1] *PSS* 48:20. "Anna" was presumably one of the proposed names of the heroine/narrator, called Masha in the final version, sometimes, as here, used as an appellative for the story itself.
[2] *PSS* 48:20.
[3] Botkin to Tolstoy, 3 May 1859. Переписка Л. Н. Толстого с В. П. Боткиным, 70.
[4] Botkin to A. V. Druzhinin, 5 April 1859. Письма к А. В. Дружинину, 57.
[5] From her unpublished diary, quoted in N. N. Gusev, Летопись 1818–1890, 199. G. Lesskis thinks Tolstoy read an early version of the story to "Granny" as early as the summer of 1857, in Switzerland, but there seems to be no documentary foundation for this claim. G. Lesskis, Лев Толстой (1852–1869), 261n.

Back at Yasnaya Polyana, Tolstoy revised the story again. He wrote to "Granny," "I am absorbed in work eight hours a day. Anna is reworking her notes, and I hope that her grandmother will like them better than in their first, ugly form."[6] Tolstoy gave the story one more thorough revision, seeming to feel at least hopeful of the outcome: "I keep thinking that something will come of it," he wrote to his friend Aleksandr Druzhinin,[7] and Botkin quotes him as saying, "If my story is not appreciated now, it will receive its due in five years' time."[8]

However, when Tolstoy read proofs for the second part, a startling emotional revolution occurred. He was overcome by *shame*. He now proclaimed that *Family Happiness* was a "disgraceful abomination" (постыдная мерзость).[9] To Botkin he wrote on May 3,

> What have I done with my *Family Happiness!* Only now, here in the country, have I collected myself and read the proofs sent me of the second part, and I saw what shameful shit it is, a stain, not only authorial, but human. It is a vile work. [. . .] I am buried as a writer and as a man. This is definite. The more so that the first part is still worse. [. . .] There is not a live word in the whole thing. And the ugliness of language, which stems from ugliness of thought, is indescribable.[10]

He wrote just as despairingly to "Granny": "When I arrived in the country, I reread my Anna, and it proved such a disgraceful abomination that I cannot collect myself from shame, and I think I will never write any more."[11]

How are we to understand this extraordinary revulsion? True, Tolstoy often had a negative reaction to work he had just finished. In 1871 he famously referred to *War and Peace* as "verbose rubbish" (многословная дребедень) and vowed never to write in that vein again.[12] But surely, this passionate repudiation of *Family Happiness* is something quite different, not only in degree, but in kind. It is a puzzle that calls for more than an offhand explanation. Tolstoy scholars have offered a variety of different solutions to the puzzle, none of which seems to me fully satisfying. They fall into two large classes: the literary-aesthetic and the biographical.

---

[6] Tolstoy to A. A. Tolstaya, April, 1859. *PSS* 60:283.
[7] Tolstoy to Druzhinin, 16 April 1859. *PSS* 60:291.
[8] Botkin to I. S. Turgenev, 6 April 1859. *В. П. Боткин и И. С. Тургенев, неизданная переписка, 1851–1869*, 152.
[9] Diary entry of 9 May 1859. *PSS* 48:21.
[10] Tolstoy to Botkin, 3 May 1859. *PSS* 60:296.
[11] Tolstoy to A. A. Tolstaya, 3 May 1859. *PSS* 60:295.
[12] Tolstoy to A. A. Fet, 1..6? January 1871. *PSS* 61:247.

Proponents of the literary-aesthetic explanation essentially agree with Tolstoy's revulsion, if without his passion. They do not like the story and consider Tolstoy's repudiation of it a sign of the sureness of his innate artistic sense. The leading exponent of this position is perhaps the greatest and most original of all Tolstoy scholars, Boris Eikhenbaum. Though usually circumspect about passing aesthetic judgments, Eikhenbaum decisively turns thumbs down on *Family Happiness*: it is "schematic and poor in material," he asserts. Eikhenbaum is simply irritated by the ambiguity of the title: are we to take it as descriptive or ironic? "It is unclear," he continues, "why the novel is written from the point of view of a woman and in the form of notes," and concludes that the progression from Masha's initial subjugation to her husband through frivolous flirtations to the final "love for my children and the father of my children" was an artificial intellectual construct, a scheme predetermined by Tolstoy's reading of Michelet's *L'Amour* (1858) and Proudhon's *De la justice dans la revolution et dans l'église* (1858). Eikhenbaum also discerns a pernicious influence of the "English family novel," especially its female variety (the Brontes). He also faults Tolstoy for using initials instead of names—Princess D., Lady S., etc—as if the author lacked the creative energy to invent complete names, although of course Eikhenbaum knew very well that the use of initials was an old device of illusionism, designed to give the reader the impression that the characters were drawn from real persons whose identities had to be protected. His "failure" with *Family Happiness*, according to Eikhenbaum, made Tolstoy realize that he was on "some sort of false path or rather at a crossroads."[13]

R. F. Christian, one of the most distinguished Western Tolstoy scholars, is in full agreement with Eikhenbaum: *Family Happiness*, he too avers, is a failure. Christian does concede that it contains fine lyric descriptions of nature and an occasional "quiet flash of humour" in the first part, but in the second

> the dialogue becomes at times inept, and there are some embarrassing passages which might have been culled from an old-fashioned schoolgirls' magazine.[. . .] There is a flavour of Turgenev at his most wistful—the past is gone, youth is over, there is no excitement in store, but only the desire for a quiet life in which passion is replaced by habit.[. . .] But the story breaks off where it should really start. Towards the end it shows all the signs of hasty composition.[. . .] It has no complexity or natural growth; and while its beautiful evocation

---

[13] B. M. Eikhenbaum, *Толстой; книга первая, 50-ые годы*, 361–63.

of the raptures of youthful, romantic love more than compensates for its sketchiness and didacticism, the story as a whole left Tolstoy so dissatisfied that he did not wish to publish it.[14]

Henri Troyat likewise finds *Family Happiness* "uneven, clumsily constructed, and lacking in originality," though he too qualifies these strictures by noting the "remarkable feeling for nature."[15]

Another common complaint against *Family Happiness*, especially by Russians in the Soviet period, is its narrowness, in particular its failure to grapple with social issues. By choosing to write from the point of view of a naïve seventeen-year-old gentry girl, a *baryshnia*, whose whole life had been spent on a country estate, Tolstoy cut himself off from the larger world and from the kind of perceptions and reflections he deemed suitable for mature male characters. Under Sergei Mikhailovich's guidance Masha does come to the belated realization that the peasants among whom she lives are real people with feelings like her own, but the topic of serfdom and the impending Emancipation does not impinge on her consciousness at all. G. A. Lesskis believes that the limitations of the female narrator were intolerably constricting for the real author. Tolstoy could not ascribe to Masha the deep perceptions of other people that were Tolstoy's stock-in-trade as omniscient author.[16] V. Ia. Lakshin concurs: "By isolating his characters from everything that did not impinge on their personal psychology and private life the writer excessively narrowed his enterprise and thus doomed his novel to failure."[17] The same point is made by S. P. Bychkov, adding that Tolstoy was then under the noxious influence of aesthetes like Druzhinin and, paradoxically, Botkin, though Botkin initially disliked the story.[18]

Perhaps the most significant negative judgment of *Family Happiness* was this initial reaction of Botkin, since it may have influenced Tolstoy himself and helped to undermine his confidence in his work. "It is all filled with a sort of cold glitter and does not touch either the mind or the heart," Botkin wrote Tolstoy. Tolstoy was wrong, however, to disparage the language, which was "everywhere excellent," the very source of the glitter. The fault of the story, Botkin felt, stemmed from lack of clarity in the original thought and in an intense puritanism of conception. The prudish

---

[14] R. F. Christian, *Tolstoy: A Critical Introduction*, 92–93.
[15] Henri Troyat, *Tolstoy*, 202.
[16] Lesskis, *Толстой*, 264.
[17] V. Ia. Lakshin, note in *SS* 3:487.
[18] Introduction to volume of letters. *PSS* 60:34.

story would be better placed in a children's magazine; it was a piece mothers could recommend to their virginal daughters without misgivings. "In places the story is boring and leaves an impression of dissatisfaction. [. . .] It smells," he concluded pungently, "of the—of an old *institutka* [graduate of a ladies' seminary]."[19]

In fact, however, the world's response to *Family Happiness* since 1859 has by no means been such a chorus of unforgiving no's as the harsh judgments cited above might suggest. Actually, the critical responses published immediately after the story's first appearance were overwhelmingly *favorable*. *Peterburgskie Vedomosti* rated *Family Happiness* "beautiful" (прекрасная) and went on, "How much grace, poetry, and attractiveness there is in Masha's coming together with Sergei Mikhailovich. Here all is poetry and life. This story is extraordinarily fine [. . .] At the time she was in love with Sergei Mikhailovich, Masha was as if a different woman and saw everything in a different light, through the prism of some sort of ineffable poetic charm, as a result of which it seemed to her that people were all good and all loved her. Such an enchanting impression was produced on us by the story itself." *Syn Otechestva* wrote of *Family Happiness*,"The idea of the story is not new, but no less interesting for that, and to explore it was evidently no easy task; but it has been beautifully carried out by the author. The awakening in Masha's heart of youthful strength, her infatuation with life, the conflict in her feelings, and later her return to recognition of her mistakes—all this is conveyed by the author with remarkable sureness and with that profound analysis of feelings that reveal in him a connoisseur of the human heart. Furthermore, it is all depicted so vividly and entertainingly, so poetically, that you read Count Tolstoy's story with real pleasure." Later, in 1862, in an article on "phenomena of contemporary literature ignored by our critics," the well-known critic Apollon Grigor'ev called *Family Happiness* Tolstoy's best work to date.[20]

Family Happiness has also found admirers in the West. Romain Rolland gave the story the ultimate French compliment: "*Bonheur Conjugal* a la perfection d'une oeuvre Racinienne."[21] One of the fullest, most

---

[19] Botkin to Tolstoi, 6 May 1859. Переписка, 71. The word unprintable in Soviet times is probably *пиздой*, "cunt." I am grateful to Yuri Slezkine for helping me identify it. In his self-lacerating mood, Tolstoy seized on it eagerly. "The ——— of an old *institutka*. Yes! C'est le mot!" he exclaimed. Tolstoy to Botkin, 11 May 1859. *PSS* 60:298. One wonders if Christian's "schoolgirls' magazine" may not be a cleaned-up echo of this passage.

[20] All these quotes are as cited in Gusev, *Материалы с 1855 по 1869 год*, 337–38.

[21] "*Family Happiness* has the perfection of a work by Racine." Romain Rolland, *Vie de Tolstoi*, 3rd. ed. (Paris: Hachette, 1911), 55.

elaborately argued celebrations of the story was written by the noted Italo-American scholar and critic, Renato Poggioli, surely a man of impeccable taste and sophistication, whose essay on *Family Happiness* was included in his posthumous book, *The Oaken Flute.* Following Rolland and seemingly unaware of the strictures of Eikhenbaum *et al.*, Poggioli pronounces resoundingly, "There is no doubt that the tale is a little masterpiece." To be sure, it is an ambiguous masterpiece, the ambiguity lying in the tension between the two parts. Of these, "the first is written in the key of a pastoral romance; the second, of realistic fiction."[22] The rest of Poggioli's essay is a detailed, elegantly worked out demonstration of this contrast, first linking the first part, though with many appropriate qualifications, to the pastoral tradition, as a reincarnation of the archetypal pairing of Adam and Eve, then showing how the idyll is transformed in the second part into a "realistic" account of the frictions, disappointments, and compromises that must mark actual human marriages. The protagonists discover, Poggioli concludes, "that passion is deemed limitless only as long as man and woman remain within the sphere of pastoral and romantic love, which is but an enchanted circle. But as soon as the lovers go beyond the boundaries of pastoral fantasy and romantic fancies, they discover that love can last and grow stronger and truer, only if and when it is circumscribed."[23]

Perhaps the most remarkable of the positive assessments of *Family Happiness* is that of its earliest and harshest critic, Botkin. Conscientiously carrying out Tolstoy's injunction to be as ruthless as possible in editing this supposedly misshapen monster, Botkin set about reading the proofs for the second part, blue pencil poised to make drastic deletions, and lo! he concluded that the story was . . . a masterpiece! "Not only did I like the second part," he wrote Tolstoy, "but I find it beautiful in all respects. In the first place, it possesses great internal dramatic interest; in the second place, it is a superlative psychological study; and finally, in the third place, there are in it profoundly perceived representations of nature. [. . .] This piece of yours is excellent in conception and for the most part excellent in execution. But it should have been thought out and developed more fully; it needed an incomparably more developed ending, not the abrupt [проглоченный, 'swallowed'] way it ends now. But even in its present form it is still a beautiful piece, the product of a serious and profound

---

[22] Renato Poggioli, *The Oaken Flute: Essays on Pastoral Poetry and the Pastoral Ideal*, 266.
[23] Poggioli, 282.

talent."[24] Unfortunately, we have no record of Tolstoy's reaction to this unexpected eulogy. No letters between him and Botkin seem to survive for the period from May, 1859, to April, 1861, and there are no further references in their published correspondence to *Family Happiness*.

It would be absurd for me to pose as supreme arbiter of the case for or against *Family Happiness*. I will confess, however, that I like the story and find it charming and delicately wrought, anticipating in many ways fuller realizations in the great novels. The young Masha has many of the qualities of the young Natasha Rostova—the exuberance, openness, and passionate desire to live to the utmost. Masha's near seduction by the sexy Italian marquis clearly anticipates Natasha's near elopement with the infamous Anatole Kuragin. The degenerate Princess D., who coaches Masha in her career as a society belle, likewise anticipates the equally infamous Hélène Kuragina-Bezukhova, the very incarnation of female corruption, in her role as mentor to Natasha. The big difference from the later novels besides length and complexity, and in my opinion the only serious weakness of *Family Happiness*, is the treatment of Masha's motherhood. The unmarried Tolstoy in 1858–59 had as yet no experience of fatherhood. He had never been close to a woman going through the primal experience of pregnancy, birth, and lactation—topics he was to invoke so powerfully in the "biological" epilogue to *War and Peace* and in *Anna Karenina*. All this was still *terra incognita*. As Eikhenbaum notes, Masha's babies are arbitrary ciphers. They appear and disappear to meet exigencies of the plot without ever coming to life or evoking any real emotion in either mother or father. And I will concede Botkin's and Christian's point that the ending is "swallowed," too abrupt, though Christian overstates the case by saying that the story should begin where it ends.

One final reversed assessment of *Family Happiness* seems to have been made by the author himself, though it is nowhere explicitly documented. Despite his claim in 1859 that the very thought of *Family Happiness* made him "blush and utter cries,"[25] Tolstoy does seem to have relented in his hatred for this story, perhaps under the influence of the praise it had received. At any rate he allowed it to be reprinted in all the collections of his works published up to and including 1880, editions he himself supervised. The shame seems to have subsided. Posterity also appears to have been benevolent toward *Family Happiness*. The story

---

[24] Botkin to Tolstoy, 13 May 1859. *Perepiska*, 75.
[25] Tolstoy to Botkin, 11 May 1859. *PSS* 60:258.

has appeared in countless Russian collections and has been translated and frequently reprinted in dozens of foreign languages. It is apparently still read with pleasure all over the world. Of course, the question that cannot be answered is whether it would be so received if the author had not also written *War and Peace* and *Anna Karenina*.

Thus it would seem that the literary-aesthetic solution to the puzzle is no solution at all. In view of the tremendously divergent assessments of *Family Happiness*'s quality and of Tolstoy's own more tolerant later attitude, it seems impossible to conclude that his extreme "shame" was simply a matter of aesthetic judgment. Something more must have been at stake. We therefore turn to biography.

It is a well-known fact, attested by Tolstoy himself,[26] that *Family Happiness* in some sense reflects the author's romance with Valeriya Vladimirovna Arsen'eva, later Talyzina, still later Volkova (1836–1909). Valeriya came from a family of local gentry, living on an estate, Sudakovo, only eight versts from Yasnaya Polyana. Tolstoy had been acquainted with her parents, and as a congenial and presumably responsible gentleman living nearby had been chosen as the official guardian (опекун) of their four children, who were left orphans by the deaths of their parents, the father in 1853 and the mother in 1856. In 1856, to be sure, Valeriya was twenty years old and hardly in need of a guardian, except perhaps with respect to finances.[27] Tolstoy's situation in relation to her is thus approximately duplicated in Sergei Mikhailovich's to Masha, except that in the story the age gap has been considerably lengthened — 36 to 17 in the story, 28 to 20 in real life. Valeriya's siblings, two sisters and a brother, have been consolidated in the story into one sister, Sonya. Valeriya played in relation to her youngest sister, age eleven, and her brother, age ten, a mentor's role similar to that assumed by Masha toward Sonya in the story. (The other sister, Olga, was eighteen and clearly needed no guardian either — she was already engaged to be married, ahead of Valeriya.) The other main character in the story, the elderly governess, Katya, also had a prototype at Sudakovo, a Franco-Italian lady named Genni Vergani, who years before had been governess to Tolstoy's sister Masha and later became governess to Masha's children.

---

[26] Tolstoy to P. I. Biryukov, 27 November 1903. *PSS* 74:240.
[27] Tolstoy's duties do not seem to have been at all burdensome: there does not seem to be a single reference in his diary or correspondence to any official act he performed on behalf of the Arsen'evs.

Tolstoy's position as guardian gave him the excuse to make frequent calls at Sudakovo, which he clearly enjoyed, and the young ladies could also come to Yasnaya Polyana, officially in order to call on his beloved "auntie," Tatyana Ergolskaya. Tolstoy's old friend Dmitry Dyakov advised him to marry Valeriya, considering her to be as attractive and appropriate a potential wife as he was likely to find, and Tolstoy took the advice seriously. "Listening to him, I also thought it is the best thing I could do," he wrote in his diary.[28] He had long aspired to find "family happiness" for himself, and indeed at 28 it seemed time to settle down.

But wasn't there something called "love" that was supposed to accompany engagement and marriage? Everyone seemed to think so, but was it true? Tolstoy was always skeptical of received opinions and accepted formulas. Maybe "love" was nothing but an overplayed fantasy of the romantics. Tolstoy had never been in love, though he had long kept his eye out for young ladies who might inspire such feelings. So with Valeriya Arsen'eva he evidently decided to undertake an experiment: see a great deal of her and monitor what happened inside him. She was young, good-looking, and friendly, and he was at least mildly attracted. Would this spark turn into flame? Time passed, encounters were many, but alas, there was no fire, despite—or perhaps because of—such close and constant introspection.

I need not recount here in detail the ups and downs of this affair, which lasted about seven months, from June to December, 1856.[29] However, I will say that the relationship strikes me, at least on Tolstoy's part, as a case of ambivalence carried to the nth power. Here are a few samples of the evidence, culled from his diaries.

June 26 (all dates are 1856): V[aleriya] was in a white dress and very nice, I spent one of the pleasantest days of my life. Do I love her seriously? And can she love for long? These are two questions I would like to answer, but I can't.

June 28. V. is terribly badly educated, ignorant, if not stupid.

July 10. V. is very nice, and our relations are easy and pleasant.

---

[28] 15 June 1856. *PSS* 47:82.
[29] It is of course discussed by all Tolstoy's biographers, most fully in Gusev, *Материалы* and most discerningly in V. A. Zhdanov, *Любовь в жизни Льва Толстого*, and P. A. Zhurov, "Л. Н. Толстой и В. В. Арсеньева (Автобиографические отражения в повести 'Семейное счастье'," 119–36. An article in English by P. Pavlov, "Tolstoy's Novel *Family Happiness*," despite its psychoanalytic trappings strikes me as exceptionally naïve and of little value.

July 12. I am afraid she is the kind of character that can't even love children.

August 12. I would like to know whether I am in love or not.

At this point Valeriya leaves for Moscow to attend the coronation festivities there. She and Tolstoy exchange letters. She writes of clothes and parties, of handsome aides-de-camp she had met. Tolstoy, at least affecting to be jealous, says of the forty aides-de-camp he knows, only two are not scoundrels or fools. She also saw something of a former piano teacher, a Frenchman named Mortier, and Tolstoy could also be jealous of him. He writes disapprovingly of her social ambitions and interest in clothes.

25 September, with Valeriia back in Sudakovo. V. is nice, but alas, simply stupid.

October 1. She is terribly empty, lacking in principles, and cold as ice.

October 19. She's gotten terribly fat, and I absolutely feel nothing for her.

October 24. Went to a ball. V. was enchanting. I am almost in love with her.

October 28. I have quite involuntarily become something like a fiancé. This vexes me.

At this point Tolstoy decided to continue the experiment, but from a safer distance; without warning he suddenly departed for Moscow and then Petersburg. For the next two months he and Valeriya carried on a voluminous correspondence. Analyses of his own feelings form a great part of the letters, interspersed with instructions about how she should improve herself by reading, exercising, and practicing the piano. (Like Masha in the story, Valeriya played the piano, apparently quite well. Tolstoy did too, perhaps better than Valeriya, but he does not bestow this talent on Sergei Mikhailovich.) Later he "fictionalizes" the relationship, casting himself as Mr. Khrapovitsky and Valeriya as Miss Dembitskaya. Khrapovitsky is "morally old," has wasted some of his best years, but has now found his calling, literature, and longs to settle down to a peaceful, moral, family life. Miss Dembitskaya, on the other hand, lives for "balls, naked shoulders, a carriage, diamonds, acquaintances with courtiers, adjutant-generals, etc." Can people with such different longings ever love each other?

As Khrapovitsky, Tolstoy tries to get down to financial brass tacks. Neither he nor Valeriya is rich. If they marry and live in Petersburg part of the year, they will have to take an inexpensive apartment on the fifth floor. Fancy dress balls are out, but they will quietly entertain good friends at home. An alternative would be to live on the third floor, keep a carriage, and dress in lace, and at the same time hide from creditors and write to the country to have the last drop squeezed out of the peasants there. In the story Masha is allowed to act out what were for Valeriya only fantasies of the high life. Despite some talk of economies, Sergei Mikhailovich seems to have sufficient resources to afford to set Masha up as a Petersburg belle and later take her to Baden-Baden.

In his letters Tolstoy continues to work his two dominant themes, microscopic analysis of his own feelings (Do I really love you?) and lectures about how she ought to behave. The ultimate involution is this complicated justification for his own didacticism: "You see, I want so much to love you that I am teaching you how to make me love you. And really, the main feeling I have for you is not yet love, but a passionate desire to love you with all my might."[30] From his letters to Auntie Ergol'skaya and to his brother Sergei it is clear that as late as December Tolstoy was still toying with the idea of marrying Valeriya.[31] If he could only believe that she had a constant nature and would always love him, he claims that he would not hesitate a minute to marry her.

Valeriya, however, was finally growing restless. She had tolerated a good deal of uncertainty and a great deal of lecturing. Whether she was in love or not, she knew that it was a young lady's urgent obligation to make the most of what opportunities she had to find a husband during the few years she was a marketable commodity. Tolstoy was an attractive man, a Count with landed property and a potential literary star into the bargain, and she kept hoping he would finally make up his mind to propose. But she did have her limits of tolerance. First she began to protest against the constant нотации и скука (reprimands and boredom) of his letters. She insisted that he would have to love her with her weaknesses intact; she was not a project for his remodeling. But finally she lost patience. She sent Tolstoy a short note telling him not to write her any more.[32] He could not resist replying to this, with a mixture

---

[30] Tolstoy to Arsen'eva, 9 November 1856. *PSS* 60:106.
[31] Tolstoy to T. A. Ergol'skaya and to Sergei N. Tolstoi, both 5 December 1856. *PSS* 60:135–37.
[32] Giving up on Tolstoy, she married one A. A. Talyzin in 1858.

of apologies and self-justification; but in his diary he wrote the truth: he was relieved. "I got an offended letter from V[aleriya], and to my shame I am glad of it."[33]

Tolstoy did feel a good deal of guilt about the way he had treated Valeriya. Auntie Ergol'skaya had reproached him for his behavior. And in reply — he usually wrote to Ergol'skaya in French, following a long established, but by then fading aristocratic rule for men writing women — he explained that he had never really loved Valeriya, but had enjoyed inducing her to love him, which he called a "méchant plaisir" (wicked pleasure). This, he admits, was wrong. "J'ai très mal agis [sic], j'en ai demandé pardon à Dieu et j'en ai demandé à tous ceux à qui j'ai fait du chagrin."[34] How much real remorse he felt may be open to question, but at least he acknowledged some fault.

But actually, had Tolstoy's treatment of Arsen'eva really been so bad? I am inclined to extenuate the offense as relatively venial in the long catalogue of men's sins against women. He did not seduce her or even attempt to; he made no false promises. His declarations of love were always shaky and qualified. He never gave her cause to feel deceived. She may have had false hopes, but he cannot be said to have encouraged them. In short, the guilt from the relationship itself does not seem to me sufficient to cause the extreme revulsion evoked by the finished story, especially in view of the time that had elapsed.

In any case, a year or more later Tolstoy wrote *Family Happiness*, to some degree based on his affair with Arsen'eva. But the story is anything but a faithful record of that experience. It first chronicles an idyllic love affair leading to betrothal and marriage, not a drawn-out display of wary ambivalence. Then, in the second part, it shows the couple actually wed — an imaginary projection of what would have happened if he had married Valeriya and lived the kind of life she wanted, the high life of Petersburg and European resorts. Even if we accept the Poggioli view of the final marital equilibrium as the most any couple can realistically hope for, the story still seems designed to prove that Tolstoy's decision not to marry Valeriya had been correct. He still hoped for more family happiness than that vouchsafed to Sergei and Masha at the end. And as for the guilt, there is little male guilt in the story at all. Sergei Mikhailovich does not toy with Masha as Tolstoy did

---

[33] Entry of 10 December 1856. *PSS* 47:104.
[34] "I acted very badly, I have asked forgiveness of God and I have asked it of all those to whom I have caused pain." Tolstoy to T. A. Ergol'skaya, 5/17 April 1857. *PSS* 60:177.

with Valeriya; he loves her unambiguously and can only watch sadly as she belatedly sows her wild oats. All the guilt is shifted onto Masha—for immaturity, bad judgment, and shaky loyalty.

Imaginary assuaging of guilt seems to have been for Tolstoy one of the fringe benefits of writing fiction. Put an alter ego character into a situation that duplicates one you lived through in real life, but have him behave better than you did, and your conscience is consoled, if not clear! Konstantin Levin in *Anna Karenina* is more compassionate with his difficult dying brother Nikolai than Tolstoy had been with *his* difficult dying brother Dmitry; and in *Resurrection* Prince Dmitry Nekhliudov goes to enormous lengths to make amends to a woman he had once seduced and who had eventually been reduced to prostitution, whereas Tolstoy had never done anything for a maid he had seduced in his aunt's house in Kazan who had likewise come to a bad end. In any case, self-justification and easing of guilt feelings about Valeriya may have been part of the reason for writing *Family Happiness* in the first place, but it would hardly account for the sudden revulsion Tolstoy experienced after it was finished and being published.

There are, however, deeper guilts in the treatment of Arsen'eva that may have come into play. In the first place, there is the "double standard," the largely unwritten Victorian codex that prescribed different—much laxer—standards of sexual morality for men than for women. As Tolstoy himself was to do later with Sofya Bers, Russian gentlemen often married girls ten or so years younger than they. These girls had no previous sexual experience, but the men were already thoroughly "sullied." They had been "married," as Tolstoy put it later, countless times, with prostitutes, lower class women, and perhaps even with high-society ladies in adulterous love affairs. At least later this sexual imbalance troubled Tolstoy greatly, but in *Family Happiness* it is kept out of sight. Not a word is uttered about Sergei Mikhailovich's prior sex life. Whatever it was, it does not matter: his love in the present is pure. Possibly this cover-up troubled Tolstoy as he reread the story.

The "puritanism" that bothered Botkin, however, seems more the fault of inexorable Victorian taboos than of Tolstoy's covering up what he should have opened up. For instance, surely Masha, the narrator, during the courtship would have had recurrent thoughts stimulated by her sexual feelings and later her anticipation of the wedding night. (Does it feel good? Will it hurt?) Later, after the marriage, the honeymoon period is represented as blissful, but not noticeably different from the months before; the effects of sexual fulfillment are not explored at all, even by indirection. But how much could any nineteenth-century writer—except, perhaps, in France—say about such topics? Actually, Tolstoy was one of the great taboo-breakers, but that role came later. Perhaps more could have been conveyed by hint and allusion, and perhaps Tolstoy's imagination failed him in this respect. No echoes from his passionate affair with his peasant serf Aksiniya Bazykina, begun in mid-1858, found their way into *Family Happiness*, as they were much later to do in *The Devil* (written 1889). The barrier may have been the same sexual taboos, perhaps enhanced by the difference in class. Could a refined lady herself experience or arouse in a partner the kind of feelings Tolstoy had known with Bazykina?

In real life there was, however, another dimension of sexual guilt that is totally kept out of *Family Happiness*. During the months he was visiting Valeriya and measuring the feelings she aroused or did not arouse in him, Tolstoy was occasionally having real sex with lower-class women—and feeling guilty about it. The diaries give a few cryptic clues:

June 15 (1856). The s[*oldatka*—a peasant soldier's wife reduced to prostitution] didn't come.
June 19. S[*oldatka*] in the evening. Disgusting.
June 25. In the evening the s[*oldatka*]. Surely the last time.
July 5. A wench [*devchonka*] came running, but I was in control and drove her off.
July 26. Took a horseback ride with voluptuous intent, but unsuccessful.

V. A. Zhdanov cites these entries, quite reasonably arguing that Tolstoy clearly was never in love with Valeriya, as some biographers had claimed. A man really in love, Zhdanov believes, would not indulge himself "out of bounds" like that.[35]

Traces of another symptom of psycho-sexual disorder also surface in Tolstoy's diary during this period: apparent episodes of impotence. There are two such entries. The one for 17 August 1856 concludes, "A woman [b(*abu*)] was brought and I"—this followed by a series of Cyrillic letters: п. с. с. б. и н. в. The exact decipherment of these initials remains somewhat in doubt, but there seems no question that they refer to an episode of what is now celebrated on the airwaves as "erectile dysfunction." This hypothesis is strengthened by the entry of September 5, which reads,

---

[35] Zhdanov, 33.

"I am tormented by the thought that I am almost i[mpotent]."[36] Impotence does not seem to have been a problem that troubled Tolstoy either earlier or later. Apart from possible physical causes, it could be a symptom of depression, perhaps brought on by emotional conflicts stemming from the experiment with Valeriya. Whatever the explanation, however, these symptoms belong to 1856, at the time when the relationship with Valeriya was developing, not to 1859, when Tolstoy reacted so violently to his own story. The connection, if any, could only lie in the cloudy region of conscious or unconscious memories.

Thus perhaps the cumulative effect of psychological pain and the fact that *Family Happiness* had resurrected the Arsen'eva affair but had not treated it honestly, confessionally, may have helped bring on the revulsion against the story. In any case, the revulsion extended beyond the story itself to encompass the writing of fiction in general. Was authorship a worthy goal for one's life, Tolstoy now asked himself, to spend it writing little love stories designed to entertain idle people? It seemed a trivial, childish occupation. By that standard it mattered little whether *Family Happiness* was good or bad. In the big world nobody cared. There were more important things in life. As he wrote to Druzhinin in October, "I am not writing and have not written since the time of *Family Happiness*, and I think I will not write. [. . .] The main thing is that life is short, and in one's mature years to waste it writing such stories as I wrote is immoral. I can and must and want to occupy myself with something real [делом]."[37] Or to Fet, at that time his closest friend, "[W]riting stories in general is pointless, especially by people who feel sad and don't really know what they want from life."[38]

As mentor and presiding shepherd of Russian literature, Turgenev was troubled by Tolstoy's defection from the ranks of literary professionals. On 25 November/7 December 1857 he wrote Tolstoy prophetically, ". . . I can't imagine what you are if not a man of letters [литератор]: An officer? Landowner? Philosopher? Founder of a new religious teaching? Government official? Businessman?"[39] And in a follow-up letter he made the accusation clear: if you are not a professional, you are a dilettante![40]

---

[36] *PSS* 47:90, 91. The editors of the Jubilee edition filled out the b[*abu*] and the i[mpotent], but left the longer encryption unresolved. I have been much helped in deciphering it by Yuri Slezkine and, via James Rice, by Lev Loseff.
[37] Tolstoy to Druzhinin, 9 October 1859. *PSS* 60:308.
[38] Tolstoy to Fet, 23 February 1860. *PSS* 60:324–325.
[39] I. S. Turgenev, *Собрание сочинений*, 12:287.
[40] Turgenev to Tolstoy, 17/29 January 1858. Turgenev, 295.

The "something real" that was to rescue Tolstoy from the frivolousness of fiction was the school for peasant children on his estate and the serious involvement with pedagogical issues that was to occupy him intermittently for some years. But luckily for us, the enormously powerful literary talent lurking within him could never be permanently denied, and before long he was hard at work on *War and Peace*.

Finally, there is one more area connected with *Family Happiness* where the biographical and the literary/aesthetic factors intersect: Tolstoy's personal and literary relations with Ivan Turgenev, his most distinguished fellow writer and his own mentor and model. The story of Tolstoy's personal involvement with Turgenev is far too long and complex to be explored here. Perhaps it can be summarized in two words: deep ambivalence. It was a tumultuous love-hate relationship, the negative side of which eventually led the two men to the brink of a duel and to a long rupture, only repaired with some effort toward the end of Turgenev's life.

But apart from his relations with Turgenev the man, Tolstoy also had to relate to Turgenev the writer, the great pioneer of realistic fiction, a figure of enormous talent and achievement ten years older than he. In 1855 Turgenev had generously befriended the somewhat uncouth young lieutenant fresh from Sevastopol, ensconced him in his apartment in Petersburg, and helped him to navigate the literary world, at the same time trying to refine his taste and help him shed his roughnesses (the literati called him a "troglodyte"). Though duly grateful, Tolstoy soon rebelled. He had somehow to shake off the "anxiety of influence," to make himself into Tolstoy, not a clone of Turgenev. His judgments of Turgenev's works become more and more harsh. Though he liked "Faust,"[41] the Turgenev story nearest in theme and manner to *Family Happiness*, "Asya," he peremptorily dismissed as "rubbish" [дрянь].[42]

Nevertheless, the spirit of Turgenev hovers over *Family Happiness*. As Eikhenbaum, Christian, Gusev, and several others have noted, *Family Happiness* is the most Turgenevesque of all Tolstoy's works. It follows the standard Turgenev formula, a gentry romance in the country against a background of lyrically perceived nature. Eikhenbaum cites

---

[41] Diary entry of 28 October 1856. *PSS* 47:97.
[42] Diary entry of 19 January 1858. *PSS* 48:4. Tolstoy also wrote to Nekrasov, "Turgenev's 'Asya' is in my opinion the weakest thing he has written." Tolstoy to N. A. Nekrasov, 21 January 1858. *PSS* 60:252. Elisei Kolbasin obligingly informed Turgenev of this opinion, along with Nekrasov's interpretation that Tolstoy's motive for it was pique at his, Nekrasov's, initial rejection and criticism of his story "Al'bert." *Тургенев и круг "Современника,"* 350.

examples of nature-description passages that could have been written by Turgenev, though interspersed with some purely Tolstoyan ones. As noted, Christian calls attention to a similarity of mood, a melancholy and resigned acceptance of the passage of youthful hopes and dreams. But surely the differences are as striking as the similarities. Turgenev would never dream of writing a story from a woman's point of view, a bold tour de force for a male writer. And most of all, Turgenev very seldom allows his lovers to marry. For Turgenev the most characteristic—and indeed most poetic—figure is the old bachelor, relating to other men the story of his "First [and presumably only] Love."[43] So perhaps in *Family Happiness* Tolstoy sought to out-Turgenev Turgenev by having a *woman* serve as narrator and carrying the story beyond the altar into conjugal life. When reading the proofs in May, 1859, Tolstoy may have felt that he had not won this contest, that despite his efforts to treat the theme differently, the story still smelled too much—not of the anatomy of an *institutka*, but of the formulas of Turgenev. Kornei Chukovsky is of this opinion. He believes that Tolstoy, with *Family Happiness*, had hoped to reestablish his (allegedly) declining reputation by outclassing *A Nest of Gentlefolk*, which he did not like. It was the realization that he had not succeeded, Chukovsky thinks, that triggered his violent reaction when reading the proofs and his professed withdrawal from literature into pedagogy.[44]

To sum up. The effort to solve our puzzle has not, alas, led to a clear, unambiguous solution. All answers seem to be negated or at least qualified. Whatever its faults, *Family Happiness* is clearly not such an artistic failure as to warrant Tolstoy's violent repudiation of the work. Likewise, his treatment of Arsen'eva, though callous and selfish, was also not nearly bad enough to provoke such shame. However, the memories of the sexual indulgences "on the side" while courting her, and the anxiety and humiliation from the episodes of impotence may well have contributed to his reaction against the story. Possibly the sanitized, fictional version of that affair might evoke some remorse as falsehood, dishonesty. If he felt guilt toward Arsen'eva, he certainly did not expiate it confessionally by writing *Family Happiness*. But after all, fiction is fiction; it follows and is judged by its own laws, and authors cannot be held accountable for the "truth" of their reproductions of actual persons and events. However, emotions do not always obey laws, and the "lies" of *Family Happiness* may still have burdened Tolstoy's conscience. More generalized sexual

---

[43] "Asya" too is essentially in this format, but the scene of narration is not realized.
[44] Kornei Chukovsky, Люди и книги, 90–91.

guilts may also have played some role. Further, Tolstoy had to emancipate himself from the specter of Turgenev, and he had hoped that *Family Happiness* was itself a step in that direction, confronting the master on his own territory and attempting to outdo him there. Yet reading the text in cold print, he may have felt that he had lost this contest. Finally, the reaction against fiction itself, the suspicion that making up stories is not a serious or worthy pursuit for a mature man—this was to be a recurrent theme in Tolstoy's life, most powerfully manifest in the crisis that followed the completion of *Anna Karenina*.

Some or any combination of these factors may have contributed to Tolstoy's reaction. As Tolstoy knew so well and demonstrated so often and so penetratingly, the human heart is a complicated place, where all sorts of impulses struggle for recognition and dominance. Just which of the competing impulses, or combination of them, was responsible for the outburst of "shame" over *Family Happiness* seems impossible to discern conclusively from this distance in time.

The Case of the Missing Mothers,
or When Does a Beginning Begin?

One of my most cherished purposes, if I am lucky enough to encounter Lev Tolstoy in the next world (whichever region thereof), is to ask him to fill in what has always seemed to me a disturbing lacuna in *War and Peace*: the two missing mothers. "Dear Lev Nikolaevich," I shall say, "will you please tell me something about Princess Bolkonskaya, the mother of Prince Andrei and Princess Marya? What was she like, when did she die, and what had been her relations with her difficult and domineering husband?" My second question, even more fascinating, will evoke the mother of Pierre Bezukhov. Was she, as the name Pierre perhaps hints, a Frenchwoman, perhaps a demi-mondaine, a dancer or chanteuse, kept as mistress by the immensely wealthy grandee and jouisseur, Count Kirill Bezukhov? Or, alternatively, was she a serf girl on one of the Count's numerous estates, a pretty lass who briefly caught the master's eye and received a summons to the seigneurial bed? And what was her later fate? If she was a Russian peasant, did she and Pierre live together, like Asya and her mother in Turgenev's eponymous story,[1] until by a sudden whim of his father the boy was catapulted upward to be educated as a gentleman? Or had Pierre and his French mother, like Alexander Herzen and his German one, always been an established, if irregular, part of the Count's household?

---

[1] A story, incidentally, which Tolstoy dismissed as "rubbish" (дрянь) [diary entry of 19 January 1858; *SS* 19:228] and "the weakest thing he [Turgenev] ever wrote" [Tolstoy to Nekrasov, 21 January 1858; *SS* 17:189.

Tolstoy's answers to these questions, if any are vouchsafed me at all, are likely to be like Pontius Pilate's: "What I have written I have written." (This phrase always sounds better to me in Church Slavic, and that is probably the way Tolstoy will say it: "Еже писахъ, писахъ.") "You are asking me," he will say, "to write a novel different from the one I wrote, and the time for that has passed." Here below, alas, these questions are clearly unanswerable, and it may be improper even to ask them; they lead only to idle speculations of the type indulged in above, efforts to out-Tolstoy Tolstoy by extending the limits of his novel. I will therefore try to rephrase the problem so as to render it critically more acceptable. Why, then, did Tolstoy deliberately refrain from introducing these two mothers as characters, if only to a ghostly, posthumous existence in the memories of their living relatives?

For the (almost) total absence of these two ladies does seem to me to constitute a genuine puzzle, though perhaps not an insoluble one. On the one hand, it would seem that they would have provided some very apt narrative or illustrative material. There could, for example, have been an account of how Prince Nikolai Bolkonsky, though doubtless only with the benevolent intention of reshaping his wife to fit his image of an enlightened gentlewoman, had harassed and humiliated the poor lady, as we see him doing later with his beloved daughter Marya, perhaps driving her into an early grave. And the story of Pierre's mother would appear to be even more promising novelistic material—a piquant romance, diverting in itself, that would also enhance our understanding of that old roué, Pierre's father, and explain why to be his sole heir he singled out *this* son from among what must have been his many bastard children. (Incidentally, it has always seemed to me a bit implausible that none of Pierre's hypothetical half-brothers or half-sisters ever comes forward to claim a share of the inheritance, even if only as a suppliant. They missed an excellent opportunity: the guilt-ridden Pierre would surely have come across with a handsome settlement!) More important, his mother's story would show us some of the formative influences on Pierre, how he became what he was. "Dear Lev Nikolaevich, how could you pass up such golden opportunities to enhance your characterizations and add narrative spice?"

Even from the point of view of "realism," that school of which this novel is usually held up as a shining exemplar: is it "realistic" that not one of three major characters, Prince Andrei, Princess Marya, and Pierre, whose inner consciousness we visit many times, ever in the course of this vast novel has a single thought about his or her mother? During the night before the battle of Austerlitz, for example, the thought of his possible death the next day impels Prince Andrei to summon up "a whole series of memories, the most distant and most cherished . . . He remembered his last farewell with his father and his wife; he recalled the time of his first love for her; he recalled her pregnancy, and he felt sorry both for her and for himself" (One.III.12). Later, lying wounded on the battlefield, he also thinks of his sister and of his yet unborn son (he seems to have advance notice that the child will be a son). Is it plausible that he found no place anywhere in this litany of loved ones for his dead mother? And would not Princess Marya, sometime during all the anguish of her guilt-ridden strife with her father, have wished her mother back to life, if only to serve as a buffer and intercessor? And even at the hectic time of her father's death, when the French army was almost at the gates of their estate, would not Princess Marya have had some thought of her mother, as his body was (we assume) laid to rest near hers? Finally, would not Pierre, especially during the enforced idleness of his captivity, when his thoughts were ranging far and wide, at least once have conjured up some tender image of his mother, even if only a fantasy rather than a memory?

In fact, the novel provides us with only the skimpiest of references to the missing mothers. The night before the birth of little Nikolai Bolkonsky, the imminent event evokes a conversation about births between Princess Marya and her old nurse, Savishna, in the course of which Savishna relates "for the hundredth time" the familiar tale of the Princess's own birth, in Kishinev, delivered by a Moldavian peasant midwife (Two.I.8). One may surmise from this tale that the late Princess had accompanied her husband, then a general, on a military campaign against Turkey, presumably during the war of 1787–1792. Furthermore, one can conclude that the Princess did not die in bearing this daughter, since in the context the point of Savishna's narrative is that a peasant midwife is as good as the fancy doctor who has been brought from Moscow to attend the little Princess Lise, a point of course confirmed (doctors in Tolstoy are always useless if not harmful) by Lise's death. Late in the novel we meet in Voronezh Princess Marya's maternal aunt Malvintseva, who benevolently, if a bit haughtily, chaperones Marya's budding romance with Nikolai Rostov; yet these renewed contacts never stimulate either aunt or niece to any reminiscences about Princess Marya's late mother. As for Pierre, the only evocation of his mother is found, as expected, during his captivity. Platon Karataev has inquired about Pierre's relatives, and Pierre evidently answers that his mother is dead, for Platon especially commiserates with him for his lack of this most comforting of all relationships (Four.I.12).

A hint of an explanation for the absence at least of Princess Bolkonskaya lies in the well-known à clef dimension of *War and Peace*: *War and Peace* as a family chronicle. We know that the prototype of Prince

Nikolai Bolkonsky was Tolstoy's maternal grandfather, Prince Nikolai Volkonsky (1753–1821). Prince Volkonsky had no son to serve as Prince Andrei's prototype, but he did have a genuine, flesh-and-blood daughter, Princess Marya Volkonskaya, later Countess Tolstaya (1790–1830), the real "missing mother" whom Tolstoy himself, born in 1828, could not remember. Tolstoy's mother in turn had not sprung like Athene from her father's enlightened skull; she too had a "missing mother" whom she likewise could not remember, Princess Ekaterina Dmitrievna Volkonskaya, née Princess Trubetskaya (1749–1792).[2] This Princess Volkonskaya, Tolstoy's maternal grandmother, seems to have left almost as little trace in history (other than the exceptional, Grade A genes she perhaps bequeathed to her illustrious grandson) as on the pages of War and Peace, to which she donated only her maiden name, now bestowed — again with the change only of an initial letter — on another family in the novel, and a far from admirable one at that. Thus the fact that there had been two generations of "missing mothers" in his own family may have suggested to Tolstoy the idea of repeating the same pattern in this novel with so many family echoes. Nevertheless, Tolstoy's limited knowledge of his grandmother need not have hindered him from developing her as a character had he chosen to do so; after all, Princess Marya herself is a creative resurrection of the unremembered "missing mother" about whom Tolstoy was still having tender fantasies even in his old age.[3]

The drafts to the novel do provide a little more information about the lost mothers. In the early draft entitled "Три поры" (Three Periods) we are told cursorily of the late wife of Prince Nikolai Bolkonsky that "She died early, he was unhappy with her . . . She wearied him, and he never loved her." (PSS 13:79) In another draft we learn that Princess Marya's mother was indeed buried in the chapel at Bald Hills.[4] And of Pierre's mother we get a glimpse of the romance we had guessed at: "The father had never in his life loved anyone as much as the mother of this Pierre, with whom he had a liaison until her death. He also loved this son, but kept him at a distance . . . He feared his son's reproaches concerning his illegitimacy." (PSS 13:245)

Limited as the information on the missing mothers found in the drafts may be, it does prove conclusively that Tolstoy in his revisions *consciously expunged* these references to them. We are therefore, it seems to me, entitled to speculate concerning his motives.

---

[2] Sergei L'vovich Tolstoi, in his *Мать и дед Л. Н. Толстого* (Moscow, 1928), 23–24, has assembled whatever facts are known about her.
[3] Diary entry for 10 June 1908 (SS 20:296).
[4] *Первая завершенная редакция романа "Война и мир"*, 365.

If we presume that both missing mothers were dead by 1805, when the action of the novel begins, they could have appeared only in the *Vorgeschichte*. Our question is thus a microcosm of a much larger one: why was Tolstoy so very abstemious about providing any *Vorgeschichte* to this great novel? For there are many other events that happened prior to 1805 which we might like to know about. How and where, for instance, was the close and long-standing friendship formed between Pierre and Prince Andrei? (When you think about it, this friendship seems even a bit unlikely. Pierre appears to have been educated in Europe,[5] whereas Andrei must have attended a military academy in Russia; it is hard to see what would have brought them together.) Likewise, we may wonder about the background of Andrei's marriage to Lise Meinen. What persuaded his father to acquiesce in that ill-advised union (presuming he did acquiesce), when he was later so adamantly opposed to Andrei's perfectly suitable engagement to Natasha?[6] One could go on with questions like these, all of them evidence of the immense curiosity aroused by the characters in this novel; we would like to know more about them, because through Tolstoy's magic we feel so close to them. But the actual text answers none of these questions of pre-history; in fact it tells us almost nothing about anything that occurred before 1805. It appears that Tolstoy was very reluctant to extend his time frame any further into the past, even via the plausible memories of major characters.

The most obvious explanation for the absence of *Vorgeschichte* would be simple economy of means. The novel is already very long, and the past, like the future, is infinite; in art time must have a stop somewhere, whether moving backwards or forwards. As is well known, in its own pre-history *War and Peace* had begun as a novel centered on a former Decembrist, returning in 1856 "white as a loon" from decades of exile in Siberia. To understand the former Decembrist, Tolstoy had to go back to the Decembrist revolt itself, i.e., to 1825; and historically to understand 1825 one had to go back to 1812, to the great victory over Napoleon, the Russian army's occupation of Paris, and the subversive ideas imbibed there by some of its young officers. Then, as Tolstoy observes in a draft preface to *War and Peace*, he found repellent the chauvinistic tone of many Russian writings about 1812 and felt ashamed "to write of our triumph

---

[5] Pierre's dreamlike recollection of his Swiss geography teacher with his deliquescent globe (Four. III.3) is one of the few prehistoric "leaks" to penetrate the 1805 barrier.

[6] In the drafts we are told that his father had strongly disapproved of Prince Andrei's marriage. Andrei had married "God knows whom," and for some time afterward his father would have nothing to do with him, but he later relented for the sake of his grandchild (*PSS* 13:78).

in the conflict with Bonapartist France without having first described our failures and disgrace."[7]

So, from 1856 Tolstoy had been forced back in time by a combination of factors: a quest for deeper understanding of his characters, showing them in their youth and formative phases, and also the quest for greater historical perspective; to these was added the wish to avoid excessive chauvinism. The regressive movement passed through four stages: from 1856 to 1825; from 1825 to 1812; from 1812 to 1807 (Tilsit); and from 1807 to 1805 (Austerlitz). Thus the whole of *War and Peace* as we now have it could be regarded as itself one gigantic *Vorgeschichte* to an unfinished novel about a returned Decembrist. In the event, of course, the year 1856 was never reached at all, and even 1825 is only a vista dimly glimpsed on the distant horizon in the Epilogue, as Pierre returns, in December 1820, from one of his conspiratorial meetings in Petersburg. A tragedy looms in the distance, but we are not to witness it, nor is there any explicit reference to it; the tragic expectation depends on the reader's extratextual knowledge of later Russian history.

There is thus a marked contrast between the explicit happy ending of the novel in December 1820, the cozy and fertile family life of the Bezukhovs and the Rostovs, and the implied tragedy: Pierre's participation in the revolt of December 1825 and subsequent exile to Siberia. Yet Tolstoy carefully refrains from any reference to these later events, even in the form of what would have been the expression by Natasha of quite appropriate and poignant anxiety. In their concluding tête-à-tête she might well have said, "What you and your friends are doing there in Petersburg is dangerous, and I am frightened: for you, for me, and for our children." Such missing worries about the future would be the counterpart in the *Nachgeschichte* of the characters' missing memories of the past. But Tolstoy has set an equally impenetrable barrier against post-history: up to 1820 and no further! This barrier is necessarily broken by our knowledge of later public events, but we can only guess at their private consequences.

In any case, within this massive *Vorgeschichte* turned novel, Tolstoy may have felt constrained to limit further agglomeration by placing 1805 and 1820 as strict frontiers. Though his characters might "realistically" be expected to remember antecedent events, for these memories to be comprehensible to the reader Tolstoy would have to accompany them with a body of explanatory matter that would have weighed down the narrative

---

[7] *PSS* 13:54. It might be snidely pointed out in this footnote that for all his wish to describe "our failures and disgrace," Tolstoy pointedly omits in this still very nationalistic book any but fleeting references to Russia's most resounding defeat at Napoleon's hands, the battle of Friedland (14 June 1807).

and further increased the novel's already formidable bulk. And mutatis mutandis, the same was true of their hopes and fears about the future.

Besides simple economy of means, a second possible reason for Tolstoy's avoidance of both *Vor-* and *Nachgeschichte* might be the deliberate wish to create mystery. Not everything should be perfectly clear, even in the bright daylight of a realistic novel. The reader's imagination should be stimulated to wonder, to guess, to pursue leads not followed up by the author, just as we all wonder about what *Nachgeschichte* lies ahead in our own lives. There were plenty of literary precedents for such deliberate mystification of a character's antecedent biography—for instance, that of Pushkin's prisoner of the Caucasus, Aleko in *The Gypsies*, Lermontov's Pechorin, and many others, to name only Russian examples.

After all, the towering, worldwide reputation of *War and Peace* shows that we clearly do not need to know about the missing mothers, or any other facts from the *Vorgeschichte*. We will never know precisely how the major characters came to be what they were, and perhaps we could not really know that anyway. In Tolstoy's view the mystery of how each unique human personality is shaped cannot be resolved by the sort of curriculum vitae that Turgenev's characters, for example, generally display on their appearance in a story or novel (ancestry, class, parents, marital status, education, occupation, etc.). To ascribe the formation of a person's character to such obvious "causes" would be to commit on a small scale the same error for which Tolstoy berates the historians for their efforts to "explain" history. Life is too complex, too multifarious to be understood in this way; there are mysteries we cannot penetrate.

A deeper reason for Tolstoy's avoidance of *Vorgeschichte* in *War and Peace* has to do with the general treatment of time in the novel. As several critics have observed, time in *War and Peace* resembles time in the *Iliad*, rigorously sequential, linear, moving only forward, never sideways (there are no "meanwhiles") or backwards.[8] Why did Tolstoy feel so inexorably

---

[8] As noted by Krystyna Pomorska; see her "Tolstoy—Contra Semiosis." The parallel with the *Iliad* of course pleases those who like to assert or stress the affinities of *War and Peace* with the epic genre, a connection evidently supposed to enhance still further the work's prestige and majesty. Without disputing the linkage here, I would only point to another celebrated nineteenth-century novel, by an author known to have influenced Tolstoy, for which no epic connections are claimed, yet which is also "relentlessly diachronic" in its treatment of time and equally abstemious with *Vorgeschichte*, namely, *Le rouge et le noir*. *Le rouge* also, incidentally, also has a notable "missing mother." Not once in that long novel does Julien Sorel have a single recorded thought about his mother, even when he is dreaming of how he might not, after all, be the son of the father he detests. The phrase "relentlessly diachronic" comes from D. A. Miller, p. 200. A similar formula, "resolutely serial," is found in Carol A. Mossman, p. 109.

chained to Chronos's chariot? I find especially suggestive the explanation put forward by the late Krystyna Pomorska: "Time so represented [i.e., in pure forward motion] is thus another instance of a 'naked fact,' of non-mediated reality, while all devices which serve to break, or 'deform,' the temporal sequence appear as means of mediation" [Pomorska, 389]. In other words, for Tolstoy strictly sequential time is a form of Truth, that deity Tolstoy worshiped so devoutly (and even naively). Since in our real lives time never moves backward or sideways, it should not do so in "true" novels either. A flashback is as artificial—and therefore false—a representation of reality as a sung dialogue in an opera.[9]

So *War and Peace* begins in July 1805,[10] with Anna Scherer's party at which we hear the news of Napoleon's annexation of Genoa and Lucca, and proceeds with "relentless" sequentiality (though with many gaps) through 1812 to an Epilogue concluding in December 1820, which marks the end of the characters' lives as we know them; of course Tolstoy's "timeless" philosophizing continues for many more pages. From what seems to him the abrupt and "unmotivated" commencement and cessation of the action, Gary Saul Morson concludes that *War and Peace* has no real beginning and no real end; it simply starts and stops, thus echoing in its structure (or lack thereof) Tolstoy's philosophical premise that neither historical events nor human lives can be represented in neat patterns of causes, effects, and conclusions [Morson, 62–63].

Here I must disagree, despite all my admiration for Morson's immensely stimulating and seminal book. Whatever the role of chance, error, and unfathomed motive in real life, in art there are no accidents. (Of course, accidents may happen to characters, but we know that the author willed them to occur.) *War and Peace* may leave much unexplained, including the "causes" of the Russian victory over Napoleon (inexplicable, from Tolstoy's point of view, though he does seem to ascribe a good deal of causal power to what we would call morale), but it has an artistically valid beginning and an artistically valid conclusion. As history, the beginning in 1805 has already been explained: a "running start" on 1812, including some less than glorious Russian engagements with the French.

---

[9] Of course, in *Anna Karenina* Tolstoy violated this commitment to the truth of linear time, veering back and forth between the Anna-Vronsky and the Kitty-Levin lines. But, we might add, Homer in the *Odyssey* did the same thing.

[10] There are, to be sure, a few discrepancies, such as the fact that the novel begins at Anna Scherer's party in *July* 1805, but that same night, when Pierre leaves Prince Andrei's house to carouse with Anatole Kuragin, it is *June*. See Iu. Birman, p. 125. As Birman suggests, Tolstoy needed the "white nights" of June to stimulate Pierre to continue his habits of dissipation despite his promise to Andrei not to do so.

As a family novel, the starting point is chosen with equal care. The action of the "peace" segments of the novel is propelled by the sexual energy of the principal characters, all of whom are in their mating years. Seeking his or her proper mate, each one will blunder and stumble through a wrong choice, suffer, undo it with enormous difficulty (and a good deal of luck), until ultimately, a thousand pages later, the "right" pairings have been achieved: Natasha/Pierre, Marya/Nikolai. Andrei and Sonia, of course, are the odd ones out. Andrei had made a wrong choice before the action begins, and though he later finds his way to the right one, he does not live to consummate it. As for Sonia, she is the "sterile flower" condemned to a life of spinsterhood.

If we consider only the novel as narrative and exclude the second part of the Epilogue (a procedure to which Morson would no doubt have objections), the ending of *War and Peace* seems to me to differ little from the traditional closure of comedy, the marriage of the good, young characters; in fact it seems much like the ending of the novel Morson chooses for contrast, exemplifying the neat closure of a well-made plot, Jane Austen's *Emma*. In both cases, the mating game, with all its false starts and false leads, has been played out and straightened out. In both cases sexual attraction and its loftier emotional ramifications have been for a time deflected and confused by considerations of status and money, by pressures from others, such as parents, and by the rules of the game as it was played in that particular society at that particular time, the rules of what men and women can and can't, should and shouldn't do. In both cases, all this is happily resolved at the end, and wedding bells peal out.

The difference, of course, is that Tolstoy cannot rest content with a wedding fadeout. Insisting on full biological truth, he must pursue the couple if not into the conjugal bed, at least to its natural products, the babies that are the proper consequence of proper mating. Life goes on; one generation succeeds another. As Pierre demonstrates, despite the lessons—too soon forgotten—of "philosophers" like "Plato" Karataev, men will continue with what they call "history," which consists of their silly wars and politics. Women, however, are closer to the ultimate realities. Natasha with her baby and its diaper and Countess (as she is now) Marya with her swollen belly—these very present mothers tower over the ending as colossal symbols, standing at the true, timeless core of life.

Truth in Dying

It has long been a commonplace of Tolstoy scholarship, duly noted in every commentary on *Anna Karenina*, that Nikolai Levin is an artistic reincarnation of Tolstoy's own brother Dmitry, who died of tuberculosis in 1856, nearly twenty years before that novel was written. It would seem, therefore, that a comparison of the fictional character Nikolai Levin with what is known about the real Dmitry Tolstoy should provide some means, however meager and inadequate, for exploring the mysterious relationship between life and art, for measuring the distance between them and studying the processes by which the one is metamorphosed into the other. In short, it should help us understand how Tolstoy's artistic machinery worked. What happens when a real blood-brother Tolstoy is transformed into a Tolstoyan character?

The metaphor "artistic machinery" is misleading, however. It implies a mechanical process: you feed reality in at one end and out comes art at the other. Yet the "whys" behind an author's varied operations in transmuting real experience into fictional representation, his innumerable decisions, great and small, of what to include and what to exclude, what to duplicate faithfully and what to alter—such decisions are anything but mechanical. They emerge from a murky region in which the author's real emotions, aroused by his real experiences, confront and tangle with the aesthetic and structural requirements these reincarnated experiences must serve in their new environment. The present study is an effort to examine one particular instance of the art-life relationship. To what extent were Tolstoy's decisions concerning the character of Nikolai Levin artistic decisions, or at least justifiable in artistic terms; and, conversely, to what extent (if any) did Tolstoy use his art not only as a means of recapturing the past but of reshaping it into a form more comfortable and agreeable to him?

To judge from the surviving drafts, Konstantin Levin enters *Anna Karenina* complete with two brothers. He also has a sister, but Tolstoy keeps this shadowy lady hidden away in some foreign abode. Perhaps rather implausibly, she is not stirred to return to Russia even for the marriage of one brother or the death of another, nor, as far as we know, does she even come to visit the dying Nikolai during his stay at Soden, where he is seen by Kitty Shcherbatskaya. (Kitty is recuperating there from being jilted by Vronsky, and Nikolai arouses her animosity both by his unpleasant habit of jerking his head and by reminding her of the brother whom she in turn had jilted.) Tolstoy clearly did not want the Levin sister physically present in his novel; her sole function, it would appear, is to own estates which Konstantin can manage for her, thus displaying both his generosity and his managerial talents. These duties also conveniently oblige him to move about in his rural neighborhood, and it is on a journey to his sister's estate at Pokrovskoe that he catches the providential early-morning glimpse of Kitty driving by in a carriage—a glimpse that fortunately restores his sexual aspirations, which had temporarily been deflected into fantasies of melting by marriage into the peasantry, to ones more appropriate to his station, that is, marriage to a lovely and virginal gentlewoman. In any event, the Levin sister is a less than vital presence in the novel. Konstantin's two male siblings, however, are both important, though secondary, characters, each with an important part in the life of their brother.

Sergei Ivanovich Koznyshev is a subject in himself, to be treated here only in the most summary fashion, as the occupant of the right-hand side of the symmetry that has Konstantin Levin looming large in the center, whole and complete, with a flawed and one-sided brother at either hand. Though in early drafts Sergei is a full-blooded Levin, Tolstoy soon demotes him to the status of a half-brother, and notably a half-brother on the mother's side, единоутробный, which gives him a different surname, rather than on the father's, единокровный, which was apparently regarded as a closer bond. This dilution of the relationship doubtless is needed to signal the fact that the respectable Sergei Koznyshev is emotionally more distant from Konstantin than the disreputable full brother, Nikolai Levin. It may also incidentally tell us that Koznyshev does not have a Tolstoy prototype: certainly neither of Tolstoy's other two brothers bears the slightest resemblance to him.

Koznyshev's principal function in the novel is to serve as a foil for his younger brother, who, though at first overawed and overshadowed by this famous writer and thinker, "known to all Russia," is ultimately shown to surpass him on every count (except, perhaps, in such ironic notoriety). At the same time, Koznyshev serves as a target for Tolstoy's own social and ideological satire. In this latter capacity he represents that hateful creature, the academic intellectual, deracinated, city-dwelling, and excessively cerebral. He is rich in book-learning but poor in spirit, a man for whom ideas are only playthings and chess problems are as absorbing as the question of the immortality of the soul. Tolstoy is really very hard on poor Sergei Ivanovich; he seems to miss no opportunity to ridicule and humiliate him. Though he expatiates on agricultural economics, Koznyshev has no roots in the soil and no farmer's feeling for how agriculture actually works. He lies abed while Levin displays both his muscular prowess and his democratic spirit in the great mowing scene. Koznyshev prates about the beauties of nature—something true country people never do; and worse still, he goes fishing, destructively driving a carriage through a meadow to reach a stream. Despite their passion for hunting—which to some of us seems a much uglier, more bloodthirsty sport than fishing—both Tolstoy and Levin for some reason consider fishing a foolish waste of time. And, as the ultimate humiliation, Tolstoy never lets Koznyshev catch a single fish!

More seriously, Koznyshev's magnum opus, a book ponderously entitled *An Experimental Survey of the Bases and Forms of Statehood in Europe and in Russia*, the fruit of six years' toil, proves a flop. To divert himself from this disappointment Koznyshev begins to beat the dubious drums of pan-Slavism, rallying Russian support for the oppressed Balkan Slavs groaning under the Turkish yoke. For this misplaced enthusiasm Koznyshev has to bear the brunt of all Tolstoy's anger against the journalistic fakery and manipulation he perceived among the promoters of that questionable cause. Perhaps the bitterest blow of all, Koznyshev is a flop with the fair sex: his Rudin-like failure to propose to Varenka, despite his intentions and all his well-considered reasons for doing so, is one of Tolstoy's great scenes, demonstrating his marvelous awareness of the frequently vast gulf between conscious purpose and unconscious wish (or fear).

And just to rub in the insult, Tolstoy has Kitty and Levin demonstrate immediately afterwards, as far as they decently could within the confines of a Victorian novel, that their relationship, by contrast, has in it plenty of physical passion. Becoming progressively disillusioned with his brother as the novel develops, Levin sums up for us the author's (and presumably our) judgment of him: Koznyshev is lacking in "life force, what is called heart." Thus he not only has wrong ideas; he is something short of being a complete man. And by comparison Levin looks all the better.

Now what about Nikolai? First of all, Nikolai Levin obviously serves at least one of the same functions for which Tolstoy has used Sergei Koznyshev: he lights up his brother Konstantin from the other side. By the time we meet him in the novel, Nikolai is already a derelict, physically, socially, economically, emotionally. He has squandered his share of their mother's estate (whereas Konstantin has carefully husbanded his); several attempts at a career have ended in failure; he has never married, but lives with a former prostitute, Marya Nikolaevna or Masha, whom—in that romantic gesture so popular in nineteenth-century fiction—he has rescued from a brothel. But in its quotidian aftermath even this noble gesture proves flawed: Nikolai treats Masha badly, despite her meekness and devotion, and at one stage of his illness drives her away, as if to prove to himself that he needs no nurse.

Nikolai is hostile to both his brothers, who, he claims, have cheated him in the division of their mother's property; but his antagonism toward Koznyshev is stronger. Koznyshev shows toward Nikolai his characteristic dryness and lack of "heart," whereas Konstantin, though troubled and uncomfortable with his difficult brother, retains with him a deep, unbreakable bond of fraternal love, trust, and acceptance, a bond that Nikolai also recognizes, though he may appear to deny it or strain it to the limit.

Finally, Nikolai represents, as does Koznyshev, an ideology of which Tolstoy disapproves: in this case, socialism. To be sure, he is never given much chance to expound his ideas. He makes a beginning of explaining the theory of surplus value, but his brother Konstantin, through whose eyes and ears we receive our impression of this encounter, tunes out Nikolai's lecture, absorbed as Konstantin is in thoughts about his brother's tragic state of health. Nikolai's ideas are made to seem almost a byproduct of his illness and thus discredited. We do learn, however, that their most concrete manifestation is a scheme for a workers' *artel'*, or cooperative guild, to be organized in a provincial village. The reader is evidently expected to dismiss this project as illusory, not so much, perhaps, because it is inherently impracticable as because Nikolai obviously has neither the resources nor the stamina to implement it.

Besides the economic and ideological contrast with Nikolai, which are both highly advantageous to Konstantin, Konstantin Levin has two other important areas of superiority to his brother: sexuality and health. Whereas Nikolai's sexual partner is a low-class ex-prostitute, Konstantin, after a temporary setback, acquires a pure and beautiful young bride, a princess or княжна; and he is clearly destined to sire a large brood of Konstantinovichi and Konstantinovny. To be sure, Tolstoy carefully avoids any impression of aristocratic or moral snobbery in his depiction of Marya Nikolaevna and of Levin's behavior toward her. Levin politely addresses her with the formal pronoun *vy*—something rare in her experience and even disconcerting—and, despite some initial qualms, he allows his wife to remain in the room with her at Nikolai's deathbed (though in her latter-day capacity as respectable matron Kitty is reluctant, despite their in-law relationship, to meet that other besmirched woman in the novel, Anna Karenina). Nevertheless, Marya Nikolaevna cannot begin to match Kitty's charms: she is pockmarked, wears tasteless clothes, and can barely read and write. And in the deathbed scene it is Kitty, not Masha, who displays so impressively that marvelous feminine sickroom know-how, utterly inaccessible to Tolstoyan males. Within a few hours she transforms a drab and smelly hotel *nomer* into a clean and cheery hospital room, ministering with unfailing tact and efficiency to all Nikolai's needs. Konstantin's superiority is thus vicariously reinforced, as it were, by his wonderful wife.

Of all the events in Nikolai Levin's life, however, the most central in the novel are his illness and death: one might almost say that his function there is to be ill and die. By so doing he confronts his brother Konstantin, emotionally as well as intellectually, with the reality of death—that supreme existential fact which his creator, Lev Tolstoy, found such an unacceptable feature of God's arrangements for us. Besides providing a stimulus for Konstantin's philosophical ruminations on mortality, the representation of Nikolai's illness and death enables Tolstoy greatly to deepen the characterization of Konstantin Levin himself, showing him struggling with the tangle of conflicting feelings evoked by this troublesome and moribund brother. In the early encounters the fraternal blood-bond, with its warm associations from childhood, plus a sense of duty, contend with shock and revulsion at Nikolai's antisocial behavior and exasperation with his constant aggressiveness; later, pity for the dying man's plight clashes with irritation at his refusal to face his predicament honestly; and in the deathbed scene, impatience with the long-drawn-out process of dying triggers a reaction of guilt and horror at discovering such an unworthy feeling in himself. (After all, to be impatient with your brother for taking so long to die seems despicable in the extreme; yet Levin cannot deny that the feeling is there.) With their searingly honest presentation of all these conflicting emotions, the chapters describing the death of Nikolai Levin, including the climactic one entitled "Death"—the only titled chapter in the novel—are among the most powerful and moving in world literature. To use Tolstoy's term, the reader's "infection" with Levin's emotions—pity, love, irritation, frustration, terror, and guilt—is complete. We too find it almost too much to bear when Levin, needed to help turn the dying man in bed, is forced to reach under the bedclothes and feel that emaciated body in all its physical reality, and when Nikolai takes Levin's hand and in a final gesture of reconciliation, gratitude, and forgiveness presses it to his lips.

Yet despite all the truthfulness in Tolstoy's portrayal of Konstantin Levin's feelings about his brother—about both his brothers, in fact—there is one familiar emotion that seems all too obviously inherent in the material as presented but is never explicitly articulated. That emotion is *rivalry*, sibling rivalry, in twentieth-century psychological jargon. Tolstoy seems to see and identify for us all Levin's emotions but this one. And yet, if we dig to the bottom of Konstantin Levin's heart as he stands by his brother's deathbed, we can hardly fail to discover there what is perhaps the most powerful and certainly the guiltiest emotion of all: *triumph*. We do not know who won the pillow fight Konstantin remembers from their childhood, but he has certainly come off the victor in all life's other contests. Where Nikolai's scorecard has nothing but black marks—poverty, a flawed and failed cause, a flawed and sullied mistress, and, finally, illness and death—Kostya's is studded with stars: relative (though not unseemly) affluence; deep roots in and efficient management of ancestral lands; sound, responsible, independent ideas about social problems; a beautiful, capable, loving young wife, whose revelation of her first pregnancy is perfectly—perhaps a little too perfectly—timed to follow Nikolai's death; and perhaps most of all, the simple triumph of remaining alive when someone else dies, that guilty triumph later to be experienced so vividly by all the associates of Ivan Ilyich. How could Levin help feeling triumphant?

Yet to feel triumphant over a brother's corpse, a brother pitied and loved despite all his failings—such a feeling, however understandable, would inevitably be followed by a rush of shame and guilt. This guilt would be a larger edition of the guilt already experienced over the feeling of impatience at death's delay. The latter feeling, however, is directly articulated by the author and recognized by the character, whereas the former must be deduced by the reader. Since Tolstoy's art places so much stress on whole-truth, dig-to-the-bottom psychological revelations, this failure to identify Konstantin Levin's feelings of fraternal rivalry and aggression might be considered an artistic flaw. If so, it might be suggested that Tolstoy's usually unerring intuition may have been inhibited here by emotional resistances stemming from his own life. He could not quite perceive this truth even about a somewhat distanced, fictional alter ego.

To pursue this hypothesis from literature into life one obviously has to look to the prototype of Nikolai Levin, Dmitry Tolstoy, and his relations with his celebrated sibling. To be sure, the difficulties are considerable: our data are limited and their objectivity questionable. Except for the barest facts of his curriculum vitae, what we know about Dmitry Tolstoy is almost entirely limited to what his brother Lev chose to record about him, either in his letters and diaries written during Dmitry's lifetime or in autobiographical writings of a later date. But we must make do with what we have.

The two principal autobiographical documents in which Dmitry plays a significant part are *A Confession* (Исповедь), written immediately after *Anna Karenina*, and the unfinished *Reminiscences* (Воспоминания), written in 1902–1906.[1] Both these sources inform us, as we are told about Nikolai Levin, that as a young man Dmitry Tolstoy went through a period of intense religious involvement during which he punctiliously carried out all the required observances—fasts, vigils, and ceremonies—of the Orthodox Church. He also "led a pure and moral life," avoiding alcohol, tobacco, and sexual relations. For this excess of puritanical zeal, according to *A Confession*, Dmitry's friends and relations, including both his elders and his brothers, made fun of him and christened him "Noah." Even in the most confessionally truthful of autobiographies, however, there are problems of *Dichtung* and *Wahrheit*, questions involving the uses made of a given episode and the coloration given it. In *A Confession* Tolstoy presents the "Noah" incident simply as an illustration of the hypocrisy endemic in this nominally Christian society: its upper-class representatives, at least, do not expect any of their number to take religion too seriously, and the passionate commitment of this earnest young man is treated with cruel mockery. In the *Reminiscences*, however, where the same memory is revived more for its own sake than as an illustration, it is presented quite differently. There the "Noah" taunt is attributed, not to friends and relations in general, but to one disagreeable fellow student in Kazan, S., who came into Dmitry's room, messed up his mineral collection, and teased him about his religiosity, adding "Noah" as the final sting. Dmitry's response, notably omitted from *A Confession*, was a burst of uncontrolled fury. He struck his tormentor in the face and menaced him further with a broom handle. The threat from this weapon was so convincing that S. took refuge in the adjoining room, which Lev Tolstoy shared with his second brother, Sergei; from there S. had to crawl out through a dusty attic to avoid mayhem at the hands of the still raging "Noah." [SS 14:460]

---

[1] I have excluded any consideration here of Dmitry Tolstoy's possible role as the model for Dmitry Nekhlyudov in *Youth*.

Dmitry Tolstoy makes only this one appearance in *A Confession*; but in the *Reminiscences* he gets the most extended treatment of any of Tolstoy's brothers. From his physical description there we can easily recognize Nikolai Levin's double: "with thoughtful, stern, large brown eyes, he was tall, thin, rather, but not very, strong, with large, long arms and a rather bent back." [SS 14:458] Most of all, we instantly spot Nikolai Levin's physical trademark, his habit of "jerking his head as if trying to free himself from a necktie that was too tight." [SS 14:459] This tic is also attested in a contemporary document, a letter to Tolstoy from his brother Sergei of 14 July 1852: "Mitenka . . . looked at me very fixedly, made with his head and neck the motion you are familiar with, and gave a shout." [PSS 59:187–88] We also recognize the same difficult character: explosive on occasion, but otherwise withdrawn and self-absorbed, perhaps a bit self-righteous in his moral rigors, and something of a loner among the four brothers. In Kazan Dmitry, unlike the other brothers, refused to learn to dance; had a threadbare plebeian friend symbolically named Poluboyarinov, whom the brothers called Polubezobedov (half-minus-dinner); and faithfully spent hours at the bedside of a poor ward of their aunt's, a woman suffering from a disease that caused her face to swell horribly, her hair to fall out, and her body to stink. This St. Julian-like display of non-squeamishness, much stressed in the *Reminiscences*, is notably missing from the moral exploits of Nikolai Levin. We can only guess at the reasons, of course. It would seem that in the self-accusing, look-how-terrible-I-was spirit of his later years, Tolstoy's strategy in the *Reminiscences* is to elevate his brother at the expense of his own earlier self, emphasizing Dmitry's moral courage and denouncing himself as one of the mockers and denigrators. In *Anna Karenina*, however, to canonize Nikolai Levin or even to represent him temporarily as Konstantin's moral superior would have upset the balance of the novel. Moreover, to celebrate Dmitry's austere Christian asceticism would have undercut the ideal of family happiness and biological fecundity that Tolstoy presents in *Anna Karenina*, via Konstantin Levin, as the solution to the ever-troublesome problem of sexuality. Later on, as John Kopper has demonstrated in a brilliant essay,[2] Tolstoy's ideals gravitated back to those of "Noah."

In the *Reminiscences* Tolstoy says that he loved his brother Dmitry with a "simple, even, natural love," a love he did not notice and does not remember, adding that such love is natural toward everyone unless offset by fear or intensified by some special attachment. For his two older

---

[2] Kopper, "Tolstoy and the Narrative of Sex."

brothers, Nikolai and Sergei, however, he, Lev, felt just this "special" love, and for Nikolai there was respect and admiration as well. "Special" love for Nikolenka and Seryozha, but only "natural" and forgotten love for Mitenka, the nearest to him in age: one is tempted to translate such subtleties into cruder language and conclude that Tolstoy liked Dmitry the least of all his brothers and perhaps did not like him much at all.

Evidence of hostility between the two brothers dating back to Dmitry's lifetime is scanty, but there are a few clues. On 13 February 1854, for instance, after passing through Moscow on his way from Bucharest to the Crimea, Tolstoy wrote in his diary that he had seen all three of his brothers, with two emotional reactions strikingly opposed: "Mitinka hurt [огорчил] me, but Seryozha gave me joy [обрадовал]." [*PSS* 46:236] Unfortunately, he gives no particulars. And a clue even more revealing, at least for those with Freudian oneiric inclinations, is found from three years earlier. In 1851, living in the Caucasus, Tolstoy wrote in his diary: "Today, December 22, I awoke from a terrible dream—the corpse of Mitinka. This was one of those dreams you don't forget. Can it mean something? I cried a lot afterwards. Feelings are truer in dreams than awake." [*PSS* 46:240] The next day he wrote Seryozha about this dream, afraid that it might be prophetic or telepathic: "What's with Mitinka? I had a very bad dream about him on December 22. Has anything happened to him?" [*PSS* 59:132] Even in this letter we can perceive a suspicious bit of censorship: to Sergei, Tolstoy writes only of a "bad dream," not a dream of Dmitry dead.

It would be wrong to maintain that Tolstoy was consistently hostile toward his brother Dmitry. Rather, his feelings were a complex mixture of the positive and negative, very much as were Konstantin Levin's toward his brother Nikolai. If irritation and antagonism, not to mention unconscious death wishes, were indeed a strong component of Tolstoy's feelings about Dmitry, however, the recollection of them would in turn evoke a reaction of guilt after Dmitry's sickness and death. And the pain of the guilt might then produce an effort to deny or mitigate the offense.

In the *Reminiscences*, written in his old age, Tolstoy professes to admire his brother Dmitry for his religious fervor and especially for his indifference to what other people thought of him, a trait he is said to have shared with the oldest brother, Nikolai; it is one that Lev Tolstoy admits he himself entirely lacked. (Indeed, acknowledging by implication that it was the thirst for fame that energized his own literary career, Tolstoy cites with approval Turgenev's observation that Nikolai Tolstoy had all the prerequisites—Tolstoy calls them defects—needed for becoming a writer except this one, vanity.) [*SS* 14:465] In general, in the *Reminiscences*

Tolstoy is clearly trying to give Dmitry every credit he can. One feels his finger on the scale in the sequence of adjectives he applies to him there: "serious, thoughtful, chaste, decisive, ardent, courageous." And to cap it all, he even as it were seeks to erase the ultimate injustice of Dmitry's early death: "How clear it is to me now that Mitenka's death did not annihilate him, that he existed before I knew him, before he was born, and that he exists now, after he has died." [SS 14:461]

Tolstoy espoused this Platonic or Hindu-like conception of immortality, of course, too late to bestow it on Nikolai Levin. But in the 1870s, in creating the character out of his memories of his brother, Tolstoy had to make countless decisions about what to include, what to omit, and what to change.

First of all, in the novel's time sequence, the *syuzhet*, Nikolai Levin appears only toward the end of his life; there is little for him to do from that point on but to sicken and die, in the process displaying his prickly personality and thus testing his brothers' charity and forbearance. But if we include all the events that precede the main action of the novel, its *Vorgeschichte*, we can compile a fairly extensive biography of Nikolai which can then be compared, item by item, with events in the real life of Dmitry Tolstoy.

After a happy childhood at Pokrovskoe, Nikolai went on to study at and graduate from the university, as Dmitry Tolstoy did at Kazan. (One might at this point cattily note in parenthesis that Tolstoy has Konstantin Levin graduate from the university, something he himself never did.) After the division of their parents' property, the youthful Dmitry Tolstoy attempted to follow the principles set forth in Gogol's much-ridiculed instructions to Russian landowners (from *Selected Passages*). Not questioning the institution of serfdom as such, he wanted to do his moral duty to his peasants, sitting in judgment on them and trying to raise their standards of behavior. This display of earnest крепостничество (paternalism toward serfs) is, of course, excluded from the characterization of Nikolai Levin, though it may remind us of the autobiographical hero of Tolstoy's much earlier "Landlord's Morning" or even of Dmitry Nekhlyudov in *Resurrection*. This exclusion, however, could be accounted for simply by the difference in time. By making his alter-ego character Konstantin Levin more than ten years younger than himself, Tolstoy moves the entire action of *Anna Karenina*, including the *Vorgeschichte*, past the Emancipation. Thus none of his characters has to confront the moral ambiguities of serf-owning, though Tolstoy has his Levin perversely sympathize, in one of the arguments at Sviyazhsky's house, with the unregenerate крепостник (former principled serf-owner) whose hardheaded realism contrasts refreshingly with the wishy-washy liberalism of Sviyazhsky himself.

In any event, Dmitry Tolstoy, like his brother Lev, did not persist very long in his efforts at benevolent serf-management. He next decided that his gentry privileges morally required service to the state. Again very much like Gogol, he bought himself a directory listing all the government departments, decided that legislation was the most important activity of government, and set out for St. Petersburg to present himself for legislative service. The reality of the bureaucracy he found there was as distant from Dmitry's idealistic dreams as it had been from Gogol's, and his bureaucratic career proved even briefer: he departed from St. Petersburg without ever serving at all. In an early draft of *Anna Karenina*, Tolstoy ascribed this same naive behavior to Nikolai Levin, having him also choose his area of service from a government directory, for which his brother Koznyshev, who through his connections could have helped Nikolai obtain a post, disparaged him as an infant and an eccentric. [PSS 20:175] The episode was later eliminated, however; perhaps this quixotic, humorous ingredient seemed out of place in the characterization of Nikolai Levin, the prevailing tones of which are irritability and gloom.

Even more out of keeping would have been another episode told of Dmitry Tolstoy in the *Reminiscences*. At one point in his search for the ideal position in St. Petersburg, Dmitry had sought advice and aid from an old acquaintance from Kazan, one Dmitry Obolensky. Dmitry Tolstoy arrived uninvited at a garden party at Obolensky's house, wearing a nankeen overcoat. Obolensky introduced him to his guests and invited him to take off his coat. This proved impossible, since Dmitry had to admit that he had nothing on underneath it! [SS 14:463] He always dressed, Tolstoy tells us, "merely to cover his body" and was totally indifferent not only to fashion but even to convention.

The sex lives of Dmitry Tolstoy and Nikolai Levin appear to coincide quite closely. Both, in their character as "Noah," lead pure, undefiled lives until their mid-twenties. At that age they both undergo a sudden transformation. Dmitry Tolstoy "began to drink, smoke, squander money, and frequent women." [SS 14:464] Nikolai Levin does the same, his associates in these diverting activities, as his brother recalls, being "the most disgusting people." In the *Reminiscences* Tolstoy puts the blame for Dmitry's downfall on a single "disgusting" individual, a family friend named Konstantin Islavin, whom he goes on to describe as an "externally very attractive, but profoundly immoral person." [SS 14:464] (It is ironic, however, that Tolstoy himself preserved for decades a warm friendship with this "profoundly immoral person," who often visited at

Yasnaya Polyana. To be sure, perhaps Tolstoy had little choice: Islavin was the Countess's uncle.)[3]

Though not by the old Tolstoy, for most of us the youthful dissipations of Dmitry Tolstoy and Nikolai Levin could be written off as fairly harmless wild oats. To be sure, at times they went rather far: Nikolai is said to have been arrested for rowdyism (буйство) and spent a night in a police station. (I have no evidence that Dmitry Tolstoy had a comparable police record.) But certain other actions are harder to forgive. According to the final text of *Anna Karenina*, Nikolai Levin is guilty of several more serious misdeeds. He took a peasant boy from a village to educate him but in a fit of rage beat the boy so badly that charges of battery were brought against him. (In the drafts it is the boy's mother who brings charges.) [*PSS* 20:174] In the *Reminiscences* the parallel incident concerning Dmitry Tolstoy is somewhat modified. There it is said that by order of their aunt and guardian, Pelageya Yushkova, when the four orphaned Tolstoy boys moved to Kazan each was assigned a serf boy as a personal servant. Dmitry's boy was called Vanyusha, and Tolstoy reports that "Mitenka treated him badly and I think even beat him. I say 'I think' because I don't remember it, I only remember his remorse for something he did to Vanyusha and his humiliating pleas for forgiveness." [*SS* 14:458] There is no mention in the *Reminiscences* of any legal case against Dmitry, and no mention in *Anna Karenina* of any remorse. Here we may perhaps stifle our psychiatric suspicions and attribute the changes to purely artistic motives. It would seem that Tolstoy, to enhance the contrast with Konstantin, wanted to make Nikolai Levin look worse than Dmitry Tolstoy. For the sake of greater simplicity and consistency Nikolai's life after the "Noah" episode is made a steady downhill slide.

To propel poor Nikolai further and faster down this slope, Tolstoy has him commit some other crimes not attested for Dmitry. During his service in the Western borderlands he beats up a foreman (старшина), and in a similar episode from the drafts he is said to have taken some tickets from a lady to exchange them and then simply stolen them.[4]

---

[3] Konstantin Aleksandrovich Islavin (1827–1903) was the son of Aleksandr Mikhailovich Islenev and Sofya Petrovna, née Countess Zavadovskaya, Princess Kozlovskaya by marriage. Princess Kozlovskaya spent most of her life with Islenev and bore him six children, but since her marriage to Prince Kozlovsky had never been legally dissolved, her children were considered illegitimate and bore the surname Islavin. Konstantin Islavin was a childhood friend of Tolstoy's. Later, Konstantin's sister Lyubov (1826–1886) married Dr. Andrei Evstafevich Bers (1808–1868) and became the mother of Sofya Andeevna Bers, later Countess Tolstaya. The "profoundly immoral" person, whom Tolstoy's children called "Uncle Kostya," thus had a double connection with the Tolstoy family.

[4] N. K. Gudzy's note in *PSS* 20:612.

Although prototype and character seem roughly similar in their overall economic behavior, Tolstoy again seems to have "heightened the colors" in his depiction of Nikolai Levin's financial dealings. At the time of his last illness, Nikolai is reduced to virtual destitution, from which he is rescued temporarily by his brothers and permanently by death. Nothing so dire seems to have been true of Dmitry Tolstoy. The financial arrangements among the four Tolstoy brothers (and one sister) are too complex to describe here in detail. After the original division of their parents' property, there were many subsequent transactions among them: they borrowed money from one another, bought and sold property, and administered one another's estates during absences, just as Konstantin Levin does for his brother and sister. It seems that all the Tolstoy brothers, very much including Lev, squandered a good deal of money, mostly by gambling; but at the time of his death Dmitry was by no means destitute, though he was short of cash. Furthermore, his general financial behavior was much less irresponsible than Nikolai Levin's. In a letter to Tolstoy of 20 October 1854, for example, he outlines his financial condition: debts amounting to 6,800 rubles, but 4,000 rubles owed to him, leaving a cash deficit of 2,800 rubles. Of the 6,800-ruble indebtedness, 4,500 rubles were owed to one Fedor Dokhturov; by the time of his death in 1856 Dmitry had repaid 1,400 rubles of this sum.[5] Thus Dmitry seems to have been making a serious effort to straighten out his affairs during his last years.

None of this effort, however, is ascribed to Nikolai Levin. Another, less creditable episode in Dmitry's financial history has, however, been faithfully transferred to the novel. In his summary history of his brother's misdeeds, Konstantin Levin recalls that after losing a large sum at cards Nikolai Levin had signed a promissory note for the money, but later claimed that he had been cheated and refused to pay. Such behavior violated the gentlemen's code outlined for us by Vronsky: gambling debts among gentlemen always take precedence over debts to tailors and such middle-class scum. Even the usually unresponsive Koznyshev is shocked by this impropriety and pays Nikolai's debt of honor for him, receiving a rude letter for his pains. Something very much like this seems to have happened with Dmitry Tolstoy, judging from a letter to Lev Tolstoy from his brother Sergei of 12 April 1853. Dmitry, Sergei writes, "keeps committing frightful stupidities... He gambled away quite a lot and in a stupid way gave promissory notes to various persons..." Later he said that "he had been forced to give the notes and doesn't want to pay. In a word, it's disgusting. He's now living in Moscow, organizing some sort of druggist's

---

[5] M. Tsiavlovsky's note in *PSS* 59:269.

shop [аптека]." [*PSS* 59:228] Tolstoy's reply to this letter does not refer to the gambling, but only to the commercial activities, which he apparently regards either as unbecoming a gentleman or simply unpromising: "I got a letter from Mitinka in which he asks me to recommend [apparently to the army] some sort of chemical supplies from his shop. Very sad."[6] In *Anna Karenina*, Konstantin Levin applies to his brother Nikolai's behavior the same epithet, "disgusting" (гадко), that Sergei Tolstoy had used to characterize Dmitry's, though, to be sure, Konstantin quickly qualifies it, reflecting that Nikolai's misdeeds seem worse to those who do not know his history and his heart as he, Konstantin, knows them.

Dmitry Tolstoy's druggist shop too almost found its way into literature, though in a poetically enlarged form. In a canceled draft for *Anna Karenina* Tolstoy has Nikolai Levin angry at his brother Koznyshev because the latter refuses to sell an estate they own in common so that he, Nikolai, can use his share to start a chemical factory (химическая фабрика) "which would bring happiness and riches to a whole province." [*PSS* 20:174] This Midas-like chemical factory was eliminated from the final version, perhaps because it lacked the ingredient of *moral* degeneration Tolstoy needed for Nikolai's prehistory.

As for the main action of the novel, the most notable change from Dmitry Tolstoy to Nikolai Levin is ideological. In the final version, as noted earlier, Nikolai is a socialist, contrasting with the academic liberalism (and, later, pan-Slavism) of Koznyshev and also with Konstantin Levin's Tolstoy-brand anarchistic, anti-urban peasantophilia. Nikolai's transformation into a socialist, however, comes rather late in the novel's genesis. It emerges as part of the novel's engagement with various social issues of the 1870s, issues with which Dmitry Tolstoy, of course, could have had no connection. In the earlier drafts Nikolai Levin's intellectual preoccupations are less up-to-date. In one version he is found translating the Bible, which he discusses animatedly, though drunkenly, with his brother. [*PSS* 20:174] The views he expresses on social questions are then more generally cynical and pessimistic—perhaps "social Darwinist"—than socialist. He applauds Konstantin's disillusionment with the zemstvos, calling such artificial institutions nothing but "lies, toys, and reshufflings of the same stupid old cards... One law," he maintains, "governs the whole world and all people as long as there will be people. If you are stronger than someone else, kill him, rob him, cover your tracks, and you are right; but if they catch you, he is right. It is not permitted to rob one man, but to rob a whole people,

---

[6] L. N. Tolstoy to S. N. Tolstoy, 20 July 1853. *PSS* 59:242.

as the Germans have robbed the French [after the Franco-Prussian war], is allowed. The man who sees this and takes advantage of it and laughs is a sage, and I am a sage." [*PSS* 20:171]

Likewise, in earlier drafts the visitor whom Konstantin encounters in Nikolai Levin's room in Moscow is not the radical ex-student Kritsky we know from the final version, expelled from the university for founding a society to help poor students and for teaching in workers' Sunday schools. Instead, the other man is simply an unsavory lawyer whom Nikolai has hired to help him collect a huge, if dubious, gambling debt.

Nikolai's socialist convictions in the final version of the novel thus appear to conflict with the general pattern observed so far, whereby Tolstoy works to make Nikolai's errors and misdeeds seem more consistently reprehensible and misguided than those of which Dmitry Tolstoy was guilty. At least most of us, surely, would regard socialism as an improvement over the social Darwinism Nikolai expounds in the earlier drafts, and one assumes that Tolstoy thought so too, even though he disapproved of the socialists for their materialism, their lack of interest in spiritual and moral values, and their assumption that society's ills were all of economic origin. One can only speculate about the reasons for this change. Perhaps social Darwinism, with its justification of unlimited mutual aggression of individuals, classes, and nations in the name of the survival of the fittest, seemed too malevolent a philosophy for Nikolai, whom Tolstoy wants us to regard as fundamentally good-hearted, however erratic and irrational his behavior may be.

It remains to compare Nikolai Levin's most important "action" in the novel, his death from tuberculosis, with the death of his prototype. Dmitry Tolstoy died in Orel on 21 January 1856, attended only by his faithful Masha and an unidentified "T.L." [*PSS* 47:65, 301] Not only was there no Kitty to brighten his room and his last days; Lev Tolstoy was not there either. Lev Tolstoy was at that time still technically in the army, stationed in Petersburg. Two weeks earlier, on 9 January, he had taken a brief leave and come to Orel to visit his dying brother, staying only one day. His diary entry for that day is laconic, but revealing. "I am in Orel. Brother Dmitry is at death's door. How the bad thoughts that used to come to me on his account have turned to dust . . . I feel terrible. I can't do anything, but I am composing a drama." [*PSS* 47:65] Back in Petersburg, Tolstoy did not learn of Dmitry's death until 2 February. His diary for that date simply records the bare fact: "I am in Petersburg. Brother Dmitry died. I learned about it today. [And continuing without a break] From tomorrow on I want to spend my days so that it will be pleasant to recollect them. Tomorrow

I will put my papers in order, write letters to [Aunt] P[elageya] I[l'inishna] and to the bailiff and will make a fair copy of 'The Snowstorm,' and in the evening, I'll drop in on Turgenev, in the morning take an hour's walk." [*PSS* 47:65] The impression is not of overwhelming grief.

There are, to be sure, expressions of grief in the letter Tolstoy duly wrote (in French) to his aunt the next day, but they seem routine and conventional:

> You probably already know the sad news of Dmitry's death. When I saw him, it was something I was already prepared for, and I would even say that it was impossible not to wish for it. I have never seen a man suffer so much as he and suffer patiently, praying to God to forgive him his sins. He died as a good Christian, and that is a great consolation for all of us; but in spite of everything you could hardly believe how painful a loss it is for me.

He added in Russian, "именно для меня" (particularly for me), as if in an effort to give some aura of sincerity to this very artificial letter. [*PSS* 60:50] Note that this passage comes after an extended discussion of where his aunt plans to live and, in that connection, of his own marriage prospects (presumably since she might think of making her home with him): "I confess to you frankly that for some time I have been thinking seriously of marriage, that involuntarily I consider all the young ladies I meet from the point of view of marriage, and that I think about it so often that if it doesn't happen to me this winter, it will never happen to me at all." [*PSS* 60:50] This proved a poor prophecy, needless to say; but the point here is that only from the topic of his dreams of marriage did Tolstoy pass on to that of Dmitry's death.

Fifty years later, looking back on this seemingly unfeeling response to the loss of his brother, Tolstoy judges himself severely:

> I was especially repulsive at that time. I came to Orel from Petersburg, where I had been going into society and was all filled with vanity. I was sorry for Mitenka, but not very. I turned around in Orel and went back, and he died a few days later. Truly, I think the worst thing about his death for me was that it prevented me from taking part in a court spectacle which was being organized at that time and to which I had been invited. [*SS* 14:464–65]

This self-accusing memory is partly confirmed, partly contradicted by the earlier reminiscences of Tolstoy's relation and confidante, Countess Aleksandra Andreevna Tolstaya. The very day Tolstoy got the news of his brother's death, she recalls, there was a party at her sister's house (not a "court spectacle") to which Tolstoy had been invited. In the morning she got a note from him to the effect that he could not come because of the news he had received. To her surprise, that evening he appeared after all. When she disapprovingly asked why, he replied, "Why? Because what I wrote you this morning was not true. You see—I came, therefore I was able to come." Moreover, according to Tolstaya, a few days later Tolstoy admitted to her that he had gone to the theater afterwards. "'And you probably had a very good time,' I said to him with even greater indignation. 'Well, no, I wouldn't say that. When I came home from the theater, there was real hell in my heart. If I had had a pistol, I would certainly have shot myself.'" Tolstaya attributes this behavior not so much to indifference or callousness on Tolstoy's part as to his fondness for conducting psychological experiments on himself. He liked, as it were, to press certain levers in his heart and then stand back and observe the results. "'I want to test myself down to the fine points,' he used to say."[7]

In any event, the picture Tolstoy draws in the *Reminiscences* of his brother Dmitry as he looked two weeks before his death is undeniably close to the image we know so well from *Anna Karenina*:

> [Dmitry] looked terrible. His huge wrist was connected to his elbow by two bones, his face was nothing but eyes, and they were splendid—serious and now inquisitive. He coughed continually and spat and did not want to die, did not want to believe that he was dying. Pockmarked Masha, whom he had bought from a brothel, with a kerchief on her head, looked after him. In my presence a thaumaturgic icon was brought at his wish. I remember the expression on his face as he prayed to it. [SS 14:464]

In his portrayal of the death of Nikolai Levin, Tolstoy may have added to his own memories of his brother's appearance and behavior some further details from the letter that brought him the news, written by the "profoundly immoral" Konstantin Islavin. It was Masha, Islavin wrote him, who came from Orel to Moscow with the news of Dmitry's death. She reported that a few hours before he died, Dmitry had at last recognized the hopelessness of his condition. He asked first for a priest, then a doctor. He wanted the doctor to make it possible for him to move to Yasnaya Polyana to die there in peace. If that were impossible, he asked to have his life prolonged by just two hours so that he could make a will.

---

[7] "Воспоминания гр. А. А. Толстой." 14.

He was very restless before death, and the doctor gave him some drops that calmed him down. He went to sleep and never woke up again. Not long before his death he asked to be buried at Yasnaya Polyana, and this was done.[8]

From these accounts it would seem that in many respects the picture of Nikolai Levin's death in *Anna Karenina* reproduces quite accurately not only the external circumstances of Dmitry Tolstoy's death, but also the dying man's behavior during his final illness. The provincial hotel, Masha, the long refusal to face the inevitability of death, the clutching at false hopes, the impassioned prayers before an icon, the demands for more doctors and more medicines, with the struggle for life subsiding into resignation only just before the end—in all this literature has faithfully reproduced life. However, precisely the most moving parts of the death scene in *Anna Karenina* are *not* taken from real memories: the deft and loving care given Nikolai Levin by his wonderful sister-in-law, Kitty, and the anguish of her husband, whose deep tenderness and pity contend with his irritation and impatience, while the stark reality of his brother's death forces him to reflect on the meaning of life itself.

In accounting for these additions, we could hypothesize that in his reconstruction of his brother's death in the novel Tolstoy was engaging in a form of retroactive wish-fulfillment. Still feeling guilty over his own callous and unsympathetic behavior at the time of Dmitry's death, he was taking the opportunity through fiction not only to relive these events but to correct them. No more would he rush back to St. Petersburg after only one day; he would sit there to the bitter end, meekly bearing all his brother's petulance and irritability, and there would be heartwarming breakthroughs of tenderness and mutual love. Such a hypothesis may well be correct, though it in no way invalidates the artistic appropriateness of these added elements in the novel.

However, these imaginary self-compensations may have been reinforced by another set of recollections from real experience. Dmitry Tolstoy's was only the first of two fraternal deaths from tuberculosis that Tolstoy had experienced long before the writing of *Anna Karenina*. The second, a far more poignant experience and more grievous loss for him, was the death of his eldest brother, Nikolai Tolstoy, some four years later, on 20 September 1860. Nikolai was the especially beloved and admired brother, a worshipped model all through the years of childhood, companion during the adventures in the Caucasus, literary consultant, and even fellow writer, author in their childhood of the celebrated myth of the green stick

---

[8] Gusev, *Материалы с 1855 по 1869 год*, 20.

on which was written the secret of how to do away with all human hostility and strife.⁹

Tolstoy did not run from the dying Nikolenka after a two-day visit; he faithfully kept a bedside vigil throughout the many long weeks that Nikolai took to expire. True, it was only in the very last phase of Nikolai's illness that Tolstoy assumed this responsibility. Earlier, Nikolai had gone abroad with Sergei to take the waters at Soden. Tolstoy himself went abroad a month later, but did not immediately join his brothers. He accompanied their sister Marya Tolstaya and her children to Berlin, sent them on to Soden, and occupied himself with his researches into educational theory, later combining these with treatments at a different spa, Kissingen in Bavaria, for illnesses of his own. (He was suffering, as he informed his "auntie" Tatyana Ergolskaya, from a terrible toothache, migraine headaches, and hemorrhoids.¹⁰) But when Sergei returned to Russia in late July, the responsibility for Nikolai, Marya, and her children fell upon Lev. In mid-August they all moved from Germany to Hyères, near Toulon, on the Mediterranean coast. A month later Nikolai died there. Tolstoy remained with him the whole time, and Nikolai expired literally in Lev's arms.

Though this experience must have been much more vivid and poignant for Tolstoy than the death of Dmitry, it left comparatively little trace in his autobiographical *Nachlass*. Though a month later he called it "the strongest impression of [his] life," it was evidently too strong for words.¹¹ He made no entries in his diary at all from the twenty-ninth of August until the thirteenth of October, some three weeks after Nikolai's death. His fullest immediate response to the event is found in his letter to Sergei of 24–25 September/6–7 October 1860:

> You must already have gotten the news of Nikolinka's death. I am sorry that you weren't here. No matter how painful it is, I am glad that it took place in my presence and that its effect on me was as it should be. It was not like the death of Mitinka, which I learned about in Petersburg when I was not thinking about him at all. This was quite another matter. With Mitinka I was bound by memories of childhood and by family ties, while this one was a genuine man for you and for me, one we loved

---

⁹ Nikolai Tolstoy's sketch "Охота на Кавказе" (Hunting in the Caucasus) was published in *Sovremennik* (no. 2, 1857), and two other works by him were discovered in his papers and published in the 1920s. (See M. A. Tsiavlovsky's note in *PSS* 59:122.) Tolstoy's diary entry for 19 January 1858 (*PSS* 48:4) testifies that Tolstoy consulted Nikolai concerning whether to leave in or exclude the tree's death from "Three Deaths." Nikolai advised him to leave it in, which he did.

¹⁰ Tolstoy to T. A. Ergolskaya, 24 July/5 August 1860. *PSS* 60:346.

¹¹ Diary entry of 13/25 October 1860. *PSS* 48:30.

and respected more than anyone on earth. You know the selfish feeling that came the last time, that the sooner the better, but now it's terrible to write that and to remember that you thought that. Until the last day he, with his extraordinary strength of character and concentration, did everything he could so as not to be a burden to me . . . As for suffering, he did suffer, but only once, a day or two before his death he said that the sleepless nights were terrible . . .

On the day of his death he asked to be dressed; and when I said that if he weren't better, Mashinka [Marya Tolstaya] and I wouldn't go to Switzerland, he said, 'Do you really think I'll get better?' in such a voice that it was clear what he felt but didn't say for my sake, and for his sake I didn't let on; however, from that morning on I seemed to know what would happen and stayed with him. He died quite without sufferings, external ones, that is. His breathing became less and less frequent, and it was over . . . I now feel what I have often heard, that when you lose such a person as he was for us, it becomes much easier to think about death.[12]

A later letter to Aleksandra Tolstaya is also revealing:

For two months I followed his fading hour by hour, and he died literally in my arms. Not only was he one of the best people I have met in my life, not only was he a brother with whom are connected the best memories of my life—he was my best friend . . . It's not only that half my life has been torn out, all my vital energy has been buried with him.[13]

And finally, one to Fet, written the same day:

I think you already know what happened. He died on our September 20, literally in my arms. Nothing in my life has made such an impression on me. He told the truth when he used to say that there is nothing worse than death. And if you really believe that it is the end of everything, then there is nothing worse than life. Why take trouble and make an effort when from what was N. N. Tolstoy nothing remains for him. He didn't say that he felt the approach of death, but I know that he followed its every step and knew for sure what was left. Several minutes before death he dozed off and suddenly awoke and whispered with horror, "What is that?" He had seen it, that swallowing up of oneself into nothingness. And if he didn't find anything to cling to, what will I find? Still less . . .

Until the last minute he didn't give in to it, he kept doing things for himself, kept trying to occupy himself, wrote, asked me about my writings, gave advice. But it seemed to me that he did this not from

---

[12] Tolstoy to S. N. Tolstoy, 24–25 September/6–7 October 1860. *PSS* 60:353–54.
[13] Tolstoy to A. A. Tolstaya, 17/29 October 1860. *PSS* 60:356.

inner inclination, but from principle . . . All those who knew him and saw his last moments say how amazingly peacefully and quietly he died, but I know how terrible and agonizing it was, because not a single feeling escaped me . . . What's the use of anything, when tomorrow the torments of death may begin with all the base vileness of lies and self-deception and will end in nothingness, in a reduction of the self to zero. What a funny joke! Be useful, be virtuous, be happy while you live, we and other people have been saying to one another for centuries; and happiness and virtue and usefulness lie in truth, and the truth which I have extracted from my 32 years is that the situation in which someone has placed us is the most terrible deception and crime, one for which we (we liberals) would not find words if a human being had placed another in such a situation. Praise Allah, God, and Brahma. What a benefactor![14]

Konstantin Levin, at the end of *Anna Karenina*, is doubtless filled with similar anger at the Creator for so cruelly condemning us all to death and extinction, though the censors (or Tolstoy's anticipation of the censors) would hardly have allowed him to express these rebellious feelings quite so bluntly. Nevertheless, the parallels are striking:

And [Levin] repeated to himself in brief the whole course of his thinking during those past two years, the beginning of which had been the clear, obvious thought of death at the sight of his hopelessly ill, beloved brother. Clearly understanding then for the first time that for him, as for every man, there was nothing ahead but suffering, death, and eternal oblivion, he had decided that one could not live like that, that one must either explain one's life in such a way that it no longer seemed the malicious mockery of some devil or else shoot oneself. But he had done neither the one nor the other. [SS 9:421]

Thus is it clear that the death of his brother Nikolai in 1860 was an overwhelming experience for Tolstoy, hurling him once more up against the question that had plagued him since childhood, of the finiteness of human life, most of all his own, and the apparent futility of all human endeavor in the face of that inexorable fact. It seems more than likely that he drew on this experience in his representation of the death of Nikolai Levin, not so much in the behavior of the dying man—for Nikolai Tolstoy was evidently much more courageous and less petulant in the face of death than Nikolai Levin (or Dmitry Tolstoy)—as in the reactions of the witnessing brother, Lev Tolstoy himself. For the death of his brother Nikolai

---

[14] Tolstoy to A. A. Fet, 17/29 October 1860. *PSS* 60:357–58.

was for Tolstoy not at all an occasion for conducting a psychological experiment in self-degradation, as he had done at the time of his brother Dmitry's death; it was the real thing.

What conclusions can we draw from this lengthy demonstration of the novel's genetic ties to the novelist's life? To be sure, the existence of these ties has long been known, but it may be of some use to have viewed their many strands in detail. Certainly, in portraying the death of Nikolai Levin in *Anna Karenina* and the response of Konstantin Levin to this death, Tolstoy did draw heavily on his own experiences at the death of his brother Dmitry, perhaps with some considerable admixture from the death of Nikolai Tolstoy. Without these experiences it seems unlikely that he could have represented Nikolai Levin's death with the consummate power he did. Tolstoy's art is introspective; his extraordinary intuitive capacities were the product of years of fascinated self-scrutiny.

However, substantial changes occur in the transition from life into art. Some of these changes seem to be externally, as it were mechanically, motivated, by the change in date and historical circumstances, since the action of the novel takes place more than a decade later than the deaths of the author's two brothers. Other changes can be viewed as necessary to produce greater symmetry, consistency, or intensity in the characterization of Nikolai Levin; at least he seems to be more consistently disagreeable and difficult than Dmitry Tolstoy was in life. Finally, some of the changes seem to originate in the author's emotional needs—in those wish-fulfillment fantasies he needed to assuage the guilt he felt over his relationship with Dmitry, over his attitude toward Dmitry's death, and perhaps over the simple fact that he had remained alive while these two blood brothers had, through no fault of their own, perished.

There is undoubtedly artistic danger when a novel, especially a novel whose strength depends so heavily on the representation of psychological truth (or what the reader accepts as psychological truth), becomes a vehicle for the author's imaginary wish-fulfillments: it runs the risk of foundering in emotional spuriousness, sentimentality. Art becomes cover-up, not revelation. If Tolstoy avoids this pitfall, it is because in the crossfire of relentless self-directed aggression he maintained toward himself, and even toward such a favored alter-ego character as Konstantin Levin, it was almost impossible for sentimentality to survive. Even if Tolstoy could not quite bring himself to name the intense fraternal rivalry that fueled his own powerful drive to overtake and surpass (догнать и перегнать) his brothers, he actually did represent it forthrightly in the person of Konstantin Levin, even to the point of triumph at his brother's deathbed. And even if

Tolstoy, via Konstantin Levin, gratifyingly represented his behavior at his brother Dmitry's deathbed as having been more devoted and sympathetic than it actually was, he was in fact only substituting his own truly devoted and sympathetic behavior at the bedside of his brother Nikolai. And if he, by the power of imagination, made his wife, Sofya Andreevna, care for a dying brother-in-law she never met, he had by the time of *Anna Karenina* seen her display comparable solicitude at countless sickbeds, including his own, and at least two deathbeds, those of their baby sons Petr, who died in 1873, and Nikolai, who died in 1875.

It would appear, therefore, that our scrutiny of the case of Nikolai Levin has succeeded only in demonstrating once more that fundamental paradox of art, especially realistic art: "truth" in art and "truth" in life are not to be equated. Fiction inevitably incorporates elements from both experience and imagination. Some experiences are reproduced intact, others are altered or recombined, and both may be interlarded with wholly imaginary events and personalities. The motives for these manipulations may sometimes be influenced by extra-literary emotions stemming from the author's own life, including wish-fulfillment, denial, and cover-up; but it must be remembered that even alterations of literal, biographical truths so influenced may prove altogether appropriate in an artistic setting, conveying deep and universal truths about human life.

Which English *Anna*?[1]

We Slavists are frequently asked by our anglophone friends, "Which translation of *Anna Karenina* shall I read?" If I am being strictly honest, I have always been forced to respond, "I don't know; I have never seriously compared the existing ones." When pressed, I have sometimes added, "I suspect the one by Louise and Aylmer Maude is probably the best. They were an English couple who lived in Russia for many years and must have known Russian well. They were educated, wrote and spoke the King's English. Moreover, Aylmer Maude was a disciple of Tolstoy, author of a thoughtful and well-written biography of the master; he knew Tolstoy well. It is hard to imagine a better set of qualifications. The Maudes' version must be the best." I must shamefully confess that even in assigning the novel in classes, I was governed more by considerations of availability and

---

[1] I am grateful for many valuable suggestions for improvements to this review article made by friends and colleagues: Robert P. Hughes, Simon Karlinsky, James L. Rice, Brian Horowitz, Anne Hruska, and C. J. G. Turner. My esteemed colleague Liza Knapp has herself written a sensitive appraisal of *Anna Karenina* translations for the MLA teacher's guide to the novel (Liza Knapp and Amy Mandelker, eds, *Approaches to Teaching Tolstoy's* Anna Karenina) which I found most valuable and stimulating. Professor Knapp has also kindly called my attention to yet another earlier toiler in this arduous vineyard, Richard Sheldon, whose thoughtful and discriminating article, "Problems in the English Translations of *Anna Karenina*," appeared in *Essays in the Art and Theory of Translation*, ed. Lenore A. Grenoble and John M. Kopper (Lewiston, N.Y.: The Edwin Mellon Press, 1997), 231–264. Professor Sheldon and I disagree on some points—Joel Carmichael wins the prize in his contest—but our very disagreements are indicative of the difficulty and elusiveness of the very process of translation, with its countless effortful approximations, painful choices, and regrettable compromises.

especially price than by any judgment of quality. In the process, however, of writing a review, commissioned by the *Tolstoy Studies Journal*, of the new *Anna* translated by Richard Pevear and Larissa Volokhonsky, I came to the conclusion that the review would be more useful if I made at least some effort to compare the new version with others currently available on the market. However, I will still keep the PV translation in the foreground of my attention.

By my count since the novel's appearance in 1877 there have been nine different English translations of *Anna Karenina*, beginning with Nathan Haskell Dole's in 1886. Some of these have been reissued many times, sometimes in revised form. The continued popularity of the book is astounding. People *en masse* keep buying and presumably reading *Anna Karenina*. No less than seven different versions are now (2005) *in print*. It seems to be worth publishers' while to keep them available, in the hope of capturing at least some of this lucrative market. The seven to choose from are the following:

1. Leo Tolstoy, *Anna Karenina. A Novel in Eight Parts.* Translated by Richard Pevear and Larissa Volokhonsky [New York] Viking [2001]. Hereafter PV.

2. Louise and Aylmer Maude, revised by George Gibian. 2nd ed. (N.Y.: W. W. Norton, 1995). Hereafter MG.

3. Constance Garnett, revised by Leonard J. Kent and Nina Berberova. (N.Y.: The Modern Library, first edition, 1965). Hereafter GKB.

4. Rosemary Edmonds, revised edition (Penguin Books, 1978). Hereafter RE.

5. David Magarshack (Signet Classics, 1961). Hereafter DM.

6. Joel Carmichael (Bantam Books, 1960). Hereafter JC.

7. The Maude translation without the Gibian corrections or appended critical articles is also on the market in the Oxford World's Classics series, but I have not included it in my discussion, on the presumption that Maude corrected is necessarily better than Maude virgin. However, Maude virgin does have good commentaries by W. Gareth Jones.

Pevear and Volokhonsky have been very active as translators from the Russian for some years now. Some of their translations from Dostoevsky have received praise from such distinguished and discriminating critics as Donald Fanger and Michael Henry Heim, their remarks emblazoned on the dust cover of their *Anna*. Pevear and Volokhonsky have also translated from Gogol and Bulgakov. One therefore approached this new translation of *Anna Karenina* with high expectations. Unfortunately, in my judgment these hopes, though not exactly dashed, must now be qualified. The PV translation, while perfectly adequate, is in my view not consistently or unequivocally superior to others on the market. I will try to justify this opinion with a series of direct comparisons of the six versions, but first I will record some initial impressions of the newcomer.

First, PV are to be commended for supplying explanatory notes, 19 pages of them, though inconveniently tucked away at the back of the book. Surely notes are needed. There are in the novel many literary references and allusions to specifics of Russian culture, society, and history that would not be comprehensible to most present-day English-speaking readers. Yet of the six translations now available, three, RE, DM, and JC, have no notes at all. Regrettably, however, PV's notes are not all they might be. They say they are partly indebted for them to the commentaries [by E. G. Babaev, though they do not mention his name] in the 22-volume "Khudozhestvennaia Literatura" Russian edition of Tolstoy's works (vols. 8 and 9, 1981–82) and to Vladimir Nabokov's *Lectures on Russian Literature*—two perfectly good sources. Yet it is most unfortunate that they were apparently unaware of the existence of the *Karenina Companion* by C. J. G. Turner (1993), which is not cited in their bibliography. Turner's book provides fuller and more accurate notes than the Russian edition and would have saved PV from errors.

PV's notes get off to a bad start right on p. 2 with *Il mio tesoro*, sung by the glass tables in Stiva Oblonsky's dream. They have the right opera (*Don Giovanni*), but the aria is surely not the one they cite, "Deh vieni alla finestra," sung by Don Giovanni himself, which contains the words *o mio tesoro*. It is rather the famous tenor aria sung by Don Ottavio in Act II, which begins, and is always known as, precisely *Il mio tesoro*. (Here, to be sure, Turner would not have helped them, since he says only that the aria is from *Don Giovanni*.)[2] Turner would, however (p. 132), have rescued them from another operatic error carried over from their Russian source (vol. 8, p. 481), which ascribes the whimsical German lines, "Himmlisch ist's," recited by Stiva (I, 11) to justify his hedonism, to the libretto of *Fledermaus*. But these lines are just not there, as Turner found after a diligent search (concerning which he and I once corresponded). The lines come, misquoted, from Heine's *Reisebilder*. I note that GKB (p. 49) also gives the correct source.

Another problem one encounters at once in considering the new translation is its textual source. PV got help with their notes from the 1981–82 edition, but was this the text they translated from? Russian texts

---

[2] In connection with *Don Giovanni*, I would like to remind readers of the excellent article by Ian Saylor, "*Anna Karenina* and *Don Giovanni*: The Vengeance Motif in Oblonsky's Dream," *Tolstoy Studies Journal*, VIII (1995–96), 112–16.

of *Anna Karenina* are not all the same. A new version was established in 1970 for the "Literaturnye Pamiatniki" edition by the joint efforts of another husband-and-wife team, Evelina Zaidenshnur and Vladimir Zhdanov, who went back to the manuscripts and corrected proofs with the particular aim of establishing a "pure Tolstoyan" text by eliminating corrections made by others, notably by Sofia Andreevna (Countess Tolstaya) and Nikolai Strakhov. (One could, of course, argue about the legitimacy of some of these restorations, since Strakhov's corrections, at least, were made at Tolstoy's behest and presumably with his approval.) One significant omission, almost surely inadvertent and restored in 1970, occurred early in the novel. It undoubtedly happened not by anyone's deliberate corrections, but through a process known as "haplography," where the copyist's eye jumps from the first of two identical words or phrases to the second, omitting what lies between. Such an omitted passage informs us that at first Stiva *did* feel some remorse about his infidelities:

> Он не мог теперь раскаиваться в том, в чем он раскаивался лет шесть тому назад, когда он впервые изменил жену. Он не мог раскаиваться в том, что . . . etc. [He could not now repent what he had repented six years before, when he had for the first time been unfaithful to his wife. He could not repent of . . .]

PV omit this passage, as do all the other translators except RE, which would indicate that PV took no account of the 1970 Zaidenshnur-Zhdanov text. It also shows that they did not translate from the 1981–82 edition from which they took their notes, since this edition reproduces the 1970 text. (The omission of this sentence in MG was duly noted by C. J. G. Turner in a valuable article, "The Maude Translation of *Anna Karenina*: Some Observations.")

The sentence does, however, appear in RE, p. 15 (in 1978 she revised her translation, originally published in 1954, in the light of the 1970 text):

> He could not now do penance for something he had reproached himself for half a dozen years ago, when he had first been unfaithful to his wife.

One could, of course, find fault with RE's rendition of this sentence. "Do penance" seems to imply a more active display of contrition than mere "repent," and although Tolstoy uses the same word, *raskaivat'sia*, twice, RE avoids the repetition and substitutes "reproached himself" on its second occurrence — a typical instance of the way well-schooled, style-conscious translators insist on rescuing Tolstoy from his awkwardnesses.

In their introduction (p. xvii) PV advertise their policy precisely of preserving the "robust awkwardness" of Tolstoy's style with its frequent repetitions. Yet already on p. 1 they violate this principle. Tolstoy writes:

> Положение это мучительно чувствовалось и самими супругами, и всеми членами семьи, и домочадцами. Все члены семьи чувствовали . . . [The situation was painfully felt by the couple themselves and by all the members of the family and by the servants. All the members of the family and the servants felt . . .]

PV translate:

> The situation was painfully felt by the couple themselves as well as by all the members of the family and household. *They* felt . . .

PV, like MG and RE, cannot bear the "robust awkwardness" of repeating "All the family members and servants felt . . . " and therefore substitute for this sequence the pronoun "they." One might also question the word "household" in the PV version as the equivalent of "domochadtsy," which here can only mean "servants," since Tolstoy clearly distinguishes them from "family members." The other translators do better with the repetition, though none is perfect. GKB have "every person in the house" for the second occurrence; DM, "all the members of the family"; and JC, "everyone in the house."

To test to my overall judgment I ran a sort of contest, taking somewhat arbitrarily chosen passages from the novel and comparing the renditions in the six English versions. Several of the selections were suggested to me by Edwina Cruise, for whose assistance I am most grateful.

1. The first passage (I, 2) presents in *erlebte Rede* Stiva's reasons why Dolly, in view of her physical deterioration and other limitations, should be tolerant of his philanderings. (It is, of course, clear to us readers that the author's attitude toward Stiva's rationalizations is ironic):

> Она [Долли], истощенная, состарившаяся, уже некрасивая женщина и ничем не замечательная, простая, только добрая мать семейства . . .
>
> PV: She [Dolly] a worn-out, aged, no longer beautiful woman, not remarkable for anything, simple, merely a kind mother of a family . . .

Here Tolstoy's order has been followed exactly, but two words trouble me. "Aged," if pronounced in two syllables, is clearly wrong; it makes Dolly much too old. It might possibly do if pronounced in one syllable, but this very ambiguity could be imputed as a fault. The other questionable choice is "kind." The novel shows that Dolly's qualities as a mother go far beyond mere "kindness": she is most of all a *responsible* parent, as her husband is not, as well as a loving one. Surely the more inclusive term "good" would have been a better choice.

> MG: She . . . was nothing but an excellent mother of a family, worn-out, already growing elderly, no longer pretty, and in no way remarkable— in fact, quite an ordinary woman.

The sentence has been recast far more than it needed to be, with the superfluous addition of the phrase after the dash, which has no equivalent in the original except the word "prostaia." Like "aged," "already growing elderly" seems to add too many years to poor Dolly's age (33), even allowing for Stiva's bias.

> GKB: She, a worn-out woman no longer young or good-looking and in no way remarkable or interesting, merely a good mother.

This version seems almost faultless: "no longer young" seems a good choice for the "sostarivshaiasia," which PV and MG have botched. However, "prostaia" is not adequately rendered by "in no way . . . interesting."

> RE: She was a good mother, but she was already faded and plain and no longer young, a simple, uninteresting woman.

Here the transpositions simplify the syntax, but at the same time change Tolstoy's, i.e., Stiva's, emphasis—Stiva by no means puts Dolly's qualities as a mother in first place. However, the word choices generally seem good, except that "plain" in the sense of "not pretty" may be felt as a Briticism unfamiliar to young Americans.

> DM: . . . worn-out, old before her time, and plain as she was, and a kind though rather simple and in no way remarkable mother

Far too much transposition, with the result that "simple and in no way remarkable" are incorrectly made to pertain to Dolly's qualities as a mother rather than as a woman. Again my strictures against "kind" and "plain" apply.

> JC: a completely undistinguished woman like her, worn-out, aging, already plain, just a simple, goodhearted mother of a family.

Again too much transposition, and again "simple" is applied to Dolly as a mother rather than in general. "Goodhearted" has the same limitations as "kind." (Incidentally, I calculate that Dolly's maternal statistics fit almost exactly those of Sofia Andreevna, who was just Dolly's age, 33, in 1877, when *Anna Karenina* was finished. She had already borne seven children, of whom two had died, and would deliver her eighth that year.)

2. Stiva has three levels of acquaintance among the rich and powerful (I, 5):

> Одна треть . . . были приятелями его отца и знали его в рубашечке; другая треть были с ним на "ты", а третья треть — были хорошие знакомые.
>
> PV: One third . . . were his father's friends and had known him in petticoats; another third were on familiar terms with him, and the final third were good acquaintances.

I had some difficulty with "petticoats," which to me are garments worn by women, not babies; but I learned that "to have known one in petticoats," i.e., since infancy, is a set idiomatic expression, current at least in Britain and enshrined in the small Oxford dictionary. All the same, it may puzzle American readers if their vocabulary is as limited as mine. More important is whether the gradation between class two, "on familiar terms," and the more distant class three, "good acquaintances," is adequately expressed. Perhaps "close friends" for "na 'ty'," and "cordial acquaintances" for "khoroshie znakomye" would be better. As the Russian text shows, instead of "final third" Tolstoy actually wrote "third third," a repetition perhaps corrected by Strakhov and restored in the 1970 edition.

> MG: One third . . . were his father's friends and had known him as a baby; he was on intimate terms with another third, and was well acquainted with the last third.

This version gets the distinction between class two and class three pretty well, but one might regret the loss of the metonymy of the "petticoats" or some equivalent.

> GKB: One third . . . had been friends of his father's, and had known him in diapers; another third were his intimate chums; and the remainder were friendly acquaintances.

Here the metonymy has been changed to a mundane garment more familiar to American babies (the original Garnett version had "petticoats"). "Chums" also seems good for Stiva's easygoing relationships.

> RE: A third . . . were his father's friends and had known him from the time he was a baby in petticoats; he was on intimate terms with another third; and the rest were his good acquaintances.

RE was the only translator to use the 1970 text, but she typically could not stomach "third third" and substituted "the rest." The insertion of "a baby" seems superfluous, but the rest is adequate.

> DM: A third . . . were his father's friends and had known him as a baby; another third were on intimate terms with him; and the remainder were his good friends and acquaintances.

Again, the "petticoat" metonymy is lost; "remainder" needlessly avoids the repetition of "third"; and "friends and" is superfluous baggage.

> JC: A third . . . had been friends of his father's and had known him in swaddling clothes; another third were on intimate terms with him; and the rest knew him very well.

A new metonymy is substituted for the petticoats, though one may still wonder how many American students have any clear idea what "swaddling clothes" are, though they may possibly remember the phrase from the Nativity story; "knew him very well" seems weak and ambiguous as an equivalent of "khoroshie znakomye."

3. The distinction between "ty" and "vy" always presents problems in English. As we saw above, all the translators render "na 'ty'" as "on intimate (familiar) terms," and that seems a reasonable solution, although it is vaguer and less vivid than the original and carries no reference to linguistic symbolism. Earlier, all the translators found the same successful solution to this problem in rendering Dolly's angry tirade (I, 4) against her errant husband. She had been using the formal "vy," as if to convey that to her he was now no more than a stranger; but in the course of the dialogue she softens a bit and shifts to the more natural spousal "ty," for which he feels grateful. All the translators render this change by having her insert the nickname "Stiva" in the "ty" passage—a very good solution. More problematic is the "ty-vy" usage in the case of Nikolai Levin's companion, Masha, the former prostitute (I, 25). Konstantin Levin, to make conversation, addresses a question to her, "Вы никогда прежде не были в Москве?" Nikolai reproves his brother for addressing Masha so formally; the only person who had ever called her "vy," he says, was the magistrate who questioned her when she was being tried for trying to escape from the brothel: "Да не говори ей *вы*. Она этого боится."

What is one to do? Apparently none of the professional translators could think of any way of translating that question so that it sounds especially formal or polite, though a possible solution did occur to me in the middle of the night: "Might I ask if this is the first time you have been in Moscow?" Only GKB confront the problem head-on, using a footnote to explain what "vy" and "ty" are. Then Nikolai can say, "Don't say 'vy' to her. It frightens her." PV have Konstantin insert the word "miss" in his question: "You've never been to Moscow before, miss?" To which Nikolai replies, "Don't call her 'miss.' She's afraid of it." It seems a creditable solution, although calling her "miss" does not seem to me quite natural. The best solution would have been to have him address her by her first name and patronymic, Mar'ia Nikolaevna, but it appears that Konstantin had never been properly introduced to her and did not know them. *We* have been informed of them by the narrator.

> MG: "You were never in Moscow before?" Constantine asked very politely . . . "Don't speak to her in that way. It frightens her."

It is hard to see how the wording of this question can be described as "very polite"; the reader must surmise that there must have been something special about Konstantin's facial expression or tone.

> RE: "You were never in Moscow before?" . . . "Only you mustn't be polite and formal with her. It frightens her."

The same strictures apply as to MG.

> DM: "You were never in Moscow before?" "Don't be so formal with her. It. Frightens her."

Same comments.

> JC: "Have you been to Moscow before?" "Don't speak to her so politely."

No better. JC also has an especially unsatisfactory way of rendering the *imia-otchestvo*, for instance, as used by Masha in addressing Nikolai Levin. "Nikolai Dmitrich" is transformed into "Mr. Nicholas," which makes her sound a bit like a black slave in the ante-bellum south. PV, incidentally, add a footnote citing Nabokov to explain the marked class difference in this usage. The low-class Masha calling Nikolai "vy" and "Nikolai Dmitrich" is quite different from the aristocratic Dolly's change from "vy" to "ty" in addressing Stiva.

4. Edwina Cruise has kindly called my attention to an instance where PV, along with others, fail to reproduce one of Tolstoy's verbal echoes, which play such an important part as linkages among different parts of the text. For example, Tolstoy uses the same words to describe the feelings aroused in Anna by Vronsky (I, 29) as she returns by train from Moscow to Petersburg (не страшно, а весело) and those experienced by Vronsky (II, 21) before the race (было и страшно и весело). None of the translators appears to have noticed the connection or reproduced it.

> PV: Anna: "not frightening, but exhilarating." Vronsky: "both terrifying and joyful."
> MG: Anna: "did not seem dreadful, but amusing." Vronsky: "both frightening and joyful."
> GKB: Anna: "not terrible, but delightful." Vronsky: "both dreadful and delicious."
> RE: Anna: "far from seeming dreadful, was rather pleasant." Vronsky: "both disgraceful and delicious" [that "disgraceful" seems uncalled-for].
> DM: Anna: "not terrifying but amusing." Vronsky: "both terrifying and joyful."
> JC: Anna: "it wasn't at all terrifying, it was gay." Vronsky: "both terrifying and joyful."

5. Professor Cruise commends PV for retaining Tolstoy's or his characters' ways of referring to people: sometimes by first name and patronymic, sometimes by surname, sometimes by first name alone, sometimes by nickname. Though foreign readers may at first have some difficulty in adjusting to this system and recognizing its symbolisms, they can be helped, as they are by PV, by providing an introductory list of characters with all their possible appellations. In the long run this seems to me better than trying to devise English equivalents. I noted above my dislike of JC's having Masha address Nikolai Levin as "Mr. Nicholas." Professor Cruise notes in particular how in Part III, Chapters 13 and 14, when Tolstoy is conveying Karenin's thoughts and feelings as he contemplates what to do now that Anna has confessed to him her infidelity, Tolstoy refers to him consistently as "Aleksei Aleksandrovich," which seems to convey a somewhat respectful attitude, as to a man of status and dignity, with whom we are already acquainted. On the other hand, in the narrator's text at this point Anna is always "Anna" and Vronsky "Vronsky"—which is how they would figure in Karenin's mind. The only change occurs when Karenin (or I should say Aleksei Aleksandrovich) addresses a servant concerning his wife; then she properly becomes "Anna Arkad'evna." How do the translators handle this usage? PV loyally follow Tolstoy throughout, except for one shift, apparently to avoid repetition, from Aleksei Aleksandrovich to "Karenin."

MG change all references from "Aleksei Aleksandrovich" to "Karenin." GKB retain "Aleksei Aleksandrovich" throughout and thus win this round. Both DM and JC consistently change to "Karenin."

6. Professor Cruise likewise called my attention to a characteristic Tolstoyan sentence (in IV, 9), a comic build-up to a rhetorical climax, in which a series of anticipatory phrases is finally resolved by a long-awaited main verb. Stiva Oblonsky, playing matchmaker but with typical unobtrusive tact, contrives to seat Kitty and Levin next to each other at a dinner party:

> Совершенно незаметно, не взглянув на них, а так, как будто уже некуда было больше посадить, Степан Аркадьич посадил Левина и Китти рядом.

How good are the translators at reproducing this effect?

> PV: Quite inconspicuously, without looking at them, but just like that, as if there were nowhere else to seat them, Stepan Arkadyevich placed Levin and Kitty next to each other.

Here the climax works well, but there is a slight expansion of Tolstoy's jest. PV's "just like that" would be appropriate only if the Russian read "a *prosto* tak, kak budto." As it stands, the phrase "tak, kak budto" means nothing more than "as if."

> MG: Quite casually, without looking at them, and just as if there were nowhere else to put them, Oblonsky placed Levin and Kitty side by side.

Almost perfect, except that Stiva's *imia-otchestvo* has been replaced by his surname.

> GKB: Quite without attracting notice, without glancing at them, as though there were no other place left, Stepan Arkadyevich seated Levin and Kitty side by side.

Also good, but "no other places left" is not quite accurate.

> RE: Quite casually, without looking at them, and as though there were no other place to put them, Oblonsky sat Levin and Kitty beside each other.

Same comment as for MG.

> DM: Quite casually, without looking at them, and as though there were no other place to put them, Oblonsky made Levin and Kitty sit side by side at the dining table.

The addition of "at the dining table" is unnecessary.

> JC: Quite casually, without looking at them but as though there were no other place for them to sit, Oblonsky seated Levin and Kitty side by side.

Again the change of Stiva's name; shift from transitive "seat" to intransitive "sit," with a different implied subject.

Note that *all* the translators avoid Tolstoy's repetition of the verb "to seat" (posadit' . . . posadil). However, all of them do, as Tolstoy did, place this single sentence in a separate paragraph, resisting the frequent temptation to straighten out Tolstoy's eccentric paragraphing.

7. Professor Cruise has also singled out what she thinks may be "the longest sentence in the novel." It occurs in V, 22, where Tolstoy is conveying the thoughts of Karenin, brooding over his predicament after a consoling conversation with Countess Lidiia Ivanovna:

> Правда, что легкость и ошибочность этого представления о своей вере смутно чувствовалось Алексею Александровичу, и он знал, что когда он, вовсе не думая о том, что его прощение есть действие высшей силы, отдался этому непосредственному чувству, он испытал больше счастья, чем когда он, как теперь, каждую минуту думал, что в его душе живет Христос, и что, подписывая бумаги, он исполняет Его волю; но для Алексея Александровича было необходимо так думать, ему было так необходимо в его унижении иметь ту, хотя бы и выдуманную высоту, с которой он, презираемый всеми, мог бы презирать других, что он держался, как за спасение, за свое мнимое спасение.

It would be too long to reproduce all the translations of this marathon sentence, but let us quote the one in PV (p. 511), which wins the round by being the only one to preserve Tolstoy's single sentence intact:

> It is true that Alexei Alexandrovich vaguely sensed the levity [this word, implying "frivolousness," does not seem quite right; perhaps "superficiality" or "lack of substance" would be better] and erroneousness of this notion of his faith, and he knew that when, without any thought that his forgiveness was the effect of a higher power, he had given himself to his spontaneous feeling, he had experienced greater happiness than when he thought every minute, as he did now, that Christ lived in his soul, and that by signing papers he was fulfilling His will; but it was necessary for him to think that way, it was so necessary for him in his humiliation to possess at least an invented loftiness from which he, despised by everyone, could despise others, that he clung to his imaginary salvation as if it were salvation indeed.

Though all the translators duly follow Tolstoy in placing this sentence in an independent paragraph, none of the others could resist the impulse to "fix" Tolstoy's cumbersome and involved syntax, to clarify and simplify. Were they right to do so? The question goes to the heart of the whole philosophy of translation. In my opinion, it is an illegitimate intrusion, where translators impose themselves as co-authors. Translators should not make themselves into editors.

MG break the long sentence into three, which perhaps makes the passage clearer, but defeats whatever purpose Tolstoy had in constructing such a complex sentence, perhaps designed to encapsulate the confusion and conflicting impulses in Karenin's mind. Like other translators but not PV, MG avoid Tolstoy's repetition of the word "salvation" at the end.

GKB: Two sentences; one "salvation."
RE: Two sentences, one "salvation."
DM: Three sentences, two "salvations."
JC: Two sentences, two "salvations."

Professor Cruise next calls attention to a passage in VI, 16, where Tolstoy has Levin use the word *nepriiatno* four times in six lines to convey the conflicting feelings aroused in him by Dolly's plan to visit Anna at Vronsky's estate, using horses hired for the trip. In the first place he is at best ambivalent about her going there at all; further, as her host he feels obliged to provide her with horses, even though his horses are needed for farm work. He is also secretly bothered by the thought that his ordinary farm horses will look disreputable by comparison with Vronsky's elegant ones, and his rivalry with Vronsky stirs in him old emotions. Rendering the word *nepriiatno* as "unpleasant," PV faithfully repeat it four times. This score is equaled only by MG. All the others translate the word differently, and none of these versions is repeated four times. GKB has "dislike" three times and "distasteful" once. RE has three variants: "disapprove," "less pleasant," and "not very nice," with one *nepriiatno* omitted entirely by the use of an implied verb: "And if I did . . . , [i.e., disapprove]." DM have three variants: "am against," "against," "resent," and "unpleasant."

JC has "disagreeable" twice, "more so" once, and omits one entirely, also by the use of implication: even if it were [i.e., disagreeable]. Of course, it could be argued that it is more important to have Levin speak normal colloquial English than to echo Tolstoy's insistent repetitions, but I would disagree, asserting that Tolstoy could have varied Levin's language just as inventively as any translator had he chosen to do so; but he did not, perhaps to show that Levin's inner conflicts render him a bit tongue-tied.

8. Another interesting passage occurs in VII, 14, where Tolstoy is conveying Levin's feelings at the time of the birth of his son. A parallel is drawn between two basic biological events, birth and death, the happy present occasion of Kitty's delivery (despite all her agony) being contrasted with the recollected sadness of his brother Nikolai's demise. Both these events are transcendental occasions for Levin, experiences that lift him out of the run of ordinary life into awareness of something higher. In this connection Tolstoy uses the verb *sovershat'sia*, "to be accomplished":

> Он знал и чувствовал только, что то, что совершалось, было подобно тому, что совершалось год тому назад . . . .Но и то горе и эта радость . . . были в этой обычной жизни как будто отверстие, сквозь которое показывалось что-то высшее. И одинаково тяжело, мучительно наступало совершающееся.

PV deserve great credit for rendering *sovershat'sia* as "to be accomplished" on all its occurrences. MG, however, like several others, translate it with "to happen." Yet Tolstoy could himself have used a more usual Russian verb, such as *sluchit'sia* or *proizoiti*. However, he chose *sovershit'sia* instead, as if to imply some element of purposefulness in these events. Tolstoy, via Levin, is asserting that birth and death are more than mere "happenings"; they have cosmic dimensions. There is also a more serious error in MG:

> But that sorrow and this joy . . . were like openings in that usual life through which something higher became visible. And as in that case, what was *not* [sic; my italics] being accomplished came harshly, painfully, incomprehensibly.

The presence of that "not" is itself incomprehensible, completely unjustified, and a most disturbing error that seriously distorts the meaning of the passage. (Professor Turner identifies another instance in MG of a totally unjustified negation: see "The Maude Translation," p. 235.)

GKB also use "to happen," and they have omitted the whole phrase beginning "And just as painful . . ." I note that this phrase was also omitted in the original Garnett translation, and Kent and Berberova did not catch the mistake.

RE, like others, writes "happen" for the first two appearances of *sovershat'sia*, but on its third occurrence she not only renders it "to be accomplished," but even manages a repetition not in the original: "And what was being accomplished now, as in that other moment, was accomplished harshly, painfully."

DM uses "to happen" three times and also loses the effect of Tolstoy's inversion in the last sentence. JC has "happen" twice and "accomplished" once; he also eliminates the inversion. PV clearly win this round.

9. One final example, the account of Anna's suicide in VII, 31.

> . . . что-то огромное, неумолимое толкнуло ее в голову и потащило за спину. "Господи, прости мне все!" проговорила она, чувствуя невозможность борьбы. Мужичок, приговаривая что-то, работал над железом. И свеча, при которой она читала исполненную тревог, обманов, горя и зла книгу, вспыхнула более ярким, чем когда-нибудь, светом, и осветила ей все то, что прежде было во мраке, затрещала, стала меркнуть и навсегда потухла.

Tolstoy begins with the horrendous image of the terrible, inexorable, crushing wheels of the train, advancing and colliding with Anna's body. She has time for one last prayer and then surrenders to the inevitable. The next sentence is ambiguous: there may be a real workman whose presence Anna dimly perceives, linking him with an ominous figure that has appeared in her life several times before, both in reality and in dreams, going back to the workman crushed by a train at the very beginning of the novel (and the beginning of her acquaintance with Vronsky); or this may be only a fantasy, a creature of Anna's soon-to-be-extinguished brain. Finally, Tolstoy invokes an entirely metaphorical candle by whose light Anna can now read, in her last moments of consciousness, the entire "book" of her life, before the candle goes out forever.

I will intersperse my comments on the translations in brackets within the texts.

> PV: . . . something huge and implacable pushed at her head [although "pushed at" may be a correct rendition of *tolknulo v*, it does not seem to me adequate to convey the collision between the wheels and Anna's head] and dragged over her [this phrase too seems to me obscure. The wheels could drag the body, but how could they drag *over* it? And the "za spinu" has been entirely omitted.] "Lord, forgive me for everything!" she said, feeling the impossibility of any struggle. A little muzhik, muttering to himself, was working over some iron." [This rendition is perhaps too literal, since *rabotat' nad chem-to* usually means to work *on* something. The "iron" possibly indicates the rails, as MG and RE render it (illegitimately, in my opinion), apparently assuming that this *muzhichok* is really present. But the word "iron" is needed, as an echo of Anna's previous encounters with this workman, real and oneiric, in which the word "iron" invariably occurs, sometimes in French: "Il faut le battre le fer . . ." The Russian term for "railroad," *zheleznaia doroga*, "iron road," is also relevant, as well as countless metaphors about

the hardness of iron.] And the candle by the light of which she had been reading that book filled with anxiety, deceptions, grief and evil, flared up brighter than ever [why not "with a brighter light than ever," as in the original?] lit up for her all that had once been in darkness, sputtered, grew [began to grow] dim, and went out for ever. [It is interesting that *all* the translators change Tolstoy's word order here, making the sentence conclude with the powerful word "forever." This is understandable if *"potukhla"* is rendered with such a low-style term as "went out"; "forever went out" seems too anticlimactic. However, "was forever extinguished" might be dignified enough.]

MG: . . . something huge and relentless struck her on the head and dragged her down [again, *za spinu* is omitted]. "God forgive me everything!" she said, feeling the impossibility of struggling. A little peasant muttering something was working at the rails [see above concerning these rails]. The candle, by the light of which she had been reading that book filled with anxieties, deception, grief and evil flared up with a brighter light than before, lit up for her all that had before been dark, flickered, began to grow dim, and went out for ever. [Quite good on the physical images, but the change from "iron" to "rails" is editing, not translating.]

GKB: . . . something huge and merciless struck her on the head and dragged her down on her back. "Lord, forgive me everything!" she said, feeling it impossible to struggle. A peasant muttering something was working above [on?] the iron. And the light of the candle by which she had read the book filled with troubles, falsehoods, sorrow, and evil flared up more brightly [with a brighter light] than ever before, lighted up for her all that had been shrouded in darkness [the addition of this shroud seems to me unnecessary], flickered, began to grow dim, and was quenched forever. [I have some qualms about the word "quench" in the meaning of "extinguish." In this sense it is marked "chiefly poet. or rhet." in the Oxford dictionary, whereas Tolstoy's *potukhla* has no such overtones.]

RE: . . . something huge and relentless struck her on the head and dragged her down on her back. "God forgive me everything!" she murmured [Tolstoy says simply "said"], feeling the impossibility of struggling. A little peasant, muttering something, was working at the rails [again!]. And the candle by which she had been reading the book filled with trouble and deceit, sorrow and evil, flared up with a brighter light, illuminating for her everything that before had been enshrouded [again that shroud!] in darkness, flickered, grew dim, and went out for ever.

DM: . . . something huge and implacable struck her on the head and dragged her down on her back. "Lord, forgive me everything!," she cried [i.e., said], feeling the impossibility of struggling. The little peasant, muttering something, was working over [on] the iron. And the candle, by the light of which she had been reading the book filled with anxieties, deceits, grief, and evil, flared up with a brighter light than before, lit up for her all that had hitherto been shrouded [again!] in darkness, flickered, began to grow dim, and went out forever.

JC: . . . something huge and implacable struck her on the head and dragged her down [the identity with MG is perhaps a little suspicious]. "Lord, forgive me everything!" she murmured [said], feeling the impossibility of struggling. A little peasant was working at the rails, muttering something to himself [the changed word order does not improve the passage, and again the concrete "rails" seems to preempt the decision as to whether there is actually a workman present]. And the candle by which she had been reading that book that is [does this added phrase imply that the book is common to all?] filled with anxiety, deceit, sorrow, and evil flared up with a brighter flame [too concrete] than before, lighted up everything for her that had previously been in darkness, flickered, dimmed, and went out forever.

None of the translations is flawless, but I am inclined to award the round to GKB: the physical events are clearer than in PV, the "iron" is preserved, and there is no shroud. My misgivings about "quench" are not strong.

One could doubtless continue, almost ad infinitum, adducing examples and passing judgment on the translations. Perhaps more illustrations would lead to different opinions. However, from the cases examined here I reach the following conclusions:

1. *None* of the existing translations is actively *bad.* From any of them the ordinary English-speaking reader would obtain a reasonably full and adequate experience of the novel. The English in all of them sounds like English, not translationese. I found very few real *errors* and only a few omissions, and of the latter most were only a few words or phrases. One's choice among the existing translations must therefore be based on nuances, subtleties, and refinements.

2. Following Professor Turner and with the addition of the disturbing error pointed out in example 8 above, I would be inclined to eliminate the Maude translation (MG) from the competition. However, the valuable additional critical matter supplied by Gibian for the Norton edition might possibly be enough to bring that version back into contention, but I doubt it. Turner has found a number of equally disturbing errors, enough, I am afraid, to disqualify the Maudes entirely. So much for my off-the-cuff recommendation.

3. I did not find either the Magarshack (DM) or Carmichael (JC) version ever superior to the others, and the lack of notes is a drawback. I would therefore eliminate them.

4. The three remaining contenders are PV, GKB, and RE. Of these RE (1978 version) has the important advantage of being based on the most up-to-date text. However, her version has no notes at all and all too frequently errs in the direction of making Tolstoy's "robust awkwardness" conform to the translator's notions of good English style.

I consider GKB a very good version, even though it is based on an out-of-date Russian text. Kent and Berberova did a much more thorough and careful revision of the Garnett translation than Gibian did of the Maude one, and they have supplied fairly full notes, conveniently printed at the bottom of the page.

5. Finally, PV, the original subject of this overgrown review. It is certainly a good translation and generally follows Tolstoy's style more closely and with less editing and "prettifying" than other versions. But one must still regret that it is not better than it is, that the Zaidenshnur-Zhdanov text was not used or at least considered, nor the Turner *Companion*.

Love in *Resurrection*
Eros or Agape?[1]

In June 1887, while a guest at Tolstoy's estate, Yasnaya Polyana, the eminent jurist Anatoly Koni told Tolstoy a remarkable story from his own practice. In the early 1870s, while Koni was serving as prosecutor for the St. Petersburg district court, a well-dressed young man "with a pale, expressive face and restless, burning eyes" had come to his office. He asked Koni to overrule a prison official who had refused to transmit without first reading it a letter to a female prisoner named Rozalia Oni. Rozalia Oni was a prostitute of Finnish origin. Convicted of having robbed a client of 100 rubles, she had been sentenced to four months' confinement. Without revealing his motives, the young man said that he wanted to marry the woman.

The young man, Koni knew, belonged to a well-known gentry family, was well educated, and held a responsible post in the civil service. Koni tried to dissuade him, saying that Rozalia could never be happy with him, but it was to no avail. Rozalia herself had eagerly agreed to the marriage. Koni refused to expedite the wedding, however, and the advent of Lent necessitated further postponement. During this waiting period Rozalia caught the typhus endemic in Russian prisons and died. As Koni sententiously put it, "The Lord drew a curtain over her life and stopped

---

[1] This essay, written for the *Cambridge Companion to Tolstoy*, was intended only as an introduction to *Resurrection* for the general reader, not as a work of scholarship presenting new information or interpretations. It is therefore less fully annotated than other articles in this volume.

the beating of her poor heart." Koni lost sight of the eccentric young man, but later a female warden passed on to him the whole story as told her by Rozalia. Rozalia's father had rented a farmhouse from the young man's aunt, a rich St. Petersburg lady. Dying of cancer, he begged his landlady to take his orphaned daughter under her protection. The lady graciously agreed and after the man's death took the girl into her household. When Rozalia was sixteen, the young man, on a visit to his aunt, had seduced her. Observing signs of pregnancy, the rich lady, scandalized, had driven her from the house. Abandoned by her lover, she turned the baby over to an orphanage and after that skidded down the moral and social ladder until she ended up in a low Haymarket brothel. Some years later, by sheer chance, the young man who had first seduced her served on the jury trying her for robbery. Realizing that he had been the cause of her downfall, he was consumed with remorse and felt morally obliged to offer her marriage in recompense.

Such was the "Koni story," under which title it figured for some years in Tolstoy's diaries and correspondence. In Tolstoy this tale touched a raw nerve: the sexual guilt and revulsion that had been tormenting him all his life, but were especially acute just at this time, the late 1880s and early 1890s. These are the feelings that inspired three important works of fiction besides *Resurrection*, written in this period: "The Kreutzer Sonata," "The Devil," and "Father Sergius." All these stories relate instances of sexual crimes committed by men against women—seduction, betrayal, sexually motivated murder. The "Koni story" fit these same well-formed Tolstoyan grooves.

The origin of these grooves no doubt lay deep in Tolstoy's past, perhaps his childhood. The most immediate, conscious source, however, may be parallel episodes from his own life. A few months before he died Tolstoy told his biographer, Pavel Biriukov, that in his university days at Kazan, while living in the house of his aunt Pelageya Yushkova, he had seduced a maid in the household who had later come to a bad end. The fact that in early versions of *Resurrection* the name of the hero was Yushkov (later modified to Yushkin) points to a connection in Tolstoy's mind with that epoch in his life. In her diary his wife mentions another case, a maid in the house of Tolstoy's sister Marya. "He pointed her out to me, to my deep despair and disgust," the Countess wrote on September 13, 1898. She was particularly incensed that Tolstoy attributed all these fine sentiments of repentance, recompense, and vows of sexual purity to fictional autobiographical heroes, whereas he himself had never done anything for the victims of his transgressions and remained, she added, addicted to "fleshly love."

In any case, Tolstoy was fascinated by the "Koni story," recognized its novelistic possibilities, and urged Koni to write it up. When Koni failed to do so, Tolstoy asked his friend's permission to use it himself. Koni readily agreed. So, after some preliminary turning the tale around in his mind, on December 26, 1889, Tolstoy "suddenly" began to write. Despite the initial enthusiasm, however, the gestation of *Resurrection* proved exceptionally long and tortured, not reaching a final text until ten years and more than 7,000 manuscript pages later.

The writing was carried out in three widely separated stages. Early drafts were sketched in 1889–91, during which time Tolstoy visited a court and prison in nearby Krapivna, angrily noting for later use what he saw and heard. He broke off work, however, partly because of his involvement in famine relief during 1891–92. But he also felt deep ambivalence about the whole project. Though one of the world's greatest novelists, Tolstoy had serious doubts about the morality of writing fiction at all. "Fiction is unpleasant," he wrote his son Lev in 1895. "Everything is invented and untrue." Moreover, Tolstoy had never been willing to view himself as a professional author, one whose job is to entertain people by writing stories for money. He needed a more serious purpose for his life. And now, since his religious conversion of 1879–81, this need for commitment had been greatly intensified. He had taken upon himself the most serious responsibility conceivable: to reform the world. He had set himself the colossal task of cleansing Christianity from all the malignant encrustations of the ages, including all miracles, mystery, and magic. Extracting from the somewhat garbled Gospels the true teachings of Jesus, he would show people how to live together in harmony and love.

This task was obviously far more important than writing novels. By 1890 Tolstoy had already set forth his message in a series of treatises: *A Translation and Harmony of the Four Gospels*, *An Investigation of Dogmatic Theology*, *What I Believe*, *What Then Must We Do?* and *On Life*. During 1891–93 he completed yet another, *The Kingdom of God is Within You*, spelling out how the commandment of Christ that we resist not evil (by violence), if actually carried out, would change the world. It would eliminate armies, wars, police, law courts, and indeed all governments, which rest on violence.

Tolstoy had thus given humankind the answers, but would they listen? Evidently not, or not much. Of course there were disciples, both Russian and foreign; Mohandas Gandhi became prominent among the latter. Tolstoy's personal image as a figure of exceptional moral stature was recognized all over the world. But that philistine world's interest in Tolstoy's treatises was slight, and itself mainly a by-product of his towering reputation as a novelist. By most people the treatises were written off, unread, as the eccentric concoctions of a wayward genius. They liked his novels, but were bored by his sermons.

Tolstoy took up the "Koni story" again in 1895–96. Now the novel began to branch out from its original sexual core into larger social questions, becoming more and more an outlet for the author's outrage against Russian society and indeed all "civilized" societies. He felt surrounded by, embedded in evil, and he had to strike out against it. His particular aim was to ally himself with, work for, educate, and uplift the peasantry, which still constituted the vast majority of the Russian population. The trouble was, however, that few peasants would read a big novel. He therefore found himself as before writing not for them, but for the Russian intelligentsia, a class he was coming more and more to dislike. "My writing [i.e., *Resurrection*] has become terribly complicated and I'm sick of it," he wrote on October 5, 1895, to his friend Nikolai Strakhov. "It is insignificant, vulgar, and the main thing is that I hate writing for the parasitic, good-for-nothing intelligentsia, from which there has never been anything but futility [суета] and never will be." So he broke off again.

A great artist himself, Tolstoy felt obliged to explain and justify the very existence of art. What is art for? Is it moral? How can we judge it? The result of Tolstoy's grappling with these questions was another formidable treatise, *What Is Art?* (1898). Despite its fulminations against sophisticated art addressed to a small elite, in which he included his own big novels, *What Is Art?* did provide for some categories of morally acceptable art. Good art "infects" the recipient with good feelings. Thus even a big novel like *Resurrection* might be squeezed through this loophole if it instilled emotions that would impel people to carry out the moral imperatives outlined in the treatises.

So in mid-1898 Tolstoy returned to *Resurrection* for the third time, now spurred on by a new motive. The religious sect known as Doukhobors (Spirit-wrestlers) were being persecuted by the government for their refusal to pay taxes or serve in the military—exactly what Tolstoy recommended for everyone in *The Kingdom of God is Within You*. Though not directly his disciples, the Doukhobors were kindred spirits, true peasant Christians. He decided to do something he had explicitly vowed never to do again, to write for money, the funds earned to be used to pay for transporting thousands of Doukhobors to Canada, which had agreed to accept them as immigrants.

By this time Tolstoy was a world celebrity, and the prospect of a new Tolstoy novel, the first since *Anna Karenina* twenty years before, was a sensation. *Resurrection* was to be serialized in Russia before coming out in book form, and immediate translations were arranged in Europe and America. So in 1898–99 the book was finished—and greatly expanded—in a hectic rush, with new texts copied, revised, recopied by family and friends, revised again, sent to the magazine, then virtually rewritten on proofs that sometimes themselves had to be run off two or three times. Finally, on December 15, 1899, Tolstoy wrote in his diary, "Finished *Resurrection*. Not good. Not corrected. Hasty. But it's off my back and doesn't interest me any more."

The novel by this time had vastly outgrown the original dimensions of the "Koni story." The primary nucleus of sexual misbehavior and repentance had expanded into a wholesale indictment of Russian society: the luxury and callousness of the privileged classes versus the poverty and hunger of the masses; the whole cruel criminal justice system; the Orthodox Church's enormous distance from true Christianity. In Soviet times some Russian commentators[2] sought to show that this larger design had been Tolstoy's intention from the beginning, that from the start he had planned a big social novel "de longue haleine" (on the grand scale), as he put it in his diary entry of September 15, 1890. The "Koni story," they claim, just happened to fit this larger scheme. This interpretation seems to me unconvincing. In the late 1880s Tolstoy may have had occasional yearnings to immerse himself in a big novel again, but in my view the "Koni story" did not grow into that novel until considerably later. One of the reasons Tolstoy gave for his difficulties with *Resurrection* was that the topic was not his own, "was not born in me." He would hardly have made that statement if he had conceived the novel from the start as a vehicle for a comprehensive social indictment.

Tolstoy aficionados will recognize that the name of the hero of *Resurrection*, Prince Dmitry Nekhliudov, is no newcomer to Tolstoy's pages. A character with that name had been prominent in several of Tolstoy's early works. Prince Dmitry Nekhliudov was an admired friend of Nikolenka Irteniev, the hero of *Boyhood* and *Youth*; he was the central character of three stories, "Notes of a Billiard Marker," "Lucerne," and "A Landlord's Morning"—all dating from the 1850s. This is not to say that the hero of *Resurrection* is a pure reincarnation of these earlier namesakes. But the revival of the name in *Resurrection* is surely of some, if only private, significance. Tolstoy adds the seemingly gratuitous detail that the sister of the *Resurrection* Nekhliudov had once been in love with Nikolenka Irteniev, now dead. Of course only readers with excellent

---

[2] For example, Konstantin Lomunov and Vladimir Zhdanov.

memories (or Tolstoy scholars), steeped in the Tolstoyan corpus, would note these linkages, but the author did.[3]

Why this particular name? Though other, more linguistically "correct" etymologies have been suggested, I read it as a thinly disguised autobiographical signal, like the Lev-in of the hero of *Anna Karenina*. In Tolstoy's mind Nekhliudov, I believe, was simply a "softened" variant of нехудой, "not thin," a synonym of толстый, "fat," of which Tolstoy is a variant.

So Dmitry Nekhliudov is a disguised Tolstoy. But not only Lev Tolstoy. Dmitry Tolstoy was the name of the brother closest to Lev in age, the brother who had died of tuberculosis in 1856, in a seedy hotel in Orel, attended by an ex-prostitute named Masha whom he had bought from a brothel. With his Paphian paramour, Dmitry Tolstoy had already served as the model for the character of Nikolai Levin in *Anna Karenina*; but the connection between a Tolstoy and a prostitute still evidently carried a creative charge for Lev Tolstoy. The "Koni story" revived it.

It should be noted that besides its "real life" connections, the theme of "rescuing" prostitutes, even by marrying them, had a long history in Russian literature. Though mocked in Gogol's "Nevsky Prospect" (1835), it was played at full sentimental volume in Nekrasov's poem "When from the Darkness of Error" (Когда из мрака заблужденья (1846), which in turn is cited as an epigraph in Dostoevsky's *Notes from Underground* (1864), a work which exposes some of the pitfalls of this gratifying plot. After *Anna Karenina*, in the 1880s Vsevolod Garshin revived the theme in his *Nadezhda Nikolaevna* (1885), and Chekhov was to invoke it in "A Nervous Breakdown" (Припадок, 1889). It was a powerful tradition.[4]

However, the most direct real-life model for the Nekhliudov-prostitute linkage is the author himself, at a much earlier age. Though he formed no long-term bond with any prostitute, Lev Tolstoy's first experience of sexual intercourse had been with one, at the tender age of fourteen, after which he had wept, standing by the bed. We might see this as an extreme case of post-coital angst, an affliction that seems to have often troubled Tolstoy later. Sex, he felt, is always a disappointment, the pleasure brief, the aftermath sad. In *Resurrection* Nekhliudov discovers that even at its best "animal love" did not give him anything like what it promised. Despite his earlier celebration of the joys of biological fecundity in the great novels, Tolstoy by 1890 had come to the conclusion that there is no such thing as "good" sex. As the "Afterword" to "The Kreutzer Sonata" explains, the

---

[3] See Donna Orwin's thorough scrutiny of the various Nekhliudovs: "The Riddle of Prince Nexljudov."

[4] See George Siegel.

procreative sex of a married couple is the least offensive kind, but even that distracts people from selfless service to God and man. It is better to live together in sexless "purity," as brother and sister.[5]

The existential stance of Dmitry Nekhliudov, as of many of Tolstoy's quasi-autobiographical heroes, is that of a young man *somehow morally superior to his environment*, who struggles to find the path of righteousness and truth despite the efforts of a vicious society to ensnare him in its net. Tolstoy himself had assumed this stance in *A Confession* (1884). In spite of its flourishes of self deprecation, *A Confession* seems remarkable for its lack of real contrition. The blame for the subject's sins is shifted to an anonymous "they," who ridicule his noble strivings and entice him with the fleshpots of carnality and greed. Similarly, in *Resurrection* Nekhliudov succumbs to the "animal" side of his nature and seduces Katiusha Maslova because "everybody," i.e., all the well-heeled young blades of his set, does such things and is even proud of them. They, however, take their pleasures free of guilt, while Nekhliudov can only temporarily suppress his self-disgust. The source of this moral superiority is never explored.

In *A Confession* there is another figure whose youthful scrupulosity is even more pronounced than the author's: the same brother Dmitry, who for a time, during the Kazan period, became deeply religious, punctiliously observing the fasts and attending church, including (Tolstoy adds in his *Reminiscences*) Holy Week services in a prison chapel near their aunt's house—no doubt something like the one depicted in the famous "defamiliarized" satire of the Orthodox Eucharist in *Resurrection*. For this excess of piety Dmitry's relatives, no doubt including his brother Lev, mocked him and called him "Noah." Later Dmitry trod the primrose path in his turn. "He suddenly began to drink, smoke, squander money, and visit brothels." His further moral development was cut short by his death, but his "purchase" of Masha seems to indicate some stirrings of conscience and sense of responsibility.

The distinction between two kinds of love, carnal and spiritual, eros and agape, had been on Tolstoy's mind for a long time. It is found in Plato's *Symposium*, a work Tolstoy singled out as having had a "great influence" on him. In *Anna Karenina* Konstantin Levin invokes the *Symposium* in his restaurant conversation with Stiva Oblonsky, the latter an unequivocal devotee of eros as opposed to agape. But the contrast of the two "loves" goes back to Tolstoy's earliest works, to the trilogy and especially *The Cossacks*, where Dmitry Olenin veers back and forth between the two. In

---

[5] Edwina Cruise argues that the sexless love Tolstoy advocates for everyone, men and women alike, is essentially feminine, maternal. See Cruise.

Anna Karenina Levin seemed to have found a reasonable balance of eros and agape in his married life, based on a deep spiritual bond with his wife, but with a healthy admixture of sensuality.[6] But in *Resurrection* any Tolstoyan tolerance of eros has disappeared. It was eros that led Nekhliudov to his criminal seduction of Katiusha, and it is eros that reigns in the cheap vulgarity of the whorehouse where "Liubka" Maslova had consorted with an endless succession of lust-ridden males: merchants, clerks, Armenians, Jews, Tatars, rich, poor, healthy, sick, drunk, sober, coarse, tender, military, civilian, university students, high school boys. Her life had been an erotic horror. No wonder her eventual marriage to Simonson is apparently to be at the opposite extreme: "Platonic," sexless.

In *Resurrection* Tolstoy decided to forgo strictly chronological exposition in favor of two beginnings in the middle of the action, followed by flashbacks. The situation in which we are at once immersed—after the famous introductory celebration of the power of spring even in the city—is a contrast of the two main characters' lives on that spring morning. The first we see is a young woman, Katerina ("Katiusha") Maslova, being escorted by soldiers from prison to the courthouse where she is to stand trial. The flashback at this point includes only the bare facts, curriculum vitae style, of the "Koni story," a "very ordinary story," Tolstoy observes: seduction, pregnancy, dismissal, downward slide into prostitution. Her crime, however, is not divulged at this point.

Very different is the morning of Prince Nekhliudov. He wakes up in a luxurious apartment. All around him are fine *things*. He wears a clean Dutch nightshirt, washes his hands, face, and "fat neck" with fragrant soap. When he dresses, everything he puts on is of the most expensive kind. Even before getting out of bed he lights himself a cigarette taken from a silver case—an act more significant than simply another attribute of his affluence. The reader will notice all through the novel how smoking as well as drinking are used to illustrate the doctrine Tolstoy had set forth in the article "Why Do People Stupefy Themselves?" (Для чего люди одурманиваются?, 1890). The purpose of alcohol and tobacco, Tolstoy believes, is to deaden the moral sense. People smoke or drink when they are doing something that goes against their moral nature. At the beginning of the novel Nekhliudov's only visible sin is the original one of being rich (and thus, according to Tolstoy, having robbed the poor); but he is also contemplating marriage to a cultivated, well-off woman in society, before which he must break off a long adulterous love affair.

---

[6] See Irina Gutkin.

We are also given Nekhliudov's curriculum vitae. He had resigned from the military service seven years before. Since then he had devoted himself to art, only to discover (as Vronsky in *Anna Karenina* had done before him) that his talent was a minor one at best. So at present he is at loose ends and is even grateful that jury duty will give a certain fleeting purposefulness to his life.

We then move to the court, which is given a savagely satirical representation. Tolstoy had never had much use for lawyers—witness the moth-infested office of the attorney Aleksei Karenin consults concerning a possible divorce. But in *Resurrection* the hostility has become much more acute. Here Tolstoy is demonstrating his conviction that we should take literally Christ's precept, "Judge not that ye be not judged." Human beings have no right to judge and punish one another. That is God's job. "Vengeance is mine, saith the Lord"—this was the epigraph to *Anna Karenina*. "Let him who is without sin cast the first stone." As a plebeian juror says, "We are not saints." Criminal courts are thus by their very nature immoral institutions.

The nature of Maslova's crime has been escalated over that of Rozalia Oni. Maslova is accused not only of theft, but of murder, carried out with two accomplices. In fact, she admits to giving sleeping powders to her customer, a rich Siberian merchant, but only with the aim of putting him to sleep so that she could escape his drunken attentions. The question of intent was crucial. The jury's agreement that she had no murderous intent is inadvertently omitted from their verdict, and the judge fails to remind them of this possibility. Because of these errors Maslova receives the harsh sentence of four years at hard labor. Thus even by the criteria of Russian law there is a miscarriage of justice. There would therefore seem to be good grounds for appeal, but of course in Tolstoy the appeals process is to be treated no less satirically than the original trial. There is no justice to be had from human institutions.

Though in general he presents the courtroom and its realia through the naive eyes of Nekhliudov, who is seeing these things for the first time (again, Tolstoy's trademark "defamiliarization"), Tolstoy has no compunctions about resorting to the god-like, "omniscient author" point of view when it suits his satirical purposes. He tells us, for example, that the presiding judge, who is supposed to represent the majesty of impartial justice, has an "open" marriage, leaving both spouses free to commit adultery *ad libitum*. The previous summer this judge had an affair with an attractive Swiss governess. This woman is just now passing through Moscow and will be waiting for him that afternoon in a hotel. Hence he is eager to conclude the proceedings with dispatch—a haste which perhaps leads him to commit the judicial error that seals Maslova's fate. Thus the law that is supposed to be so impervious to human foibles is shown to be just the opposite, caught up in the tangle of extraneous human passions. A lawyer "of genius" is admired by all because he has managed to do an old lady out of her property in favor of an unscrupulous merchant who has no right to it at all. (As the novel's god, Tolstoy knows the absolute wrongness of this decision.) There is posturing everywhere: the lawyers with their pretentious speeches, the priest who sanctimoniously administers the oath, the chief judge who so enjoys the sound of his own voice. A particular irony is that the prosecutor who so indignantly demands the severest punishment for this pernicious prostitute has himself come to court without sleep after a night on the town with friends, ending at the very brothel where Maslova had worked.

The trial is of course the scene where Nekhliudov's "resurrection" begins. The sight and recognition of Maslova force him to resurrect the suppressed memories of his relationship with her, as later he will force her to do the same.[7] Nekhliudov's memories provide motivation for a major flashback, to the time of his first visit to his aunts and his acquaintance with Katiusha. Then an earnest young man of nineteen, a reader of Herbert Spencer, and concerned about the morality of land ownership, he is also still a virgin and cannot imagine sex outside of marriage. He and Katiusha fall in love, an innocent, "pure" love, so much so that the aunts are worried that he might even take it into his head to marry this peasant. Three years later he comes again as a young officer, thoroughly corrupted by the military ethos. His "animal self" is now in command; he smokes and drinks.

Ironically, the seduction of Katiusha takes place at Easter time. The celebration in the village church of Christ's resurrection is represented with charming lyricism, as it was felt by both these young lovers, without any of the derisive satire with which the Orthodox liturgy is mocked later. The lovers are still chaste; their kiss after the ritual exchange—"Christ is risen!" "Verily He is risen!"—is rapturous but innocent. This is the zenith of their love. The seduction scene follows, symbolically accompanied by the noise of breaking ice in the river. As usual, Tolstoy is especially attuned to body language. Katiusha's lips said no, but her "whole being" said "I am all yours." The scene aroused the indignation of Countess Tolstaya, disgusted that her aged husband would propagate such salacious fantasies. "He describes the scene of the adultery of maid and officer with the relish of a gourmet eating a tasty dish," she fumed.

---

[7] See Marie Semon.

The memories of his callous abandonment (and payment!) of Katiusha are bitter to Nekhliudov, and he resists their emergence as long as he can. But, as Tolstoy believed, our consciences are the voice of God within us, and Nekhliudov was already a man of relatively high moral standards. He forces himself to make the ultimate commitment, not just of money and support for an appeal of her sentence, but the offer of marriage.

Though there are later some temptations to backsliding, Nekhliudov thus essentially completes his "resurrection" early in the novel. He commits himself to marry Maslova, and if she will not have him as a husband, at least to stay near her and do everything he can to make her life more endurable. His soul has been purged, and he is on the right path. Nekhliudov can then expand the scope of his benevolence beyond Maslova. An old connection with a female revolutionary named Vera Bogodukhovskaya is revived, and through her he takes on the cases of other upper-class revolutionaries along with those of mistreated common criminals he hears about from Maslova. He becomes a sort of prisoners' ombudsman, using his money and connections to alleviate the suffering caused by the tsar's system of courts and punishments.

For Maslova, however, the process of resurrection has only just begun. At their first meeting after the trial Nekhliudov perceives her as a "dead woman" in whom all natural emotions have been stifled. His appearance and support are the catalyst that initiates the revival, but it will take some time to work itself out, assisted not only by Nekhliudov, but by a series of fellow prisoners, especially the upper-class revolutionaries with whom she is allowed to associate on the journey to Siberia. Inspired by the example of the virginal Marya Shchetinina, she learns to abandon all "coquetry," all effort to exploit the power eros gives her over men. Earlier, vodka gives her the boldness to vent her anger against Nekhliudov, charging that his beneficence is nothing but an effort to use her once again, this time as a means of purifying his soul. But his moral influence is still powerful, and she soon gives up the anodynes of tobacco and alcohol.

Ultimately, both she and Nekhliudov are redeemed by agape. Putting aside their own needs and interests, they involve themselves in the problems of others, always trying to serve, to help. They thus escape from the prison of self. Life, even in a literal prison, becomes freer and richer. This is the core of Tolstoy's sermon: love thy neighbor, not as thyself, but instead of thyself.

Nekhliudov's sexual reformation is accompanied by a social and economic one, which points to one of the larger topics of *Resurrection*, the cruelty and immorality of the entire social structure. Having repudiated his own class and attained the point of view of the "patriarchal peasantry," as Lenin put it in his articles on Tolstoy cited *ad nauseam* in Soviet times, the writer tried to see the world through peasant eyes. Though serfdom had been abolished decades earlier, the peasants' poverty was as dire as ever. The problem, as they saw it, was not overpopulation, low investment, and backward agricultural methods, but the land squeeze. Their numbers increased, but their land holdings did not. Peasants saw the solution as giving them the rest of the land, the gentry's land, and Tolstoy agrees. Tolstoy's utopia was a simpler world of universal subsistence agriculture, where all would raise their own food, and there would be no exploitation and no class divisions. Cities too would disappear, because cities are nothing but places where the exploiters concentrate their power and spend the wealth extracted from the countryside.

Tolstoy does not envisage the possibility of forcible seizure of the land by an aroused peasantry—what actually happened in 1917. He wants the landowners voluntarily to surrender their ownership, as Nekhliudov had done with a small estate he had inherited from his father. He had been inspired by the American reformer Henry George (1839–97), a thinker Tolstoy greatly admired, who maintained that the root of social evil is private ownership of land. However, Nekhliudov's problem in dealing with the much larger estates he had inherited from his mother (and also from the maiden aunts) was more difficult. The peasants are at first resistant and suspicious, but they eventually come to recognize his good will and good sense. With these estates, however, Nekhliudov cannot quite go the whole distance. He is willing to rent land to the peasants on much less onerous terms and to reduce drastically his own standard of living. But he still must have money, both to live on, still in relative comfort, and to carry out his various agape-inspired enterprises. Nekhliudov never *earns* any money at all, nor does he seem to have any thought of doing so. The aristocratic mentality dies hard.

Tolstoy's picture of upper-class life is unrelentingly satirical. After the trial Nekhliudov goes to dinner at the house of his prospective fiancée, "Missi" Korchagina. The luxury is ostentatious and the young lady attractive, both physically and culturally. But Nekhliudov is now alienated, his moral energies absorbed in his thoughts about Maslova. He sees the Korchagins with changed, "defamiliarized" eyes. The father is a brute, a former governor known for his fondness for flogging and hanging criminals. The mother is an absurdly vain, self-indulgent invalid. She flatters Nekhliudov in the hope of ensnaring him as a husband for Missi, but it is too late; he has moved on.

Nekhliudov's pursuit of an appeal of Maslova's sentence takes him to St. Petersburg, the glittering imperial capital, which had long been an object of Tolstoy's dislike. Here the prince deals with a succession of the very highest officials, to whom his princely connections give him access. They are paraded before us, one after the other, like a high-class version of the parade of bribers in Gogol's *Inspector-General*. Tolstoy, via Nekhliudov, finds scarcely a redeeming feature in any of them. They are pompous and greedy, oblivious to the cruelties their offices sponsor, and in addition they are mentally vacuous. Silly fads flourish among them, such as spiritualism (ouija boards) and the we-are-all-saved harangues of a sentimental German preacher. (Another evangelical, an Englishman, appears in Part III, sanctimoniously passing out Gospels to pugnacious prisoners and admonishing them to observe the nonviolent precepts of Christian morality. In a passage coming perilously close to mockery of his own cherished turn-the-other-cheek doctrine, Tolstoy has the prisoners dissolve in laughter when one of them asks the Englishman, "When he smacks me on the second cheek, which one do I turn then?")

Maslova's appeal of course fails, despite its obvious justification. Here the court's decision is determined not even by the usual pettifogging legal technicalities, but by rivalries and prejudices among the judges. Nowhere among all this high officialdom is there a trace of humanity or compassion. The only Petersburg character with at least a remnant of soul is Nekhliudov's old friend Selenin, whom Nekhliudov had known in his student days as a thoughtful and morally upright young man. Selenin has now, however, been disastrously corrupted by the compromises inherent in a Petersburg career.

The most famous recognizable Petersburg character in *Resurrection* is Toporov, the Chief Procurator of the Most Holy Synod, to whom Nekhliudov appeals on behalf of some sectarians who have been arrested for holding non-Orthodox prayer services. Toporov is an obvious caricature of the celebrated Konstantin Pobedonostsev, an arch-conservative who was Chief Procurator for decades and a close adviser to Alexander III. Tolstoy portrays him as a complete cynic, who without any personal belief promotes Orthodoxy as a means of brainwashing the masses. Though Toporov grants his petition (for reasons of expediency), Nekhliudov regrets even having shaken the man's hand.

In Nekhliudov eros has not yet been totally squelched; his "animal self" is still alive. He is briefly tempted by the prospect of a love affair with "Mariette," an old acquaintance now married to a high official. Mariette uses all her wiles, physical as well as psychological, but in the end Nekhliudov's newly won virtue holds out. The last straw is the perceived comparison with a vulgar prostitute who importunes him on the street. The difference between the two women, he now understands, is only a matter of class, not of substance.

With Nekhliudov back in Moscow, Tolstoy's indictment intensifies. One of the most searing representations of senseless cruelty in the penal system is the picture of the departure for Siberia of a large group of prisoners. On a day of intense summer heat the victims are lined up in the sun, counted, counted again, and finally marched through the streets of Moscow to the railway station. Several prisoners die of sunstroke or heat exhaustion; all suffer. It is one of those instances, as Nekhliudov analyzes the causes, where it is impossible to pin responsibility for the misery. Every official is just doing his job, following orders; but the result is suffering and death. Official, legal duties make people impervious to the human law written by God in their hearts, just as pavement makes a road impervious to rain.

The third part of *Resurrection* deals with the journey to Siberia of the party of prisoners to which Maslova belonged, with Nekhliudov accompanying them as closely as he can. Here Tolstoy was not writing from personal knowledge, but from accounts read or heard from those who had experienced such journeys, perhaps beginning with Dostoevsky's *Notes from a Dead House*, which had always been the Dostoevsky book Tolstoy admired most. One of his sources was the famous *Siberia and the Exile System* (1891) by the American George Kennan, who had also visited Tolstoy in 1886. The horrific account of the execution of a Pole and an adolescent Jew is based on an unpublished memoir by a witness. From these materials the power of Tolstoy's imagination and talent enabled him to create a vividly realized picture of the "great road" to Siberia, trod by so many wretched prisoners.

A major novelty in this section of the novel is the first appearance in Tolstoy's corpus of real revolutionaries. Their portraits are varied and reflect Tolstoy's marvelous capacity to perceive all human beings in their unique individuality; but they also serve as vehicles by which he can convey his judgment of them and their cause. He mostly likes them as people, though he disapproves of their methods. Through Maslova, Tolstoy recognizes that revolutionaries from the educated upper classes were almost by definition good people, because they had voluntarily sacrificed their own comfort and status for the sake of others. He also seems to acknowledge that inculcated upper-class behavior is just humanly better than the coarseness and frequent brutality of the common folk. The revolutionaries do not use foul language and are polite and considerate of one another. It is a revelation to Maslova that people can actually be kind to one another; and it plays a major part in her "resurrection."

Tolstoy is not, however, blind to the negative qualities also found among the revolutionaries. His portrait of the "famous" Novodvorov, though only lightly sketched, shows clearly the authoritarian Lenin type, vain and sure of himself, cynical in his view of revolutionary ends and means. "The masses always adore only power . . . ," he says. "The government has power—they adore it and hate us; tomorrow we will have power—they will adore us." Characteristically, he claims the support of "science" for his doctrines.

Tolstoy of course fundamentally disagreed with all the revolutionaries, soft as well as hard, on the grounds that violence only begets more violence. The assassination of Alexander II (the "event of March 1") had clearly made matters worse for everybody; the government only intensified its oppressions. Nekhliudov argues the author's theoretical case, saying of the authorities, "They too are people," when the dying tubercular Kryltsov, overflowing with rage and frustration, imagines himself empowered to drop bombs on those "human bedbugs" from a balloon. In Tolstoy's ideal solution the rich and powerful, persuaded by his treatises, will voluntarily surrender their privileges and authority; but the novel itself does not make this utopia seem likely. Nekhliudov is absolutely unique in his class; one cannot imagine the Petersburg grandees voluntarily surrendering anything.

The original "Koni story" plot—Nekhliudov's remorse and efforts to make amends to Maslova—had essentially been resolved by the end of Part I. The rest of the novel is thus almost plotless, if regarded in conventional narratological terms. The only remaining "plot" question was whether their marriage would actually take place, and if it did, what sort of a relationship it would be. An early draft had them not only marry, but escape from Siberia to London. But ultimately Tolstoy decided otherwise, thus making the structure even looser, more focused on larger social issues. After her spiritual resurrection Maslova resolutely rejects Nekhliudov's offer of marriage. Her motives are perhaps not entirely clear. Does she, as some critics maintain, still love Nekhliudov and genuinely wish only to set him free, knowing that the cultural gulf between them was too wide to be crossed? Or has she really come to love the devoted, non-erotic Simonson?

In any case, the novel seems to end rather abruptly, with Maslova, now pardoned (through Selenin's efforts), but committed to following Simonson wherever he had to go, and Nekhliudov set free to pursue his criminological interests. Though Tolstoy has had little to say about Nekhliudov's religion, he is given a religious send-off. We know only that in his youth he had been a seeker like Selenin, already free from the "superstitions of the official church," and that he believes that God has written the law of love in people's hearts. Therefore, the novel's sudden fadeout in a long series of Gospel quotations seems scarcely justified.

That at any rate was the judgment of Anton Chekhov. Though he liked the book, calling it "a remarkable work of art," he objected that "The novel has no ending . . . To write so much and then suddenly make a Gospel text responsible for it all smacks a bit too much of the seminary."

In its day *Resurrection* was read with excitement all over the world, argued over, condemned, and exalted. In the terrible century that has elapsed since then, Novodvorov's utopia was realized in Russia, only to create the hell of the gulag archipelago, far worse both in numbers and in cruelty than the tsarist hell described by Tolstoy. Fortunately, that Soviet hell, too, has at last faded away. Perhaps we can now take the didactic message of *Resurrection* more serenely and usefully—as a plea that human beings should allow the agape in their hearts to govern their relations with one another.

As for the novel itself, quite apart from its "message" and despite its heavy didacticism, it has retained its standing and its popularity as a major work of literary art, perhaps not quite of the same supreme stature as its two predecessors, but a book that can still immerse us, as only Tolstoy could do, in an imagined world of human beings and human life that seems as real as if it were our own.

Could the Master Err?
A Note on "God Sees the Truth but Waits"[1]

"God Sees the Truth but Waits" (Бог правду видит да не скоро скажет, 1872), originally written for Tolstoy's *Primer* (*Азбука*) for children, is easily recognized as an expanded version of a fable related by Platon Karataev in the closing pages of *War and Peace*. The basic plot nucleus remains the same. The main character, a merchant, is wrongly convicted of murder and robbery, knouted, and serves many years in a Siberian prison.[2] There he by chance encounters the true murderer. Eventually the latter is moved to confess the crime to the authorities, but before the necessary documents have made their way through the bureaucracy to effect the innocent man's release, death has already claimed him.

In Karataev's version the true culprit is moved to confess simply by hearing the old merchant's story, related to a group of fellow convicts. What

---

[1] This article owes a great deal to the thorough and incisive criticisms of Gary Jahn, who is the major non-Russian authority on Tolstoy's *narodnye rasskazy*, those stories primarily addressed to uneducated, non-intelligentsia readers, including children. Professor Jahn is the author of a fine article on this story ("A Structural Analysis of Leo Tolstoy's 'God Sees the Truth but Waits'") a much more substantial study than the present note, which attempts only to call attention to certain puzzles and anomalies connected with the story. Professor Jahn and I have agreed to disagree on certain questions, but I am delighted that he has consented to present his points of view in the form of a rejoinder to this note. Let the readers be the jury.
I am also grateful for assistance to my colleagues Olga and Robert Hughes.

[2] Earlier, the anti-legal, anarchistic Tolstoy places in Karataev's mouth the characteristic aphorism, "Где суд, там и неправда" (Where courts are, there is injustice), *War and Peace*, Four: I:12.

moves him is not so much the narrative of the suffering and deprivation the old man has undergone as the fact that despite his innocence of the crime for which he was convicted and despite his virtuous life and benefactions to the poor, he has come to accept his fate as a just retribution exacted by God for his sins and those of mankind (*за свои да за людские грехи страдаю*, PSS 12:155). His pronouncement of sacrifice, common guilt and atonement affects the murderer so powerfully that he falls on his knees before the merchant and begs his forgiveness. The reply is, "God will forgive you. We are all sinners before God, and I am suffering for my own sins." It is this declaration that impels the man to confess, and as expected in Tolstoy, human "justice" fails to right the balance.

Karataev's special ecstasy in relating this finale, which is communicated to Pierre, seems to come from the conviction that there is a moral order in the universe presided over by God, one that lies quite beyond human measurement and especially beyond any effort to impose morality here on earth by laws and punishments. We all share the universal guilt. (This was also a favorite idea of Dostoevsky.) Platon may also sense his own impending death, as he is soon to be executed by the French for the crime of being unable to walk any further, and may regard it, like the old merchant's, as a payment for the sins of mankind, another episode in the mysterious operations of divine justice.

This otherworldly moral conclusion perhaps remains the same in the expanded version of 1872, although its anonymous and "objective" narrator cannot impart to the conclusion Platon's mystically ecstatic emotion. The hero of "God Sees the Truth," Ivan Aksenov, although he has committed no crime at all, says to the now repentant murderer, "God will forgive you; perhaps I am a hundred times worse than you" (Бог простит тебя; может быть, я во сто раз хуже тебя). He says this after he and the murderer have wept together, following which he "suddenly felt a lightness in his soul" (И вдруг у него на душе легко стало). The point here may be slightly different from the Karataev version, stressing not so much the common, shared guilt of us all, but rather universal human sinfulness, so vast and so complex that it far exceeds any human measurements of crime, since sins of thought may on God's balances weigh as heavily as sins of deed.

In any case, the change of narrator from the peasant philosopher Karataev to the author Lev Tolstoy also involved a partial change of genre. The Karataev version may be called a parable or a fable, i.e., a schematic narrative designed to illustrate a moral truth. The new version, though still retaining some of basic features of a fable, also shows a strong pull in the direction of Tolstoyan realistic fiction. It becomes a *story*. Tolstoy's creative imagination, always fertile, was put to work fleshing out the fable.

He added a plethora of details, providing a much more rounded, fully developed representation of the characters and events than in Karataev's very schematic outline. The chief actors are given names and distinct personalities, the settings made more concrete and vivid, and the plot augmented by several new episodes.

To make the action more dramatic and the psychology more convincing, Tolstoy added a whole new dimension to the Siberian confrontation of the two antagonists. In real, Tolstoyan life merely hearing the old man's story would clearly not be enough to move the miscreant to repentance and confession. So a new episode was added. The true murderer, now named Makar Semenov, plans to escape from the stockade by digging a tunnel. Aksenov witnesses the digging and thus acquires the power to wreak vengeance on his enemy by denouncing him to the authorities — a more interesting psychological conflict than the total self-abnegation and acceptance of the Karataev version. Aksenov is now really tempted. He recalls his wife, his children, the twenty-six years of life with them that were stolen from him, and the suffering he has endured, and he wants revenge. When Semenov threatens to kill him if he tells about the digging, Aksenov replies, "You killed me long ago. And whether I report you or not, that will be as God affects my soul." (Ты меня уже давно убил. А сказывать про тебя буду или нет, — как Бог на душу положит. *PSS* 22:429)

This sets the stage for a dramatic "moment of truth," when the prison commandant asks Aksenov, known as a particularly docile, obedient and truthful prisoner, if he knows who dug the tunnel. Responding to a higher truth, Aksenov answers, "I did not see it and do not know" (Я не видал и не знаю. *PSS* 22:430) It is this salvific act that moves Semenov to confess.

However, in the preliminary narrative before this climactic scene there are details that look very much like authorial errors on Tolstoy's part, perhaps the result of haste. The story was written fast, in early April, 1872, and perhaps not revised as carefully as was the writer's usual practice[3]. The first of these flaws is perhaps not strictly an error at all, but only a case of psychological implausibility. It does not seem to me believable that Aksenov's wife, with whom he is shown to have had a warm and affectionate relationship, would not have communicated with him at all during his twenty-six years of incarceration. To be sure, he had been deeply hurt to find after his arrest that she would even entertain the thought that he might have committed the horrible deed. But surely she would have come around to his side when he assured her that he was innocent. And afterwards, within the limits of what was permitted, she would surely have tried to keep him

---

[3] See commentary by V. S. Spiridonov in *PSS* 21:655.

informed about her life and their children's.⁴ But Tolstoy cannot allow it. "From home no one wrote letters to Aksenov, and he did not know whether his wife and children were alive." (Yet later he did somehow learn that his wife had died, and there is no explanation of this contradiction.) Even at the expense of psychological plausibility, Tolstoy needs the starkness of Aksenov's isolation, the individual totally alone with his God, as a graphic representation of man's ultimate existential state. We all must face death and eternity alone.

The second "error" is more technical and more direct. It occurs when Tolstoy tells about the day after Aksenov has observed Semenov digging the tunnel and been threatened by him. The text reads as follows: "The next day, when the convicts were led out to work, soldiers noticed that Makar Semenov was scattering [or had scattered] earth; they began hunting in the stockade and found the hole. The commandant came to the stockade and began asking everyone who had dug the hole." (На другой день, когда вывели колодников на работу, солдаты приметили, что Макар Семенов высыпал землю, стали искать в остроге и нашли дыру. Начальник приехал в острог и стал всех допрашивать: кто выкопал дыру? (*PSS* 22:429–30).)⁵

The question immediately arises, why did the soldiers not report that they had caught Semenov emptying dirt, or noticed that he had done so? Tolstoy offers no explanation. If they refrained out of some desire to protect Semenov (class solidarity?), surely this motive would require explanation and elucidation. Anyway, such an interpretation seems most

---

4   Just how much communication was permitted is unclear to me. Many of the exiled Decembrists were allowed some correspondence with relatives. Dostoevsky received no letters at all from his brother Mikhail or any other relative during the first four years of his exile, when he was in *katorga* (forced labor). Mikhail petitioned "long and zealously" for permission to write, but was refused. Dostoevsky, however, did send one letter to Mikhail through official channels, and others were carried by individuals. See commentary in Dostoevsky 28(1), 451. Aksenov seems to have been in *katorga* for all 26 years of his imprisonment; so perhaps he was not allowed to receive any letters at all. But one would expect that over so long a time his wife would have found some way of getting news to him. And as noted, he did somehow find out that she had died.

5   The choice in translation between "was scattering" and "had scattered" rests primarily on whether one reads the aspect of высыпал as imperfective, with stress on the last syllable, or perfective, with stress on the first. But either way, Makar Semenov is part of what the soldiers observed, though the perfective/pluperfect version does put the emptying of dirt before the soldiers' noticing, thus reducing the ambiguity somewhat. My colleague Olga Hughes, a native speaker of Russian, is willing to absolve Tolstoy of carelessness on this basis. However, I still think Tolstoy could have done a better job with this sentence, making clear that the soldiers saw only the incriminating dirt, not the man, e.g., Солдаты приметили ту землю, которую Семенов (раньше) высыпал., or, using a participle instead of a "which" clause, Солдаты приметили землю, высыпанную Семеновым.

unlikely. The very fact that the soldiers followed up the evidence of the scattered earth by hunting for the hole clearly implies the opposite. Like any normally indoctrinated soldiers, they were doing what was expected of them, fulfilling orders, enforcing the rules. It seems much more probable that Tolstoy simply slipped here when he inserted Semenov's name in the sentence about the dumped earth. The whole sequence would be perfectly believable if the soldiers simply discovered scattered dirt, not connected with any individual, investigated, found the hole, and reported it. Who had dug it remained a mystery.

It is puzzling that this apparent error went so long unnoticed and uncorrected. The text of "God Sees the Truth but Waits" was reprinted many times after its original publication in the journal *Beseda* (No. 3, 1872) — in the *Primer*, in the *Third Russian Book for Reading*, in various editions of the Collected Works published by the Countess, and in many cheap pamphlet editions published by the firm Posrednik (The Intermediary) for consumption by the common folk. In all of them the questionable sentence remains intact.[6]

The only alteration made in the text stemmed from quite different considerations. Vladimir Chertkov, Tolstoy's disciple-in-chief, who bore much of the responsibility for the Posrednik editions, worried about the story for different reasons, more serious than a technical error in the plot. He wrote Tolstoy on 31 January 1885:

> I have long been troubled by your story "God Sees the Truth." When the commandant asks about the digging and says to Aksenov, "Old man, you are truthful, tell me before God who did it," Aksenov answers, "I did not see it and do not know." But in fact he both saw and knew. Consequently he is resorting to a deliberate lie in order to save his comrade. Moreover, this very act gives the impression of being the greatest deed of his life. But this act could remain such even if he were freed from deceit. Aksenov could say that he did not dig the tunnel and remain silent about whether or not he knew who did. (*PSS* 85:141)

Tolstoy was convinced by this argument. He replied to Chertkov as follows:

> To the elimination of the passages you wrote about I very gladly and gratefully agree. Only do it yourself. If I started to do it, I would redo everything, and I need the time for other things. (*PSS* 85:139)

---

[6] Actually, the error was already present in the only surviving manuscript variant, in which the character is not yet named. "The next day the soldiers noticed that the new convict was spreading earth. They began to search in the stockade and found the hole." На другой день солдаты приметили, что новый колодник высыпал землю, стали искать в остроге и нашли дыру. (*PSS* 21:475)

A new speech was written for Aksenov, though by whom is a question:

> "I cannot say, Your Excellency. God does not permit me to tell. And I will not. Do what you like with me; I am in your power." No matter how hard the commandant struggled with him, Aksenov said nothing more. Thus they never found out who had dug the tunnel. ("Не могу сказать, ваше благородие. Мне Бог не велит сказать. И не скажу. Что хотите со мной делайте — власть ваша." Сколько ни бился с ним начальник, Аксенов больше ничего не говорил. Так и не узнали, кто подкопался. *PSS* 21:334)

Whether written by Tolstoy or not, this text obviously had his approval and is later than the one in the *Primer* and the Collected Works.[7] Nevertheless, the editors in charge of the Jubilee Edition did not use it in their supposedly "canonical" version, which retains Aksenov's unnecessary lie. I do not agree with this decision.[8] The "I won't tell" text is the latest one approved by the author, and according to standard textological principles it should stand as canonical.

The question remains, who wrote the new "I won't tell" version, Tolstoy or Chertkov. On this point Professor Jahn and I differ; I say Tolstoy, he says Chertkov. A strong argument in his favor is Tolstoy's "Do it yourself" letter to Chertkov of 5–6 February 1885, quoted above. To counter this evidence that Chertkov, following Tolstoy's authorization, proceeded to write the new sentence himself, one would need strong arguments. I believe such arguments exist.

First (and weakest), the editor of the Tolstoy-Chertkov correspondence, Liubov' Gurevich, says (*PSS* 85:140) that Tolstoy determined (установил) the new, "I won't tell" version as the final text. The word *ustanovil*, however, is ambiguous: does it mean "wrote" or simply "approved"? I of course vote for "wrote."

Second, later that year, in a letter of 15–16 October 1885 (*PSS* 85:267) despite the "Do it yourself" prescription and his fear of wasting time on the story, Tolstoy himself did supply a new subtitle for the story (though for

---

[7] True, there were later editions of the *Third Russian Book for Reading* and of the Collected Works, but there is no evidence that Tolstoy took any part in these publications.

[8] In the commentary to the story by V. S. Spiridonov in the Jubilee edition (*PSS* 21:654) there seems to be an implication that the revised Posrednik text was Chertkov's and only had Tolstoy's passive assent: "These changes were introduced into the text of the story by V. G. Chertkov with Tolstoy's consent" (655). But the only evidence for this is Tolstoy's "Do it yourself" letter of 5–6 February. Spiridonov then does point out that the Posrednik ("I won't tell") text was used in the Sytin edition of the Collected Works, edited by P. I. Biriukov (Moscow, 1913). He then says simply, "In this (the "I don't know") version it [the story] is printed in the present [Jubilee] edition." He does not argue the point or explain how this decision was reached. In my opinion, the decision was incorrect.

some reason it was never used): "A Story of How an Innocent Man Died at Forced Labor for Another Man's Sin and Forgave the Perpetrator."

Third, and to me most decisive, is simply *style*. The new, "I won't tell" version sounds to me unmistakably Tolstoyan. It is *perfect*. The psychology is right, the language is right. Chertkov just could not have written that passage; he did not have that kind of talent. He was hardly even a Salieri to Tolstoy's Mozart. So, I believe, Tolstoy must have written the new version and sent it to Chertkov for insertion.

In addition, the new version just seems to me artistically *better*. Aksenov would have thought just like Chertkov: lying is a sin (even in the name of a higher, divine truth). And there was no need to lie; he could just refuse to tell. If the commandant threatened him, he would be no more intimidated than he was by Semenov's threats. "I am in your power." He was quite ready for martyrdom if that was to be the consequence of his refusal.

To return to Tolstoy's alleged error, in all the published texts, book and pamphlet alike, the soldiers still observe Semenov spilling (or having spilled) dirt and yet never report him. All except one. Louise Maude, wife of Tolstoy's English disciple, friend, and biographer Aylmer Maude, translated "God Sees the Truth" into English in 1900. She apparently noticed the obvious discrepancy and undertook to fix it, but as far as we know without clearing the new version with the author. In her translation Makar Semenov's name has been removed from the troublesome sentence, which now reads, "Next day, when the convicts were led out to work, the convoy soldiers noticed that *one or other of the prisoners* [my italics] emptied some earth out of his boot. The prison was searched and the tunnel found" (Tolstoy 1928, 8–9.) (Incidentally, Louise Maude also used the revised, "I won't tell" version of Aksenov's speech.) Aylmer Maude wrote Tolstoy asking Tolstoy for his written approval of his wife's (Mrs. Maude's) translation, a document apparently demanded by her publisher. Tolstoy replied in early September, 1900, "I would write Luiza Iakovlevna my authorisation [English word], but I don't know how to formulate it. Send me the form." (*PSS* 72:449)

Very likely Tolstoy never reviewed Mrs. Maude's translation at all, but was quite ready to write his "authorisation" simply out of friendship and trust. There is also no evidence that the Maudes ever called Tolstoy's attention to the correction Mrs. Maude had made in translating Tolstoy's text. Thus the Russian original remains uncorrected to this day.

Afterword (2007)

In reprinting this exchange it seemed only fair to leave it intact, just as it appeared in 2004. Since that time the eloquence and cogency of Gary

Jahn's arguments after further reflection have led me to concede some, though not all, of his points. In the meantime Jahn's case has also been reinforced by arguments adduced by Alexander F. Zweers in 2006. I will therefore try to summarize here my conclusions as of 2007.

1. I still think Tolstoy "erred" in inserting the name Makar Semenov in the sentence, "... Когда вывели килодников на работу, солдаты приметили, что Макар Семенов высыпал землю..." Even though the Russian tense and aspect system make it possible to read this sentence as meaning that the soldiers perceived only the result of Semenov's action, not the action itself, I do not believe that reverence for Tolstoy's genius requires us to accept every sentence he composed as absolutely the best way of saying what he meant. I still contend that it would have been better to make "earth" (землю) the object of the soldiers' noticing, rather than a clause containing the name of the perpetrator.

2. I am now willing to concede that in the absence of weightier evidence than I adduced that Tolstoy himself composed the new Posrednik version of Aksenov's reply to the commandant, we must attribute that version to Chertkov. Tolstoy's "You do it" letter is decisive in this respect.

3. However, the question of which version should be regarded as "canonical" remains open. Even if Chertkov wrote the new version, Tolstoy clearly authorized it and made no effort to change it in later editions. It therefore has Tolstoy's imprimatur. The usual textological principle is that the *latest* version approved by the author should be considered canonical. As I note, the editors of the Jubilee Edition provide no arguments for their decision to use the earlier version; they just did it. Maybe they just liked it better, as Gary Jahn does, or perhaps they prefer the earlier version because it is "pure Tolstoy," uncontaminated by the sanctimonious Chertkov. In any case, their decision is clearly at least debatable.

4. Gary Jahn may be right that at the time he was being questioned by the commandant, Aksenov had not progressed far enough in his religious development to speak so confidently of a dialogue with God (Мне Бог не велит сказать). However, at that moment he *has* already progressed far enough to resist the opportunity to take vengeance on his enemy by denouncing him. Instead, he answers with the protective lie, "Я не видал и не знаю." This seems to me, as it did to Chertkov, a spiritual act of a high order, (apparent) forgiveness of one's enemy, even though perhaps he had not yet come to the point of accepting his own punishment as deserved or of perceiving the universal guilt of mankind.

5. Jahn may be right that if openly defied with a "I won't tell" statement, the commandant would take more decisive measures to force Aksenov to talk. However, we are told earlier that the commandant had respect for

Aksenov as an especially compliant prisoner, and Aksenov's invocation of God might also have affected him. I therefore find it plausible that after arguing and even pleading with Aksenov, the commandant would realize that further pressure was useless and do nothing more.

Was the Master Well Served?
Further Comment on "God Sees the Truth but Waits"

Gary R. Jahn, University of Minnesota

Hugh McLean draws our attention to certain problematic passages in Leo Tolstoy's "God Sees the Truth but Waits." I am very pleased to have been asked to contribute some remarks of my own to complement, and to contend with, those of Professor McLean. I am delighted at the attention given to a story which I (and Tolstoy himself—in *What Is Art?*) count among his best. I am sure that both McLean and I will be content to let readers judge for themselves of the issues we raise. Probably the interested reader is best advised to begin with McLean's paper.

I turn first to McLean's contention that Tolstoy suffered a bad lapse in continuity in writing the sentence: "На другой день, когда вывели колодников на работу, солдаты приметили, что Макар Семенов высыпал [perfective ВЫсыпал or imperfective высыПАЛ] землю, стали искать в остроге и нашли дыру." He maintains that according to this sentence there would be no need for the authorities to open an investigation since the soldiers saw Makar scattering the earth from his excavation. I am quite willing to admit that this sentence is potentially ambiguous, especially considering the complexity of translating it into equivalent English. An exact translation, taking into account the sequencing of tenses in reporting actions in Russian, would be:

"On the next day, after the convicts had been taken to their work, the soldiers noticed that Makar Semenov had scattered dirt about, began to search the prison, and found the hole."

We as readers already know that it was Makar who had scattered the dirt around, but the soldiers do not—what they notice is the result of Makar's action [if perfective], not the action itself. They see that dirt has been scattered about. Still, one admits that perhaps in Russian and certainly in English translation this will be confusing, especially if there is a less than pedantic attention given to the sequence of tenses. It is not surprising, then, that a translator (McLean cites the translation of Louise Maude) might express this not word for word but through equivalence, thus: the soldiers noticed that someone had scattered dirt around. In my opinion this need not necessarily be seen as evidence of the translator tacitly correcting an authorial lapse; it could as well be simply the result of accommodating the lack of clear perfectivization in the verbal system of English.

It seems to me that for Tolstoy's text to be an unambiguous mistake or a source of confusion in Russian (rather than simply a difficulty for the English translator) the Russian sentence would have to have been: Солдаты приметили, что Макар Семенов ВЫСЫПАЕТ землю (using the present tense to indicate that when the soldiers noticed this, the action was in progress, rather than the past tense, which indicates that the action had taken place prior to its being noticed by the soldiers and that Makar at that moment was no longer performing this action). If we suppose that the verb form in question is the past tense *imperfective* 'высыПАЛ' (and there is no reason on the face of the passage not to suppose this), no significant distinction enters the argument. Whether the soldiers noticed that Makar "had been scattering" [habitually, for a while, or whatever] or "had scattered" the dirt around, the point remains that he was no longer doing it when the soldiers noticed that the dirt had been scattered. In all likelihood a sentence certain to produce the confusion which McLean ascribes to it would read: Солдаты приметили, КАК Макар Семенов ВЫСЫПАЕТ землю.

On the whole, however, I willingly admit that one cannot make an indisputable case that this sentence could not have been improved. I may, then, be running the risk of "parturiunt montes, nascetur ridiculus mus" if I offer two further passages from the story in support of the contention that Tolstoy was well aware of the issues of tense and aspect and in fact used these as I have suggested. Near the end of the story, after Makar has broken down following his confession to Aksenov, we read: "Когда Аксенов услыхал, что Макар Семенов плачет, он сам заплакал . . ." This sentence is grammatically analogous to the one in dispute, but Tolstoy here clearly means to say that Aksenov hears Makar's weeping and he uses the present tense (плачет) to specify as much. Conversely, in the earlier sentence: "На другую ночь . . . он [Аксенов] услыхал, что кто-то подошел и сел у него в ногах," the use of the past tense perfective clearly establishes that Makar's approach and seating himself were already completed by the time Aksenov "sensed" that someone was there with him, sitting on his cot. Since Tolstoy seems clearly to have been conscious of the distinctions entailed by the selection of aspect/tense in these two examples, I see no reason not to assume that he was likewise aware of them in the sentence under discussion. Finally, in the disputed sentence we also have the clause "когда вывели колодников на работу," so that the sentence seems to specify not only *what* the soldiers saw but also *when* they saw it—*after* they had led (perfective) the convicts out to work. If so, then the soldiers did not see Makar himself scattering the dirt, since he has told Aksenov that he scattered the dirt *while* they were being taken out to work (высыпает [землю] на улицу, когда их гоняют на работу). At a minimum I would stoutly resist any claim that it is *clear* that this sentence represents a stylistic, logical, or grammatical error on Tolstoy's part, or a lapse in continuity. After all, if we think that this sentence represents a mistake on Tolstoy's part, and if we know that a whole series of changes were made to the story some 15 years after its first publication in the early 1870s for the Posrednik version of the mid-1880s, it is strange that those who produced those fairly numerous and significant emendations seem NOT to have thought that this particular sentence was also in need of being changed.

This brings me now to the point which McLean raises with respect to one of the emendations introduced into the first Posrednik edition. He resurrects the textological question (discussed at length in the Jubilee Edition [hereafter as JE], vols. 21 and 85) of the changes introduced into the story at the time that it was published by Posrednik in the mid-1880s. There were quite a number of these changes, but McLean is concerned with only one of them—that in which the 1870s version's simple denial by Aksenov, when questioned by the authorities, that he knows anything about the escape hole that had been discovered in the prison is replaced by a longer text designed to enable Aksenov not to tell what he knows without telling a direct lie. The paper recounts the background of this (and the other) changes. It is quite right and well documented that it originated in the discomfort of V. G. Chertkov that a lie leads to "the greatest spiritual feat of the hero's life." Tolstoy writes to Chertkov telling him to go ahead and make the changes, and so the Posrednik edition (and all later versions of the story brought out by D. I. Sytin, who published and distributed the Posrednik materials) replaced Aksenov's original response: "Не видал и не знаю" (hereafter, the "I don't know" version) with this one: "Не могу сказать, ваше благородие. Мне Бог не велит сказать. И не скажу. Что хотите со мной делайте—власть ваша" (hereafter, the "I won't tell" version). The editors of various later editions of the story, led by V. S. Spiridonov in the Jubilee Edition, have generally concluded that this change (and the others) was concocted by Chertkov and agreed to by Tolstoy, quite possibly without full knowledge in advance of the details of the emendations.

Such is the known background. McLean makes the case that Tolstoy wrote this emendation himself. I remain unconvinced, however, by the arguments he provides. Tolstoy's letter to Chertkov giving permission for changes to be made seems clear and unambiguous to me. The relevant passage says: "На исключение тех мест [Chertkov had also asked permission to excise some passages from "Кавказский пленник" for the same edition] о которых вы писали, я очень радостно согласен и благодарен. *Только делайте сами. Если бы я стал делать, я бы все переделал, а время нужно на другое"* (emphasis mine). Absent other evidence, I see nothing here to suggest that Tolstoy made these changes himself; rather the reverse, in fact. It seems clear that Tolstoy wanted to, indeed was glad and relieved, to take no active part in the revision which he authorized. I wouldn't go so far as to say that it is *impossible* that Tolstoy made these changes himself, only that there is no compelling documentary reason to think so.

Prof. McLean candidly acknowledges that his contention that the "I won't tell" version of the passage is to be preferred is speculative and rests primarily on his feeling that this version is in fact superior to the earlier version—he believes that it has the hallmarks of the master's style, it is perfectly formed, it fits the context in which it is found more aptly than the earlier version, and it is well beyond the talents of Chertkov.

I can agree that the passage is in part characteristically Tolstoyan, especially the latter half of it: "Сколько ни бился с ним начальник, Аксенов больше ничего не говорил." However, the first part (for our purpose the more relevant part) strikes me as a false note in the story. "Мне Бог не велит сказать. И не скажу. Что хотите со мной делайте — власть ваша" strikes me as sanctimonious and premature, given the context in which the words are uttered. These words imply that a perfect link of communication between Аксеnov and the deity is already at this point in existence, that Aksenov has already reached that state of exalted spirituality in which Tolstoy has clearly placed him by the story's end. But the text tells us that during his interrogation by the warden of the prison Aksenov is in a state of confusion: "У Аксенова тряслись руки и губы, и он долго не мог слова выговорить." In fact, his condition is presented as similar to that in which he finds himself in the first half of the story when being questioned by the police and confronted with the bloody knife which was found in his pack: "Аксенов хотел отвечать, но не мог выговорить слова."[9] We are also told that during the two weeks between Aksenov's dawning realization that Makar was the murderer of the merchant and his interrogation by the warden he has been beset by powerful feelings of resentment, anger, and the desire for revenge:

[9] It may be worth noting that when Aksenov finally does answer, he responds to both the policeman and the warden in the same way: "не знаю." In both episodes Aksenov is confused, but in the first his confusion arises from fear and anxiety; in the second from uncertainty about what to do.

И такая скука нашла на Аксенова, что хоть руки на себя наложить. — "И все от того злодея!" — думал Аксенов. И нашла на него такая злость на Макара Семенова, что хоть самому пропасть, а хотелось отомстить ему. Он читал молитвы всю ночь, но не мог успокоиться.

It seems clear that so far from being in a state of communion with the deity, Aksenov is presented as being profoundly upset. Yet, according to the revision insisted upon by Chertkov and favored by McLean, Aksenov here responds to the warden with the calm fearlessness of a saint, perhaps even a would-be martyr: "God does not command me to tell. And I will not. Do with me as you will; the power is yours." Indeed, the suggestion that Aksenov expects the warden to "do with him as he will" presents a further anomaly: why does the warden *not* do something. It strikes me as lacking in verisimilitude that the warden seems to accept what is, after all, open defiance from one of his prisoners with nothing more than some additional attempts at persuasion ("сколько ни бился с ним начальник"). If, in any context of "normal" or "real" life the convict Aksenov had told the warden "Well, I know who did it but I'm not going to tell you," the sequel, it seems to me, could hardly have been what the story reports. Wouldn't the warden have had to deal with great severity with this open challenge to his authority? Wouldn't there have been threats, beatings, solitary confinements to bend the stubborn Aksenov to the warden's will? Verisimilitude would seem to require this. For this reason, too, I find it difficult to believe that Tolstoy himself wrote that emendation. Most likely, to me, is the following: Chertkov was bothered that Aksenov tells a lie in the story; he asks Tolstoy to consider making a change; Tolstoy writes back to him to say "Go ahead, but do it yourself"; Chertkov takes out the offending passage and replaces it with a slightly reworked version of an earlier passage in the story (Makar has told Aksenov that if he tells, Makar will exact a terrible revenge; Aksenov replies: "I shall tell or not, as God directs."[10])

Thus the stylistic reasons for my preference for the earlier ("I don't know") version of this passage over the later one ("I won't tell"). Beyond these, however, I believe that there is a significant thematic point at issue here as well. We might reflect for a moment on the question "Why did Chertkov feel so strongly that the passage was in need of emendation?" In asking Tolstoy to emend the text of the story Chertkov began by indicating his anxiety over two passages in "Kavkazskii plennik" which he felt were

---

[10] This manner of speaking is quite in the spirit of the particular context. Makar is threatening Aksenov, and Aksenov, filled with hatred and anger toward Makar, is in no mood simply to knuckle under to these threats. He responds so as to leave Makar in doubt as to whether he would tell or not.

such as to cause the impressionable readers of this popular edition [лубочное издание] of the stories to go, if only slightly, morally astray:

> "... Я наверное знаю, что эти два места [in "Kavkazskii plennik"] должны вызывать в таких читателях одобрительный смех и, следовательно, давать им еще один толчок в том уже слишком господствующем направлении, которое признает, что несравненно практичнее при достижении своих целей не слишком строго разбирать средства (*PSS* 85:140).

He is concerned that the story should convey the message that sin is sin, and there are no two ways about it. He goes on to say that he is even more concerned about the passage in "God Sees the Truth": "скажу вам, . . . о том, что меня давно мучает в вашем рассказе *Бог правду видит*." He describes the passage which we have been discussing here, concluding by citing Aksenov's answer to the warden: "Я не видал и не знаю" Chertkov continues: "А между тем он видал и знает и, следовательно, прибегает к сознательной лжи ради спасения своего товарища, между тем самый этот его поступок производит впечатление высшего подвига его жизни" (*PSS* 85:141).

Thus, what upset Chertkov was that the "conscious lie" told by Aksenov to "save his comrade" is presented in the story as "the highest spiritual feat" of his life. Plainly, Chertkov has construed this moment as the story's climax, the point at which Aksenov enters into that state of spiritual exaltation which marks him at the end of the story.[11] Chertkov was appealing for a response from Aksenov that would match the sanctity of this moment, something more appropriate than a "conscious lie." He felt

---

[11] Some of the other changes introduced into the Posrednik edition are significant in this respect, as suggesting that Aksenov has already attained spiritual enlightenment at the moment when the warden confronts him. For example, where the original version has Aksenov in prison buying and reading *The Lives of the Saints* (Четьи минеи), the revision for Posrednik substitutes the Gospels (Евангелие), possibly suggesting that in prison Aksenov had become fully Christ-like rather than merely a simulacrum of Christ, as were the saints. Again, in the passage where Makar confronts Aksenov and warns him under threat of death not to tell about the tunnel, the original version notes that Aksenov was "shaking from head to foot with злость" (the word is difficult to translate—something like 'hatred and the desire to hurt'). The revised version seeks to show an Aksenov not quite so much in the grip of his ill feelings by omitting this phrase altogether. He therefore seems much more removed from his own painful memories than he was in the original. Finally, at the point in the story which I have identified as climactic the original version has Aksenov say "Perhaps I am a hundred times worse than you" followed by the sentence: "И вдруг у него на душе легко стало" ("And all at once the burden was lifted from his soul [lit. it became light (i.e., without weight) on his soul]). In removing this sentence, the person who carried out the revision was clearly removing an important indicator that this was, in fact, the climactic moment of the story as Tolstoy wrote it.

perhaps that Aksenov's righteous truthfulness in the revised version would be such a response. In agreeing that the revision is to be preferred to the original, McLean seems also to agree to the proposition that at this moment of spiritual triumph a lie, even a kindly one, would be a false note.

The flaw in Chertkov's reasoning (aside from neutrally characterizing Makar, whom Aksenov hated and despised, as "his comrade" or "fellow prisoner") is that this is *not* the story's climactic moment nor does it mark Aksenov's attainment of his "highest spiritual feat." It is clear, in fact, that when, on the night after the interrogation, Makar comes to Aksenov, the latter is still in the grip of a very human confusion and fear. He says: "Что надо? Уйди! А то я солдата кликну." When Makar makes it clear that he has come to confess and beg forgiveness, Aksenov is no longer anxious, but he remains aloof and unforgiving, saying: "Тебе говорить легко, а мне терпеть каково! Куда я пойду теперь? Жена померла, дети забыли. Мне ходить некуда." In short, he is still at this point far from spiritual elevation, burdened with resentment and regret. It is only when he hears Makar burst into tears that a remarkable change overwhelms Aksenov. He, too, begins to weep, and when Makar again beseeches his forgiveness, Aksenov replies: "'Бог простит тебя; может быть, я во сто раз хуже тебя. И вдруг у него на душе легко стало." It is only now that he achieves his "highest spiritual feat," and the essence of that achievement is in his recognition that his "saintly" life in prison has not led to spiritual enlightenment and calm, that he has remained perhaps "a hundred times worse" than Makar.

I agree with McLean that the point of the story is that at the end of it Aksenov comes to believe that his punishment was deserved, and it is this punishment and suffering which finally alerts him to the fact that he is, in some real sense, perhaps really "a hundred times worse" than Makar. Like Makar he has still, after 26 years, not come to a full recognition of his spiritual nature. The path to this understanding has been long. It begins around the time of his arrest and trial when, suspected even by his wife and with his appeal denied by the Tsar, he decides to "hope only in God." It continues through the establishment of the saintly persona which he develops while in prison. He accustoms himself to *say* that he is in prison on account of his own sins ("по грехам своим"), but that he hasn't yet really accepted this or sincerely felt it is shown by the sharp resurgence of anger, sense of loss, and desire for revenge that overwhelms him when he becomes certain that Makar was the real villain. Even after 26 years of self-denial and rigorous piety he is nowhere close to the realization that he himself is the "real" villain. Only after he has been touched to the heart by Makar's tears and understood that he and his tormentor are as one does he arrive at his true and final spiritual destination.

"God Sees the Truth but Waits" is, in my opinion, a miniature theodicy—an explanation of the existence of evil in God's world. The cruel injustice done to Aksenov turns out to be only an apparent evil; its real effect was to lead him to a true understanding of his fate and himself. Only by this difficult path does he come to experience genuine joy. From this point of view, deciding whether "I don't know" or "I won't tell" is the better reading of the passage in question is really a matter of deciding which of them fits better with the state of Aksenov's spiritual condition at the moment of the interrogation. The original version of the passage is, as Chertkov said, a lie—morally imperfect but practical and very much of this world. It would be appropriate to one who had not yet quite found the way to his spiritual self. The pious truth of the revised version is noble, self-sacrificing to the point of inviting martyrdom, and appropriate to one for whom the world was already of no account. I suggest that the reader's understanding of where Aksenov is at the relevant moment on his spiritual journey is the key determinant of which of the two versions better suits the story.

I see the interrogation and Aksenov's response to the warden as one more step on the protagonist's road to spiritual enlightenment rather than as an evidence that he has already arrived. I therefore prefer the original version of the passage in question as more appropriate to one who is shown to be still filled with anxiety, confusion, hatred, and despair. Aksenov will not get where Tolstoy wants him to go until he realizes that he and Makar are related as like unto like rather than as victim and tormentor. The text makes a point of the fact that Makar finds himself in prison on a false charge. He finds it ironic that he has been unjustly convicted for an action that was not a crime, having escaped punishment for the many crimes he *had* committed. In other words, Makar, like Aksenov, was unjustly convicted and sent to prison, but, unlike Aksenov, he freely admits that he is far from guiltless and that, therefore, his punishment is appropriate. Aksenov remains in the clutch of his belief in his own innocence until almost the last moment. It is only the tears he shares with Makar at the end that unites him to Makar and occasions the realization that everything he had lost, the suffering he had endured, really didn't matter at all.[12]

---

[12] Tolstoy will use a close variant of this ending in *The Death of Ivan Ilich*. There Ivan remains in the grip of his illness until he finally realizes that his life, with which he had been so contented and of which he had been so proud, was really "не то" ("not the right thing at all"). At that moment, precipitated by touching by chance the hand of his son, the protagonist enters upon a spiritual life in which pain and death are no more.

II

TOLSTOY the THINKER

A Woman's Place . . .
The Young Tolstoy and the "Woman Question"[1]

> Не дай мне Бог сойтись на бале
> Иль при разъезде на крыльце
> С семинаристом в желтой шале
> Иль с академиком в чепце!

A dialogue

A. Tolstoy was a dyed-in-the-wool misogynist. Among his pronouncements on the subject of women are such gems as this:

> For seventy years I have been steadily lowering and lowering my opinion of women, and I must still lower it more and more. The woman question!—How could there not be a woman question! Only not about how women should control life, but how they should stop ruining it.[2]

B. How could Tolstoy be a misogynist? He was the creator of some of the most enchanting, admirable, lovable heroines in world literature: Natasha Rostova, Marya Bolkonskaya, Kitty Shcherbatskaya, and even, despite her sinfulness, the great Anna Karenina herself. Tolstoy understood women and loved them.

This particular "woman question," was Tolstoy a misogynist or not, has been vigorously debated among Tolstoy scholars, some of them employing sophisticated and ingenious—perhaps a bit too ingenious—arguments, usually in an effort to claim Tolstoy as a feminist ally despite his occasional venomous outbursts.[3] The present article, however, will not venture far into that crossfire. Instead, it will examine only a small patch of this heavily

---

[1] I would like to express my grateful appreciation to colleagues who have read drafts of this article and suggested improvements: Donna Orwin, Robert Hughes, Brian Horowitz, and James Rice.
[2] Diary entry of 20 November 1899. *PSS*. 53:231.
[3] E.g., Ruth Crego Benson, Barbara Heldt, Amy Mandelker.

mined territory, namely, the attitudes and sentiments of the young Tolstoy, up to about 1870, not toward women in general, but toward the so-called "woman question."

By the time Tolstoy came on the literary scene in the mid-1850s the "woman question" already loomed large among the many "questions" that then agitated Russian society, as it awakened from the long, freezing night of Nicholas I's reign and began to contemplate the possibility of reshaping its own institutions in more rational and humane ways. The woman question as then conceived had essentially two dimensions, a social-intellectual and a sexual one.

On the social-intellectual plane the revolutionary view was advanced that though their muscles might be weaker, women's brains were just as good as men's, perhaps even better.[4] They should therefore enjoy the same opportunities as men for educating those brains; furthermore, following that education they should have the same opportunities to participate in public life as men, in the professions, in business, in government service. Of course, it should be noted that in Russia even for men education, particularly higher education, was available only to a tiny minority. The "woman question" was thus largely an "upper-class woman question," referring to women from backgrounds similar to those of educated men.[5]

On the sexual plane, women's liberation likewise meant equality between men and women, freedom of choice: a woman should be as free as a man to choose a spouse (and even to propose marriage). She should never be forced into marriage against her will. Full liberation also meant elimination of the famous "double standard." The same rules of morality should apply to both men and women, and if women should be "pure" at marriage, so should men. (This doctrine had obvious problems in view of the fact that at the time of marriage men were often a decade or more older, as Tolstoy himself was, than their teen-age brides. Furthermore, it was widely believed that frequent sexual release was essential to men's health, though no parallel need was ascribed to women.) More ardent and romantic reformists wanted even more, or perhaps something quite different. They insisted that sexual relations should always be an expression of *love*. Both women and men should be guided by their hearts, and in the quest for the perfect mate they should be free to change sexual partners

---

[4] The latter is my wife's (not too serious) contention, based on the fact that among *all* our fellow mammals the females bear all alone, without any help from their frivolous and irresponsible mates, the complex and demanding job of nurturing and rearing offspring.

[5] This aspect of the historical woman question has been very well studied in several important works, e.g., Richard Stites, Dorothy Atkinson, Alexander Dallin and Gail Warshovsky Lapidus; G. A. Tishkin; Tishkin, ed., *Feminizm*.

at will. This "free love" position was associated with the flamboyant figure of George Sand, whose novels and whose own life presented vivid models of a woman's active pursuit of happiness through love. A troublesome problem, however, remained that of *family.* What was to become of the offspring of these sexual unions, who bore responsibility for them? Could a woman at the same time be a mother, a lover—and, perhaps, a lawyer?

Tolstoy obviously had encountered many of these age-old problems long before, first from observations of family life, his own and others', and in the course of numerous sexual encounters with lower-class women. As a fashionable "question," however, as formulated by others, he discovered feminism only when in late 1855 he arrived in Petersburg from the Crimean War. Already a published and admired author, he was immediately accepted into the *Contemporary* circle and befriended by such established luminaries as Turgenev, Nekrasov, Goncharov, Grigorovich, and Ostrovsky. What he heard seems to have been a shock to him.

First of all, the *Contemporary* circle often met at the apartment of the poet Nekrasov, the magazine's chief editor. Nekrasov was openly living with another man's wife, Avdotya Panaeva; and her legal husband, Ivan Panaev, was also a member of the group, thus anticipating the role of the complacent, "understanding" cuckold later propounded as a model in Chernyshevsky's *What Is to be Done?* Tolstoy had not encountered this sort of "Bohemian" sexual laissez faire before. The common adulteries he knew about in high society were carried on, Betsy Tverskaya style, discreetly, behind a façade of decorum. The dirt and dogs of Nekrasov's abode only intensified the impression of moral disorder.

Actually, Tolstoy's early experiences with George Sand's writings had been quite favorable. Back in 1851, he had read the novel *Horace,* agreeing with his brother Nikolai that the main male character was like himself: "nobility of character, loftiness of views, love of glory, and complete incapacity for all work."[6] (Surely the diagnosed trait of perennial idleness seems strange from the author of ninety volumes of writings, not to mention other labors, but they then all lay in the future.) Three years later Tolstoy read another, unidentified Sand novel, which he found "splendid."[7] But in February, 1856, at a dinner at Nekrasov's, Tolstoy let loose a diatribe against Sand, shocking his politically correct friends. To cite Grigorovich's memoirs, "Hearing praised a new novel by George Sand, he [Tolstoy] proclaimed that he hated her, adding that the heroines of her novels, if they existed in reality, as a lesson [to themselves and

---

[6] Diary entry of 4 July 1851. *PSS* 46:66.
[7] Diary entry of 27 August 1854. *PSS* 47:24.

others] should be tied to a chariot of shame and driven through the streets of Petersburg."[8] The friends' shock was especially great because this outburst occurred in the presence of Panaeva, known as an admirer of Sand and of course guilty of the same sins as the presumed love-seeking Sand heroines. Looking back in 1909 and conveniently forgetting his own early raptures, Tolstoy said, "What a slut! [Какая стерва!]. In my time I never felt anything but disgust toward her [Sand], whereas Turgenev was enraptured by her, regarded her with respect."[9]

In any case, it is clear that by 1856 Tolstoy's convictions had crystallized at the opposite pole from the popular George Sandism. He already had a strong belief in the sacredness of family life and in marriage as a permanent and irrevocable commitment. The notion of "free love" was a sacrilege.

In that same year, 1856, Tolstoy conceived at least casts of characters for several never completed "comedies," one of which bore precisely the title "Free Love." Its dramatis personae include a gentlewoman of about thirty "with striking clothes and coiffure"; her paralyzed (and openly cuckolded) husband, very fat and lazy; the lady's twenty-two-year-old lover, "a slender dandy with a monocle and a great number of bracelet charms"; and the lady's sixty-year-old uncle, a "figure of distinction, a well-mannered society dignitary," who is also his niece's incestuous lover. The plot, so far as it can be surmised, concerns the lady's designs on a handsome, 18-year-old Georgian prince, a project her husband disapproves of, not on any grounds of morality or spousal honor, but because the uncle may be annoyed by it, and they depend on his money. It is noteworthy, however, that this imagined world of flagrant sexual depravity is not associated with the Bohemian intelligentsia or even with Petersburg, that perennial locus of evil in Tolstoy's novels, but situated in the country, on a true gentlefolk's nest. It seems that all Russia was infected with the noxious virus of George Sandism. Extreme and absurd as this unborn play may be, we may perhaps recognize in these depraved characters the ancestors of the infamous Kuragin family in *War and Peace*. In 1856 such demons of degeneracy already haunted Tolstoy's imagination.

In that same year, in the extraordinary preface to "Two Hussars"—a 192-word single sentence—Tolstoy managed to insert a seemingly gratuitous animadversion on "liberal women philosophers" in the midst of an invidious comparison of the contemporary world of the 1850s with the less contaminated one of fifty years before, the world he was to resurrect

---

[8] A. V. Grigorovich, 133.
[9] D. P. Makovický [Маковицкий], Entry of 6 April 1909.

so vividly in his great novel. One wonders if he had ever encountered any such petticoat "philosophers," but the image, even if only invented, obviously repelled him—an ugly, incongruous, and somehow threatening excrescence.

The theme of emancipated, educated women did not surface again until 1862. By that time much water had passed under Tolstoy's—and Russia's—bridges. After what he mysteriously regarded as the "disgrace" of "Family Happiness" (1859),[10] Tolstoy had loudly proclaimed his withdrawal from literature, donning alternate personae as gentleman farmer, schoolmaster, and educational theorist. Emancipated, intellectual women were very distant from his rural hideout at Yasnaya Polyana.

Real love had come at last, however, in 1862. Cupid's arrow struck, and after a whirlwind courtship Tolstoy was duly joined in marriage to the eighteen-year-old Sofya Andreevna Bers. The marriage was a turning point in many ways. As a husband and soon a father, Tolstoy reclaimed himself as a writer. The farm was neglected, the school abandoned, and he proclaimed, "I am now a writer with *all* the strength of my soul."[11] The novel on the Decembrists which he had been clandestinely and desultorily working on started growing an enormous preface—*War and Peace*.

It was a glorious transition, destined to lift Tolstoy to the ranks of the immortals. But the curious fact is that even now, right in the midst of his own lyric family happiness and his deep, immensely creative immersion in the grandeur of the Napoleonic era and the Fatherland War, Tolstoy still felt an irresistible impulse to vent his pent-up feelings about the woman question. From his file of unrealized projects dating back to 1856 he resurrected the drafts of another anti-radical, satirical comedy. Rechristening it "An Infected Family," he now brought this work to completion and took it to Moscow, hoping to get it produced at the Maly Theater.[12] The production project came to nothing, and the play was not published until 1932. The two drafts that survive, however, show that he devoted to them considerable time and energy. Whatever its literary faults, this little read or studied play remains Tolstoy's most articulated response to the woman question; it must therefore be considered here in some detail.

---

[10] " . . . such a disgraceful abomination that I can't collect myself out of shame." Tolstoy to A. A. Tolstaya, 17–31 October 1863. *PSS* 60:295. See "Buried as a Writer and as a Man."
[11] Tolstoy to A. A. Tolstaya, 17–31 October 1863. *PSS* 61:24.
[12] In Moscow Tolstoy read the play to Ostrovsky, who did not like it at all, though for Tolstoy's ears he tempered his criticisms. It proved too late in the season to have it produced that year, and by the following year Tolstoy had lost interest in the project. The finished manuscript is lost, and we are therefore limited to earlier surviving drafts. On these matters see commentary by V. F. Savodnik in *PSS* 7, 389–413; N. N. Gusev, *Материалы с 1855 по 1869 год*, 617–24; K. N. Lomunov.

Tolstoy was clearly not nearly as detached as he claimed to be from the literary squabbles and controversies of Petersburg. Though he once went to sleep at Turgenev's estate while reading in manuscript his host's *Fathers and Children*[13] Tolstoy was well aware of the polemics that had ensued after the publication of that novel, which had introduced the word "nihilist" into the popular vocabulary and the character Bazarov as a formidable specimen thereof. But the real *casus belli*, the spark that ignited Tolstoy's powder keg, was the publication of that epoch-making novel, Chernyshevsky's *What Is To Be Done?*, written by a man he had once called that "bedbug-stinking gentleman."[14] That scandalous book, destined to become a virtual Bible for generations of young Russian radicals,[15] struck Tolstoy as an absolute abomination, the very epitome of everything dangerous and hateful in the radical ethos. All his indignation and revulsion against it were to be embodied in this bombshell of a play.

Though its author assumed a stance of Olympian remoteness from the ephemeral concerns of newspapers, which he claimed seldom to read, *An Infected Family* is itself profoundly journalistic in conception and execution. Its characters are caricatured stereotypes, embodiments of abstractions, of predetermined, ideologically dictated attitudes toward current problems. Emancipated or would-be emancipated women are very much present, but they are not the only walking formulas in the play. Central is a formerly tyrannical, old-school land- and serf-owning gentleman and paterfamilias, Ivan Mikhailovich Pribyshev, now struggling to adjust to the Emancipation and to reinvent himself as a liberal and progressive. There are also several male radicals, notably the ex-seminarian Aleksei Tverdynsky, tutor to the Pribyshevs' adolescent son, Petrusha, and Anatoly Venerovsky, a very self-assured, doctrinaire, and long-winded leftist who incongruously earns his living as a tax collector (акцизный чиновник) and will play a major part as suitor to the Pribyshevs' eighteen-year-old daughter, Liubov' or Liuba. By way of moral stabilizer there is a shrewd old peasant nurse, a lone pillar of down-to-earth common sense and traditional values in the midst of everyone else's delusions and rhetorical bombast. But the woman question in various guises lies at the play's core.

---

[13] Gusev, *Материалы*, 438.

[14] "Клоповоняющий господин". Tolstoy to Nekrasov, 2 July 1856. *PSS* 60:74. Turgenev, Druzhinin, and Grigorovich also used this epithet for Chernyshevsky. Gusev thinks it was coined by Grigorovich. Gusev, *Материалы*, 72n.

[15] Irina Paperno has written a brilliant study of the impact of this novel on generations of young Russians: *Chernyshevsky and the Age or Realism: A Study in the Semiotics of Behavior.*

The leading emancipated woman is Ivan Mikhailovich's niece, Katerina Matveevna Dudkina, a true *nigilistka* (though this word is never used). She is 26 years old—a dangerous, almost "over the hill" age for a nineteenth-century unmarried woman. She exhibits the expected physical accouterments of her species: her hair is cut short, she wears glasses, and she smokes. (Later in Tolstoy smoking is always a sign of moral weakness, but here it may only be an affectation, a demonstrative defiance of the taboo that restricted tobacco to men.) She wears a short dress and carries a serious magazine (science!) under her arm, which she brings to breakfast and begins to read without greeting anyone.

Katerina is a rival of her cousin Liuba for the hand of Venerovsky. Katerina had known him before in Petersburg, presumably as his lover, but Liuba has the advantage of a much bigger dowry and is also more physically attractive. Katerina of course cannot acknowledge either of these as valid male matrimonial motives. Money, she says, could not matter to Venerovsky. "Venerovsky doesn't care whether I have a million or nothing as long as our views of life are identical." To this the sharp old nurse responds tartly that to Venerovsky Liuba's "five hundred souls are very identical, and your thirty are not identical at all." (For all its many flaws, this play does have some good lines.) Further, when the nurse suggests that Venerovsky's attraction to Liuba might be that of a he-goat, Katerina indignantly replies, "Love as you understand it is an attraction of the flesh, and you are too undeveloped and animal-like to understand me."

Liuba herself now appears at this extended breakfast and reveals herself to be a lively, animated young woman, affectionate with her parents, but with a will of her own. Out picking mushrooms with some servant girls, she had encountered Venerovsky and had with him a serious conversation, the contents of which she will not yet reveal. She already shows a trace of feminist indoctrination emanating from her cousin. When her father questions the propriety of her walking unchaperoned in the woods with a young man, she answers, "What a retrograde attitude! Right, Katen'ka?"

Of course it turns out that the nurse is proved prescient: Venerovsky asks for the hand not of Katerina, but of Liuba. Despite his explanations in a much too long soliloquy, his motives are not entirely clear. (In general, this character seems put together out of too many disparate and conflicting pieces to be believable.) He feels some real misgivings about marriage to "an undeveloped woman, corrupted by her milieu" and even about marriage itself; but on the other hand, the lure of financial security plus the magnetism of attractive female flesh are strong enough to overcome any such inhibitions. He can justify his actions by the thought that he is "extracting this young woman, a fine girl, from the stultifying and immoral conditions in which she has been living." Venerovsky knows that Katerina will be deeply hurt by his betrayal, but to a friend he justifies his choice on the simple grounds that although Katerina is "an emancipated woman," she is just not sexually attractive. He does admit that in the past he and Katerina had had "certain relations," but he claims that "as an honorable man, understanding a woman's freedom," at the time he had made clear to her that he assumed no obligation as a result of those relations. Love should be free.

Before Katerina learns of Venerovsky's proposal to Liuba, she performs the ultimate act of the fully liberated, George Sandist female: *she proposes to him.*

> "Venerovsky!" [she says]. "I have plumbed the depths of my consciousness and become convinced that we must unite. Yes. I leave it up to you in what forms this union should take place. If you think it necessary, in view of the crowd and of both your and my undeveloped relatives, to go through the ceremony of matrimony, no matter how repugnant it is to my convictions, I give my assent in advance and make this concession. [. . .] We will be the prototype of new relations between man and woman. We will be the realization of the idea of the century."[16]

Poor Venerovsky has to reply to this principled *profession d'amour.* He first offers her (and himself) the compliment that she had shown "a high degree of development" by making such a wise choice of lovers as himself. But he must tell the truth: he cannot accept her proposal. He has made another choice. Katerina is deeply wounded, but she is constrained by her George Sandist ideology to admit that he was within his rights. Katerina now learns from her uncle the terrible truth that Venerovsky's "other choice" is her naïve and underdeveloped cousin, Liuba, and she is appropriately shocked and disillusioned. She had thought better of him.

It is now Venerovsky's job to emancipate his fiancée, Liuba, who has readily accepted his proposal. He lectures her pompously about equality of women and about mutual freedom in marriage, but is a bit taken aback when she agrees all too readily: "Yes, why not get married a second time?

---

[16] This speech also illustrates the stilted pretentiousness of the radicals' language as Tolstoy parodies it. A parallel example of nihilist language, not stilted, but sickeningly cloy, is Venerovsky's use of the word "миленькая" (little darling) as a term of endearment for Liuba. (She doesn't like it.) This usage is clearly a direct carry-over from *What Is To Be Done?*, where Vera Pavlovna habitually calls Lopukhov "Миленький." Many more examples of such parodic language are cited in the excellent discussion of the play by Boris Eikhenbaum 1931, 211–222, especially 215.

[. . .] Well, if I suddenly get tired of one husband . . ." At this he quickly interrupts, but he later reiterates her point, affirming "the right to separate, without reproach or bitterness." "The chief obstacle to the development of individuality in general," he instructs her, "is the family, especially for you. [. . .] It is the dirt that besmirches you." To think of papa and mama as dirt is a bit too much for the naturally affectionate, insufficiently emancipated girl, and she raises mild objections. She also forces Venerovsky, much against his will, to go through the repugnant ceremony of receiving her parents' blessing—on their knees—and followed by a kiss.

From that point on the plot rather founders on the inconsistencies in Venerovsky's character. If he is marrying Liuba for gain or simply for lust, one would think he would consider it politic to observe the usual wedding customs, regardless of his radical contempt for them: her father still holds the purse strings. But no, he seems to make every effort to offend her family. It is only her father's blind conviction that Venerovsky's rudeness is somehow up-to-date and modern that prevents a serious rift. Nevertheless, the wedding ceremony apparently does take place, off stage, and Liuba and Venerovsky become legally husband and wife.

Custom requires the bride's relatives, minus her parents, to visit the groom at his abode and be entertained there with champagne. They are to return to her parents for a ceremonial supper before going abroad on their honeymoon. But Venerovsky's apartment is a mess, no proper preparations have been made, and the usual wedding gaiety is sadly missing. Worse, Venerovsky has decided that they must leave at once, skipping the supper entirely—another gratuitous offense to her parents, who, along with their guests and some musicians are left waiting in vain for the newlyweds to appear. In the midst of their consternation a lackey brings Ivan Mikhailovich three letters, which are then read aloud, since he is too upset to read them himself. (From the dramatic point of view, of course, this mode of epistolary revelation is much too static and tame—a peripeteia by proxy.)

Letter One is from Katerina, who announces in stilted language her plan to live in a commune where "men and women cohabit on new, original bases" (to which one of the guests whispers in Ivan Mikhailovich's ear the unprintable name of such institutions). Letter Two is from the tutor Tverdynsky, who acknowledges that he owes 32 rubles for service not performed, but adds loftily that he will pay the money some day. Letter Three is from Petrusha, the son and heir. Petrusha announces that he has now "acquired a very big development." Abreast of the latest ideas, he has decided to move to Petersburg, "to study science at the University if the professors are good." And of course his father will send him the means of living in Petersburg.

At last "enlightened" and stripped of his illusions, Ivan Mikhailovich sets forth post haste after his errant offspring. The last act, from the point of view of "progressive" ideas, is a triumph of reaction, Tolstoy's revenge on Chernyshevsky. Ivan Mikhailovich catches the two parties of runaways at the nearest posting station. Liuba is by now thoroughly disillusioned with her husband, who alternates pompous lectures with lascivious advances. She wants nothing more than to go home with her dear papa. Petrusha, who earlier had managed to get drunk, is hauled off to the well for a bath of cold water and perhaps later a dose of the birch rods his father has brought along for his edification. And poor Katerina has suddenly (and not very convincingly) undergone a complete metamorphosis. Her exalted dreams of a life of equality in a Petersburg commune have been shattered, apparently by her disillusionment in Venerovsky and his ideas and some unwelcome, "he-goat" advances by her new prospective lover, Tverdynsky. However implausibly, she is now fully penitent, ready to return a contrite dependent to the Pribyshev estate. The infected family has been fully cured.

As a work of literature "An Infected Family" is undoubtedly a failure, as many others have observed, including Tolstoy himself, although inconsistently.[17] It is therefore something of a puzzle why a man of Tolstoy's immense talent could produce anything so weak. Evidently his vaunted ability to imagine his way into a character's soul failed him in this case; not one of the play's characters, except possibly the old nurse, is a truly believable human being. Perhaps Tolstoy's unfamiliarity with the dramatic form was partly responsible: it is a genre he did not master, or even attempt again, for another twenty years. But perhaps he was simply blinded by his ideological rage.

Tolstoy had never liked Chernyshevsky. His aristocratic contempt for the ill-mannered ex-seminarian had been intensified back in the 1850s by the publication of Chernyshevsky's famous master's thesis, which had questioned the very value of art as a human activity. To that dislike had now been added a much stronger impulse, the scandal of *What Is To Be Done?*. In that shocking novel his antagonist had attacked what Tolstoy

---

[17] As early as 1864 Tolstoy wrote his sister that "my comedy seems to be bad" (Tolstoy to M. N. Tolstaya, 24 February 1864. [*PSS* 61:37]). His later judgments, however, varied. In his old age he once referred to "my bad comedy" (cited Lomunov 89), but on another occasion said, "I remember it was not bad." (cited Gusev 620). Charles A. Moser deems the play "incredibly bad" (p. 61). Even the usual Tolstoy-olator Konstantin Lomunov admits that the play has serious weaknesses of structure, though its worst sin is its "anti-democratic" political orientation (Lomunov 108–109). Tolstoy's play is also often listed together with a series of "anti-nihilist" novels written in the1860s and very discerningly studied in Moser's fine book. Of course it is not a novel, but it uses many of the same stock figures.

revered as one of the most sacred, biologically hallowed institutions of human life, the union of man and woman for the procreation of children.[18] Such blasphemy was a Carthage that had to be destroyed.

The stillborn "Infected Family," of course, did not accomplish this end. Perhaps assimilating belatedly Ostrovsky's criticism, however muted, perhaps from his own latent aesthetic sense, Tolstoy made no further attempt to have the play produced, did not retrieve the final manuscript, and consigned the drafts to archival oblivion. His animus against radical ideas on the woman question did, however, survive and found a much more durable and eloquent outlet—in *War and Peace*. That capacious novel provided for Tolstoy a general escape through imagination from the distasteful, increasingly bourgeoisified, emancipated Russia of the 1860s back into what seemed the cleaner, more orderly, more heroic time of the Napoleonic wars; it also was a vehicle for indirect pronouncements on the woman question—indirect, because mostly embodied in positive artistic images rather than discursive pronouncements or negative caricatures.

In *War and Peace* there are no women philosophers. The women characters know their place. It is an honored and honorable place, to be sure, and it carries with it important and arduous duties. First, each young woman must successfully negotiate the difficult mating game and find the right man with whom to unite her life. The central heroine, Natasha Rostova, requires some 1,000 pages to accomplish this feat, suffering along the way some bad luck (the artificially prolonged engagement to Andrei Bolkonsky and his later death) and a near escape (abduction by the iniquitous Anatole Kuragin). But she at last reaches the goal, marriage to the "right" man, Pierre Bezukhov, and in the Epilogue we see her in the next proper task of a woman, as a responsible and loving mother caring for her child.[19] The second "good" heroine, Marya Bolkonskaya, follows a somewhat similar course, culminating in a fruitful marriage to Nikolai Rostov. More intellectual than Natasha, Marya adds a strain of thoughtful religiosity and high ethical standards which she succeeds in imposing on her unintellectual and impulsive husband.

The third "good" female character in *War and Peace* is Sonya, the "sterile flower," who is destined for a seemingly unfulfilled life of

---

[18] It has been noted that there are no children in *What Is To Be Done?* and no families. Vera Pavlovna somehow forgot to dream of how children would be nurtured in the ideal new society.

[19] Stites cites the interesting—and quite typical—case of Lenin's friend Inessa Armand, who at the age of fifteen had been appalled to find that on marrying Natasha Rostova had become a mere самка (something like a brood mare), not a человек (human being) (Stites, 255). Many of my students have had the same reaction.

spinsterhood. But that too is a role provided for in Tolstoy's solution to the woman question. In his famous (unsent) letter to Nikolai Strakhov of 1870 and in several other pronouncements he has a perfect assigned role for such maiden aunts: as assistant mothers. Maternal duties are many and onerous, and a maiden sister or sister-in-law can most usefully lessen the burden. There is a place for everybody.[20]

War and Peace also offers, in Hélène Kuragina, a powerful image of a "bad" woman, infected, of course, not with the radical ideas of fifty years later, but with something like their equivalent, acting as if she had read both George Sand and *What Is To Be Done?*, Hélène is the epitome of female depravity. She has committed incest with her brother; she marries Pierre for his money without any sense of commitment; adultery for her is a natural way of life; and perhaps worst of all, she does something, not very clearly explained (an abortion?), to prevent herself from becoming a mother.

Of course, one should not exaggerate the importance to the formation of *War and Peace* of Tolstoy's negative response to the woman question and to Chernyshevsky's novel. Tolstoy's creative impulse was complex, rich, and many-sided, and the immense power of his imagination enabled him to create a fully realized world, peopled by complex human beings with diverse motivations. But still, is it not possible to see in the female characters of *War and Peace* Tolstoy's demonstrative answer to the woman question as he perceived it, a powerful antidote to the odious prescriptions of Chernyshevsky's novel? Surely Russian women, and women in general, can find in *War and Peace* Tolstoy's vividly realized prescriptions—for what is, and what is not, to be done.[21]

---

[20] See Tolstoy to N. N. Strakhov of 19 March 1870 (*PSS* 61:231–34), a letter written to express Tolstoy's enthusiastic concurrence with Strakhov's hostile review of J. S. Mill's *The Subjection of Women*. If they need gainful employment, women past menopause and those without husbands may become midwives or housekeepers—much more suitable and feminine occupations than working as secretaries or telegraph operators. Tolstoy also acknowledges the importance of one other profession for women, a dishonorable one, to be sure: prostitution. Prostitution is an essential institution, according to Tolstoy, because it provides a necessary safety valve, an outlet for the enormous sexual energies of all those unmarried men who otherwise would disrupt family life. As Eikhenbaum points out (Eikhenbaum 1960, 137), Tolstoy probably derived this idea from his reading of Schopenhauer.

[21] The connection between *War and Peace* and the "woman question" was first adumbrated in Eikhenbaum 1960, 114.

Tolstoy and Jesus

A memorable passage in Maxim Gorky's reminiscences of Tolstoy contains the following iconoclastic observation:

> О Буддизме и о Христе он говорит всегда сентиментально; о Христе особенно плохо — ни энтузиазма, ни пафоса нет в словах его и ни единой искры сердечного огня. Думаю, что он считает Христа наивным, достойным сожаления и хотя иногда любуется им, но — едва ли любит. И как будто опасается: приди Христос в русскую деревню — его девки засмеют![1]

> [On Buddhism and about Christ he always speaks sentimentally; about Christ especially badly — there is neither enthusiasm nor feeling in his words and not a single spark of emotional fire. I think he considers Christ naïve, perhaps deserving of pity, and although he sometimes admires him, he hardly loves him. And it is as if he is afraid that if Christ were to come to a Russian village, the peasant girls would make fun of him.]

To pious Tolstoyans, and even to many less than pious admirers of Tolstoy the Tolstoyan, such a statement must have seemed shocking, cynical, a vicious calumny. After all, Tolstoy could be said to have devoted to Jesus most of the last thirty years of his life, from the completion of *Anna Karenina* until his death, i.e., to the formulation and propagation of what he considered Jesus's authentic teachings. Tolstoy had proclaimed

---

[1] Cited from Л. Н. Толстой в воспоминаниях современников, 2 (Moscow, 1978) 474.

himself the spokesman of a new, true, liberated "Jesus" Christianity, a Christianity based on what Jesus actually said, not on myths about his life, death, and supposed supernatural deeds. It was to be a myth-free Christianity, cleansed at last from the encrusted errors, falsehoods, and distortions of the ages, beginning with those perpetrated by that arch-deceiver and sell-out, Saint Paul. Surely there must have been passion to sustain such a long and arduous enterprise of demolition, purgation, and reconstruction: the many volumes of treatises and tracts, the vast correspondence, the nurturing and encouragement of disciples from all over the world. Was it all only a façade, a guilt-inspired mask behind which lurked that unreconstructed, primeval pagan sorcerer whom the same Gorky saw sitting by the sea at Gaspra, seeming to command the waves that lapped at his feet and of an age with the rocks that surrounded him? What did Tolstoy really feel about Jesus?

One recalls Dostoevsky's famous statement that if forced to choose between Christ and the truth, he would unhesitatingly choose Christ.[2] Would Tolstoy do the same? It seems unlikely. For it was truth which Tolstoy had melodramatically proclaimed, at the end of "Sevastopol in May" (1855), that he loved with "all the power of his soul" (всеми силами души). [*PSS* 60:293] If Jesus and the truth may be incompatible polarities, as Dostoevsky seems to imply, then Tolstoy's soul would have to opt for the truth, and with all its power. This supposition is confirmed by a more explicit statement, written in 1859 to summarize the results of an earlier religious quest:

> Я нашел, что есть бессмертие, что есть любовь и что жить надо для того, чтобы быть счастливым вечно. Эти открытия удивили меня сходством с христианской религией, и вместо того, чтобы открывать сам, стал искать их в Евангелии, но нашел мало. Я не нашел ни Бога, ни Искупителя, ни таинств; а искал всеми, всеми силами души, и плакал, и мучился, и ничего не желал, кроме истины. [Tolstoy to A. A. Tolstaya, April 1859. *PSS* 60:293]

> [I found that immortality exists, that love exists, and that one must live in such a way as to be eternally happy. These discoveries surprised me by their affinity with the Christian religion, and instead of trying to make discoveries myself, I began searching for them in the Gospel, but I found little. I found neither God, nor the Redeemer, nor the Sacraments; and I sought them with all, all the strength of my soul, and I wept and suffered and wanted nothing but the truth.]

---

[2] Dostoevsky to N. D. Fon-Vizina, February 1854. Ф. М. Достоевский, *Письма*, под ред. А. С. Долинина (Moscow and Leningrad, 1928) 1:142.

However, perhaps in the long run Jesus and the truth would prove not wholly incompatible, and perhaps something salvageable of God and the truth, if not the Redeemer and sacraments, could be found in the Gospels, if sought with sufficient diligence. Some twenty years later Tolstoy would undertake a systematic search for them. His search is called *Соединение и перевод четырех Евангелий* (A Union and Translation of the Four Gospels).

To translate and harmonize the Gospels, and then to compose a synthetic "Gospel" of one's own, as Tolstoy did, is necessarily to engage oneself with the biography and to some extent, at least, the personality of Jesus. What does Tolstoy's biography of Jesus reveal about his feelings toward his subject? Did Tolstoy's stupendous talent as a writer of realistic fiction enable him, in his life of Jesus, to bring his hero to life in a second *Resurrection*, to make of him a vivid personality worthy to stand immortally alongside such other great seekers of truth as Pierre Bezukhov, Andrei Bolkonsky, Konstantin Levin, and Dmitry Nekhliudov?

I

The nineteenth century was an age when secular biographies of Jesus were in vogue. David Friedrich Strauss's sensational *Leben Jesu* had first appeared in 1835, and its Gallic twin, the equally sensational and infinitely more readable *Vie de Jésus* by Ernest Renan, had appeared in 1863. The techniques of *Quellenforschung* and comparative philology were being applied to the Scriptures in a less inhibited way than ever before, and it now seemed to many that these sacred texts, far from having been dictated verbatim by the Holy Spirit, were just as much a product of their place and time as other human artifacts. Moreover, they were just as much a series of literary constructs, made by a variety of persons at different times and with various motives, bearing at least as ambiguous a relation to the reality on which they drew as other human literary products—even novels written in the age of realism.

In many respects Tolstoy's *Union and Translation* would seem to belong to the same tradition, to respond to the same impulses as those that impelled Strauss and Renan. Like them, Tolstoy was a rationalist. He had already denounced at length the dogmatic theology of the Orthodox Church, and with a vehemence that might have qualified him for admission, had he lived into Soviet times, to the League of the Militant Godless. He too had long sought an earth-bound religion freed from myth and mystery; as early as 1855 he contemplated dedicating himself to the foundation of such a new faith:

> Основание новой религии соответствующей развитию человечества, религии Христа, но очищенной от веры и таинственности, религии практической, не обещающей будущее блаженство, но дающей блаженство на земле. [Diary entry for 4 March 1855. *PSS* 47:37]
>
> [The establishment of a new religion corresponding to the development of mankind, a religion of Christ, but cleansed of faith and mysteries, a practical religion, not promising future bliss, but giving bliss on earth.]

Specifically, Tolstoy did not believe, and at least since childhood had never believed, that Jesus was the Son of God in any sense different from that according to which we are all God's children. He did not believe that Jesus was the Jewish Messiah, and he considered naive and foolish all attempts to identify episodes from his life as fulfillments of Old Testament Messianic prophecies. Finally, he did not believe in any of the supernatural events recounted in the Gospels, including the resurrection. In all this Tolstoy was quite in tandem with Strauss and Renan. Yet in fact Tolstoy's attitude toward those rationalist exegetes was quite as hostile as his attitude toward the Metropolitan Makary, author of the Orthodox theology textbook Tolstoy had so savagely reprobated in his *Critique of Dogmatic Theology*.

Barbs against Renan are scattered profusely through Tolstoy's writings, beginning as early as the drafts for *War and Peace*, where Renan is linked — in the plural — not only with Strauss, but with other liberal thinkers of the nineteenth century who, Tolstoy thought, were unable to reconcile their belief in causal determinism with their need to assert individual moral responsibility. [*PSS* 15:243] Here Strauss and Renan are included among leading nineteenth-century "positivist" thinkers: Karl Vogt (1817–1895), George Henry Lewes (1817–1878), John Stuart Mill (1806–1873), and Maximilien Paul Emile Littré (1801–1881). In *Anna Karenina* Renan and Strauss, again in the plural ("the Renans and Strausses"), are linked with the Russian painter Aleksandr Ivanov (to whom we shall return) as exponents of an undesirably realistic, historical attitude toward Christ [*PSS* 19:34]; and in the drafts to the novel Anna herself is said to have lost her faith partly as a result of reading Renan. [*PSS* 20:547] But in *What I Believe* (В чем моя вера, 1883) Tolstoy states more clearly the essence of his objections to Strauss and Renan. In the first place, their attitude toward Jesus is condescending and sentimental. Jesus and his doctrine, say the Strausses and Renans, are an appealing product of the largely oral culture of some primitive inhabitants of Galilee in the first century A.D., but "for us, with our culture, they are only the sweet dream 'du charmant docteur,' as Renan says." [*PSS* 23:330] But most of all, the Strausses, Renans, and all "freethinking interpreters" as a class have absolutely no interest in putting Jesus's ideas into practice and using them to change their world, the world of the supposed lofty culture of nineteenth-century Europe, "with its designs of prisons for solitary confinement, alcazars, factories, magazines, brothels, and parliaments. And since Christ's teachings reject all this life, from Christ's teachings nothing is taken except words."³

Despite the seeming parallelism, there is thus a radical difference of mentality between Tolstoy and the "freethinking exegetes." Tolstoy is an

---

³ *PSS* 23:330. The phrase вольнодумные толкователи is on page 361. I have not been able to find the phrase "charmant docteur" in Renan and am inclined to doubt that it is there at all, since Renan makes a clear distinction between Jesus, a man without any formal education, and the docteurs, the learned scribes, lawyers, Pharisees, and Sadducees with whom he disputed. The phrase became fixed in Tolstoy's mind, however: he cites it again in *The Kingdom of God is Within You* (1893), with the same ironic contrast between the "inhabitants of Galilee, who lived 1800 years ago, half-savage Russian peasants . . . and the Russian mystic Tolstoy," on the one hand, and on the other, European culture with its "Krupp guns, smokeless gunpowder, colonization of Africa, subjugation of Ireland, parliaments, journalism, strikes, constitutions and the Eiffel Tower." [*PSS* 28:37]

In Renan's book on Marcus Aurelius the only thing that caught Tolstoy's eye was the characteristically "French" praise of the high art of tailors, hairdressers, and cosmeticians: "La toilette de la femme, avec tous ses raffinements, est du grand art à sa manière" [*PSS* 30:16], a statement Tolstoy considered the height of degenerate absurdity. Likewise, Renan's play *L'Abesse de Jouarre* Tolstoy considered "striking in its lack of talent and especially its coarseness." [*PSS* 30:297] Curiously, the only work by Renan Tolstoy could admire at all was his *L'Avenir de la science; pensées de 1848*, a work of Renan's youth not published until 1890. This work Tolstoy found "все блестит умом и тонкими, глубокими замечаниями о самых важных предметах, о науке, философии, филологии, как он ее понимает, о религии . . ." [all gleams with intelligence and subtle, profound remarks on the most important matters, on science, philosophy, philology, as he understands it, on religion.] Nevertheless, like all scholars of our time, Renan is a "moral eunuch"; he lacks "серьезность сердечная, т. е., ему все, все равно; такой он легченый, с вырезанными нравственными яйцами, как и все ученые нашего времени, но зато светлая голова и замечательно умен." [Tolstoy to N. N. Strakhov, 7 January 1891; *PSS* 65:216] [seriousness of the heart, i.e., he just does not care at all; he is such a eunuch, with amputated moral testicles, like all the learned men of our time, but on the other hand he has a luminous mind and is remarkably intelligent.] Tolstoy never seems to have engaged with Strauss as actively as he did with Renan, but he dismisses him on similar grounds: "Так Страус критикует все учение Христа, потому что жизнь немецкая расстроится, а он к ней привык." [*PSS* 24:406] [Thus Strauss criticizes Christ's entire teaching, because German life would be dismantled, and he is used to it.]

activist, a moralist, a social reformer; in the Gospel teachings he finds ideas applicable today, ideas capable of changing the world. If these teachings, at last freed from ecclesiastical doubletalk and made the central focus of religious life, were adopted widely and put into practice, the world would really change, as if miraculously: there would be no armies, no wars, no police, no law courts, no governments, no private property, no rich, no poor, and perhaps even no disorder in sexual relations, as people strove more and more to attain the ideals of chastity articulated in the Afterword to "The Kreutzer Sonata." Tolstoy seems to have really believed—or perhaps only desperately wished to believe—in the attainability of this utopia. At any rate, it was the goal that gave meaning to his life. As he wrote (in somewhat imperfect English) to his English disciple John Coleman Kenworthy, "I choosed [sic] this vocation . . . because it is the sole work in this our life, that is worth to work for."[4]

The Strausses and the Renans, however, had no such goal and made no such commitment. They were, Tolstoy asserted, passive in relation to social evil, not interested in social or moral reform. Instead, just for fun, as it were, they set themselves the puzzle of the quest for the historical Jesus, the real man who actually lived and set forth all those teachings Tolstoy admired so much. This historical quest not only did not interest Tolstoy, he considered it evil, since it distracted people from what was really important. Essentially it was only an intellectual game, a pastime, like the chess problems Sergei Koznyshev in *Anna Karenina* works at with as much—or as little—passion as he does at the problems of Russian statecraft he so pompously pretends to solve.

As early as 1857 Tolstoy had noted this tendency of people to distract themselves from the teachings of Jesus by concerning themselves with insignificant details of his biography: "Дали людям учение счастья, а они спорят о том, в каком году, в каком месте и кто дал им это учение." [*PSS* 47:205] [People were given a teaching of happiness, and they argue about in what year, in what place and who gave them this teaching.] Renan's great discovery, Tolstoy comments ironically, was that there was a man called Jesus who sweated and attended to other natural functions.[5] But who cares? Even the supposed resurrection is for Tolstoy a biographical detail of little interest: "Какой интерес знать, что Христос ходил на двор? Какое мне дело, что он воскрес? Воскрес—ну и

---

[4] Tolstoy to John Coleman Kenworthy, 15 May 1894. Quoted in Kenworthy, *Tolstoy: His Life and Works* (London and Newcastle-on-Tyre, 1902) 240; see also *PSS* 67:127.

[5] See Tolstoy to N. N. Strakhov, 17–18 April 1878; *PSS* 62:413.

Господь с ним! Для меня важен вопрос, что мне делать, как мне жить." [What interest is there in knowing that Christ went out to relieve himself? What do I care that he was resurrected? So he was resurrected—so what! Good for him! For me the important question is what am I to do, how am I to live.][6]

Furthermore, the liberal historians, according to Tolstoy, do not even understand the basic historical problems they set out to solve. Jesus Christ was remembered and admired and indeed deified not because he was born and lived in a particular place at a particular time, but because he preached ideas, moral ideas, that people recognized as profoundly right. But the historians only concern themselves with trivia:

> Задача, которую им [т. е., либеральным историкам, Н. McL.] предстоит решить, состоит в следующем: 1800 лет тому назад явился какой-то нищий и что-то поговорил. Его высекли и повесили, и все про него забыли, как были забыты миллионы таких же случаев, и лет 200 мир ничего не слыхал про него. Но оказывается, что кто-то запомнил то, что говорил, рассказал другому, третьему. Дальше, больше, и вот миллиарды людей умных и глупых, ученых и безграмотных не могут отделаться от мысли, что этот, только этот человек был Бог. И тогда все понятно. Но, если он не был Бог, то как объяснить, что именно этот простой человек признан всеми Богом?
>
> И ученые этой школы старательно разыскивают все подробности об условиях жизни этого человека, не замечая того, что сколько бы ни отыскали подробностей (в действительности же ровно ничего, кроме того, что у Иосифа Флавия и в Евангелиях не отыскали), если бы они даже восстановили всю жизнь Иисуса до мельчайших подробностей и узнали, когда и что ел и где ночевал Иисус, вопрос о том, почему он, именно он имел такое влияние на людей, остался бы все-таки без ответа. Ответ не в том, в какой среде родился Иисус, кто его воспитывал и т. п., и еще менее в том, что делалось в Риме и что народ был склонен к суеверию и т. п., а только в том, что проповедывал этот человек такое особенное, что заставило людей выделить его из всех других и признать его Богом тогда и теперь.[7]

[The problem which they {i.e., the liberal historians, H. McL} have to solve consists of the following: 1800 years ago a certain beggar appeared and said something. He was flogged and hanged and

---

[6] From the memoirs of I. M. Ivakin, a Greek scholar who was tutor to Tolstoy's children; cited in *PSS* 24:980.

[7] From "Краткое изложение Евангелия," *PSS* 24:812–813.

everyone forgot about him, as millions of such cases have been forgotten, and for 200 years the world heard nothing about him. But it turns out that someone remembered what he had said, told somebody else, and then a third person. Further on more and more, and lo! billions of people, intelligent and stupid, learned and illiterate cannot free themselves from the thought that this man, and only this man, was God. And if so, everything is understandable. But if he was not God, how to explain that everyone recognized this simple man as God?

And scholars of that school hunt energetically for all the details about the conditions of the life of this man, not noticing that no matter how hard they looked (and in fact they found absolutely nothing but what is in Josephus Flavius and the Gospels), and even if they had recovered Jesus's entire life down to the most minute detail and discovered when and what Jesus ate and where he spent the night, the question of why he, and precisely he, had such an influence on people would still remained unanswered. The answer lies not in what milieu Jesus was born to, who educated him and so forth, and still less in what was happening in Rome or that people were inclined to superstition, etc., but only in what this man preached that was so special that it made people single him out of all the others and acknowledge him as God, both then and now.]

II

Tolstoy's differences from "the Strausses and Renans" thus seem reasonably clear and consistent. The liberal exegetes are sentimental; they are morally inert; and their obsession with unimportant biographical details is distracting. However, as noted above, in *Anna Karenina* Tolstoy links these misguided foreign biographers of Jesus with the Russian painter Aleksandr Ivanov. "It's all the Ivanov-Strauss-Renan attitude toward Christ and religious painting," says Vronsky's friend Golenishchev, whom Vronsky and Anna encounter by chance in Italy. Golenishchev then pronounces certain strictures against the painting *Christ Before Pilate* by the artist Mikhailov, a character in the novel, in which Jesus is represented as ostentatiously Jewish, "with all the realism of that school."

> Я не понимаю, как они могут так грубо ошибаться. Христос уже имеет свое определенное воплощение в искусстве великих стариков. Стало быть, если они хотят изображать не Бога, а революционера или мудреца, то пусть из истории берут Сократа, Франклина, Шарлотту Корде, но только не Христа. Они берут то самое лицо, которое нельзя брать для искусства. [*PSS* 19:34]

[I do not understand how they can make such crude mistakes. Christ already has his fixed embodiment in the art of the great old masters. Consequently, if they want to represent not God, but a revolutionary or a sage, let them take from history Socrates or Franklin or Charlotte Corday, but certainly not Christ. They take the very person who must not be made a subject of art.]

In an argument with Mikhailov, Golenishchev, perhaps to spare his opponent's feelings, attributes these faults to the real Ivanov, not to Mikhailov himself, but the point is not lost on his interlocutor:

"Он у вас человекобог, а не Богочеловек . . . Но возьмем хоть Иванова. Я полагаю, что если Христос сведен на степень исторического лица, то лучше было бы Иванову изображать другую историческую тему, свежую, нетронутую."
"Но если это величайшая тема, которая представляется искусству?"
"Если поискать, то найдутся другие. Но дело в том, что искусство не терпит спора и рассуждений. А при картине Иванова для верующего и для неверующего является вопрос: Бог это или не Бог? И разрушается единство впечатления." [*PSS* 19:42–43]

["You have a man-God, and not a God-man . . . But let's take Ivanov. I believe that if Christ is reduced to the level of a historical person, it would be better for Ivanov to take a different historical topic, a fresh, untouched one." "But if this is the greatest topic that art is offered?" "If you search a bit, you will find others. But the fact is that art does not tolerate argument and discussion. And Ivanov's picture makes both believer and non-believer ask: is this God or not? And the unity of impression is destroyed."]

One would hesitate to ascribe Golenishchev's views to Tolstoy, especially since Golenishchev, who has adopted a "lofty, intellectually liberal line" since graduating from the aristocratic Corps of Pages, is clearly presented as rather stuffy and pretentious, incapable of understanding the genuine creativity of Mikhailov, a fellow artist with whom Tolstoy obviously sympathizes. But in fact we can find statements by Tolstoy, speaking *in propria persona* about Aleksandr Ivanov, very similar to those of Golenishchev about both Mikhailov and Ivanov. For instance:

Картина Иванова [the famous "Явление Христа народу"] возбудит в народе только удивление перед техническим мастерством, но не возбудит никакого ни поэтического, ни религиозного чувства.

> [Ivanov's picture (the famous "Appearance of Christ to the People") will arouse in people only amazement at its technical mastery, but will not arouse the slightest poetic or religious feeling.][8]

> Написать яблениe Христа народу — искусство, и написать голых девок — тоже искусство. [To paint the appearance of Christ to the people is art and to paint nude girls is also art.] [Tolstoy to N. A. Aleksandrov, 1882. *PSS* 30:210]

> Одними явление Христа народу считается верхом искусства, другими голые купальщицы считаются верхом искусства. [By some people the appearance of Christ to the people is considered the height of art, and by others naked women bathing are considered the height of art.] [Variant of Aleksandrov letter. *PSS* 30:433]

And Golenishchev's argument that art should avoid controversial subjects is repeated almost verbatim in a letter by Tolstoy to Pavel Tretiakov written in 1890:

> Но изображать, как историческое лицо, то лицо, которое признавалось веками и признается теперь миллионами людей Богом, неудобно: неудобно, потому что такое изображение вызывает спор. А спор нарушает художественное впечатление.

> [To represent as a historical person an individual who has been recognized as God for centuries and is so recognized now by millions of people is unsuitable: unsuitable because such a representation evokes argument. And argument destroys the artistic impression.] [Tolstoy to P. A. Tret'iakov, 30 June 1890. *PSS* 65:124]

When we look at the Ivanov painting, however, surely it is not the "realism" of the Christ figure that strikes us. Jesus appears in the distance, pointed to with excitement by John the Baptist, alone, majestic, mysterious, and certainly in no way ostentatiously Jewish. Conceivably one might make such a statement about two of the neophytes, perhaps a father and son, who are just emerging from the water; but perhaps what really bothers Tolstoy about this celebrated painting is the artist's obvious interest in naked flesh ("naked women bathing," though none of the figures is clearly female). At any rate, in his own mind Tolstoy locked Ivanov irrevocably into an association with Strauss and Renan as a classic exemplar of a wrong, controversy-arousing treatment of the Jesus subject.[9]

---

[8] "Ясно-полянская школа за ноябрь и декабрь месяцы," *PSS* 8:113.

[9] Direct association of Ivanov with Renan, at least with regard to the representation of Jesus, is anachronistic and impossible, since the *Vie de Jesus* appeared only after

However, the arguments Tolstoy adduces against Ivanov—excessive realism, controversiality—he does not seem to apply to other Russian painters of the time, especially those with whom he enjoyed personal relations. Notable among these are Ivan Kramskoi, with whom Tolstoy made friends in 1873 while Kramskoi's great portrait of him was being painted, and Nikolai Ge, who became an ardent disciple and close friend in the 1880s and 1890s. Although depictions of Jesus by both these artists seem markedly and "realistically" to stress the human qualities of Jesus the man, Tolstoy nevertheless lavishes on them high praise. Kramskoi's *Христос в пустыне* [Christ in the Wilderness], a picture showing a very human, very troubled man in deep meditation, "is the best Christ I know," Tolstoy wrote to Tretiakov.[10] And with reference to the paintings of Ge, Tolstoy developed a whole theory of "Jesus art."

According to Tolstoy, attempts had been made by various painters to escape the inevitable dilemma in representing Jesus: is he God or a historical person? Some chose one course, some another, still others tried to avoid all dispute by simply taking the subject as one familiar to all and caring only for beauty. But the problem remained unsolved. Next came attempts both to demote Christ the God from heaven and Christ the historical personage from his pedestal by treating him as an ordinary person engaged in the activities of ordinary life, but giving this ordinary life a religious, even a somewhat mystical aura. Such was Ge's painting *Miloserdie* [Mercy], painted in 1879–1880 and subsequently destroyed by the artist. But then, in *Christ Before Pilate*, a painting on the very same subject used by Mikhailov in *Anna Karenina*, Ge found the solution, and Tolstoy is ecstatic in his praise. Note also how he allows his own novelistic talent to expand upon the figure of Pontius Pilate:

> И вот Ге взял самый простой и теперь понятный, после того как он его взял, мотив: Христос и его учение не на одних словах, а на словах и на деле в столкновении с учением мира, т. е. тот мотив, к[оторый] составлял тогда и теперь составляет главное значение явления Христа, и значение не спорное, а такое, с к[оторым] не могут не быть согласны и церковники, признавшие его Богом, и историки, признающие его важным лицом в истории, и христиане, признавшие главным в нем практическое учение.

Ivanov's death. However, Ivanov was indeed influenced by Strauss and in fact made a special journey from Rome to Germany to converse with him. See Михаил Алпатов, *Александр Иванов* (Moscow, 1959) 198–199.

[10] Tolstoy to P. M. Tret'iakov, 14 July 1894 (*PSS* 67:175). Pavel Sigalov wittily suggested to me that a more appropriate title of this picture would be "Жениться ли мне или нет?"

На картине изображен с совершенной исторической верностью тот момент, когда Христа водили, мучили, били, таскали из одной кутузки в другую, от одного начальства к другому и привели к губернатору, добрейшему малому, к[оторому] дела нет ни до Христа, ни до евреев, но еще менее до какой-то истины, о кот[орой] ему, знакомому со всеми учеными и философами Рима, толкует этот оборванец; ему дело только до высшего начальства, чтоб не ошибиться перед ним. Христос видит, что перед ним заблудший человек, заплывший жиром, но он не решается отвергнуть его по одному виду и потому начинает высказывать ему сущность своего учения. Но губернатору не до этого, он говорит: Какая такая истина? И уходит. И Хр[истос] смотрит с грустью на этого непронизываемого человека.

Таково было положение тогда, таково положение тысячи, миллионы раз повторяется везде, всегда между учением истины и представителями сего мира. И это выражено на картине. И это верно исторически, и верно современно, и потому хватает на сердце всякого, того, у кого есть сердце. — Ну вот, такое-то отношение к христианству и составляет эпоху в искусстве, п[отому] ч[то] такого рода картин может быть бездна. И будет. [Tolstoy to P. M. Tret'iakov, 30 June 1890; *PSS* 65:124–25]

[And so Ge has taken the simplest, and now, after his taking it, understandable topic: Christ and his teaching not in words alone, but in words and deeds, in conflict with the teaching of the world, i.e., that topic, which constituted then and constitutes now the chief meaning of the phenomenon of Christ, and a meaning not controversial, but such as cannot help being acceptable to churchmen acknowledging him as God, and historians considering him an important figure in history, and Christians who believe the main thing about him is his practical teaching.

With perfect historical accuracy the picture depicts that moment when after being led around, tortured and beaten and dragged from one jail to the other and from one office to the other, Christ was brought before the Governor, a most genial individual, who cared nothing for Christ or for the Jews and still less about any supposed truth this ragamuffin was telling him about, a person who knew all the learned men and philosophers of Rome. He cared only about higher authorities and not to make a mistake in their eyes. Christ sees that the man before him is full of error, swimming in fat, but he does not decide to reject him on the basis of appearance alone and therefore begins to expound to him the essence of his teaching. But the governor has no time for that. He says "What is truth?" and leaves. And Christ looks with sadness on this impenetrable person.

Such was the situation then, and such a situation has been repeated thousands, millions of times everywhere and always when the teaching of the truth confronts representatives of this world. And this is depicted in the picture. And it is true historically, and true today, and therefore grips the heart of anyone who has a heart.—Well now, such a relation to Christianity constitutes an epoch in art, because there can be a mass of pictures like this. And there will be.]

Tolstoy also had high praise for Ge's *Повинен смерти* (Sentenced to Death, 1892) and *Распятие* (The Crucifixion, 1894), the latter certainly as "realistic" as could be imagined, concluding:

"Лет через 100 иностранцы попадут, наконец, на ту простую, ясную и гениальную точку зрения, на которой стоял Ге . . . и мы все будем восхищаться." [Tolstoy to P. M. Tret'iakov, 14 July 1894; *PSS* 67:175; Tolstoy to V. V. Stasov, 4 September 1894; *PSS* 67:216].

[In 100 years foreigners will arrive, at last, at the simple and clear point of view to which Ge's genius brought him . . . And we will all exult.]

III

The question now arises, to what extent was Tolstoy able to apply these principles to his own representation of Jesus in the *Union and Translation of the Four Gospels*? Certainly one principle was scuttled from the start: the avoidance of controversy. Art should not arouse спор и рассуждения (argument and discussion), but Tolstoy's book on the Gospels is one angry спор [argument] from beginning to end, with virtually all previous translators and interpreters of the Bible—Orthodox, Catholic, Protestant, and secular. Perhaps Tolstoy could except his Gospel book from the "no controversy" rule on the grounds that it is not intended as "art." But certainly the other prescriptions are applied with a vengeance. What is important in the Gospels are the teachings of Jesus. They are all that matters, and the Gospels have therefore been rigorously squeezed and pruned and pressed so as to eliminate from them any biographical details that might lessen the impact of the teachings. Nevertheless, the Gospels are, after all, presented in the form of a narrative biography of Jesus, however sketchy and incomplete, and in his version Tolstoy did not feel justified in abandoning this format altogether, thus making of the Gospels simply a treatise on morals, an extended version, so to speak, of the Sermon on the Mount. Some remnants are therefore left in which Tolstoy had an opportunity to apply his own novelistic talent to the life of Christ.

Literary recreation of Jesus's life and personality was, of course, far from being Tolstoy's primary objective; nor was his modus operandi with the Gospels anything like that of a trained philologist, although he makes a great show of his newly acquired Greek. Tolstoy's mind is anything but open as he approaches his task. He starts with what seems to him absolute, incontrovertible knowledge of what Jesus said and even what he meant. Even that formulation perhaps should be restated: not what Jesus actually said or meant, but what he ought to have said and meant. Thus Jesus per se is not even very important; what is important are the ideas Tolstoy has extracted and edited from the words attributed to him. (Although Tolstoy does not explicitly make the point, he may also have recognized that the name of Jesus attached to these ideas gave them an impact they might otherwise lack.) In the Gospels this distilled essence, the nucleus of pure, original Christianity, the undefiled teachings of Jesus, has been surrounded by a large mass of extraneous matter—myth, legend, unnecessary biographical detail, all haphazardly put together by those four rather incompetent evangelists. Subsequently, even this already half buried and disfigured nucleus of truth was further distorted and traduced by people who claimed to be Jesus's disciples, especially Saint Paul. So Tolstoy's undertaking with the Gospels is not only to "harmonize" them into one book, but in the process to press out of them everything that does not belong there, i.e., everything that does not enhance and elucidate the core teachings of Jesus. At one point Tolstoy admits that the "personality of Jesus" has no interest for him. [*PSS* 24:537] Nevertheless, some biographical details do remain, and from these we can perhaps form some idea of Tolstoy's image of Jesus the man.

Like Strauss and Renan, Tolstoy must of course reject or rationalize the birth legends. No manger, no shepherds, no star, no Magi. Of the virgin birth there is left only the germ of what might have become another adultery novel: "Была девица Мария. Девица эта забеременела неизвестно от кого. Обрученный с нею муж пожалел ее и, скрывая ее срам, принял ее. От нее-то и неизвестного отца родился мальчик. Мальчика назвали Иисус." [*PSS* 24:48] [There was a young woman named Mary. This young woman became pregnant by some unknown man. Her betrothed husband took pity on her and concealing her shame, accepted her. From her and an unknown father a boy was born. This boy was named Jesus.] Thus the whole purpose of the virgin birth story was to cover up the shameful fact of Jesus's illegitimacy.

Tolstoy subsequently uses this interpretation for another purpose, even though it involves him in a psychological implausibility he surely would never have allowed himself as a novelist. Though he had credited Joseph with considerable magnanimity in accepting and marrying a fiancée pregnant by another man, Tolstoy by implication transforms Joseph into a mean and vindictive adoptive father, one who never allowed the boy Jesus to forget the disgrace of his origin. In consequence, Jesus became accustomed to thinking of God as his only father; hence the appellation "Son of God," which has caused so much confusion and error.

This explanation emerges from Tolstoy's treatment of the one episode from Jesus's childhood the Gospels provide, the story of his tarrying in the Temple in Jerusalem at the age of twelve to converse with the "doctors," after his parents had left for home. When they returned, worried and agitated, two days later and found him there, he replied, in what seems a quite typical style of rather obnoxious, pre-adolescent sassiness, "How is it that ye sought me? Wist ye not that I must be about my Father's business?" (Luke 7:49) According to Tolstoy, who makes no real attempt to recapture the emotional dynamics of this scene, Jesus says this because he was keenly aware of the fact that he had no earthly father. In Tolstoy's interpretation, the boy Jesus was "заброшенный ребенок, видевший вокруг детей, у которых у каждого есть плотский отец, и не знавший себе отца плотского, признал отцом своим—начало всего—Бога." (*PSS* 24:52) [An abandoned child, who saw around him children each of whom had a fleshly father and who had no fleshly father himself recognized as his father—the source of everything—God.] According to Tolstoy, Jesus was doing no more than following Malachi 2:10: "Have we not all one father? Hath not one God created us?"

Later hints of discord between Jesus and his immediate family (e.g., John 2:4 or Matthew 12:46–50), which Tolstoy the novelist would surely have exploited, are passed over in silence. But Christ's general admonition (Matthew 10:37) that religious commitment must take precedence over family attachments is duly incorporated into Tolstoy's own Gospel, perhaps with some awareness of its relevance in his own case:

> Учение мое как огонь запалит мир . . . сделается раздор в каждом доме. Отец с сыном, мать с дочерью, и семейные сделаются ненавистниками того, кто поймет мое учение. И будут убивать их. Потому что тот, кто поймет мое учение, для того не будет ничего значить ни отец, ни мать, ни жена, ни дети, ни все его имущество. Кому отец или мать дороже моего учения, тот не понял учения. [*PSS* 24:356]

[My teaching like fire will enflame the world . . . There will be strife in every house. Father and son, mother and daughter and families will hate the person who understands my teaching. And they will kill them. Because the person who understands my teaching will care nothing for father, nor mother, nor wife, nor children, nor all his property. The person for whom father or mother is dearer than my teaching has not understood the teaching.]

Lacking material from which to construct a Bildungsroman of Jesus's formative years (had he cared to write one), Tolstoy must move directly, as his sources do, to Christ's ministry. The actual ministry, however, is preceded by two symbolic events of preparation: the baptism by Saint John and the temptation in the wilderness. Of the first Tolstoy says almost nothing, since he disapproves of rituals in general, and the occasion is further spoiled in his eyes by the supernatural accompaniment, the voice from heaven:

событие это неестественное и непонятное. Стихи эти ничего не прибавляют к учению, но напротив, затемняют его. [*PSS* 24:59]

[This episode is unnatural and incomprehensible. These verses add nothing to the teaching, but on the contrary, obfuscate it.]

During the forty days of fasting in the wilderness, Jesus of course underwent the three temptations of Satan, so powerfully invoked in *The Brothers Karamazov*. Tolstoy draws none of Dostoevsky's lofty theological conclusions (which hardly stand up anyway, since elsewhere in the Gospels Jesus, far from repudiating them, clearly does invoke "miracle, mystery, and authority"). For Tolstoy this is simply a period of prayerful, spiritual preparation for a difficult task, especially an effort to make spirit master over flesh. The figure of Satan is nothing more than a personification of Jesus's own doubts and hesitations, the voice in him of corporeality. For this Tolstoy adduces an interesting novelistic argument: if Satan had been a real presence, the evangelists would naturally have described him, and yet of such description there is not a word. Therefore, Satan is not a speaking character, only a personification. Tolstoy also discards the official church interpretation, that Jesus rejected the temptation to perform unnecessary or unseemly miracles.

In reality, the temptation was only the age-old conflict, which Tolstoy knew so well, between the spirit and the flesh. After such a long bout of fasting, Jesus was at last forced to recognize that although the spirit should rule, the flesh also has its legitimate demands, and these should be accepted, for they too come from God. By eliminating all the supernatural content of the story, Tolstoy also avoids issues that have troubled some ecclesiastical commentators, such as whether it was proper for Jesus to travel in the company of Satan, if that is what he did, to the pinnacle of the temple or the top of the mountain, perhaps magically, rather like Faust with Mephistopheles.

The marriage at Cana can serve as a perfect example of Tolstoy's principles of exclusion. Here is an anecdote, a biographical detail that serves no instructive purpose and is unseemly in addition. Out with it!

> Событие это в Кане Галилейской, описанное так подробно, есть одно из самых поучительных мест в Евангелиях, поучительных по отношению к тому, как вредно принимать всю букву так называемого канонического Евангелия за что-то священное. Событие в Кане Галилейской не представляет ничего ни замечательного, ни в каком бы то ни было отношении значительного. Если чудо, то оно бессмысленно, если фокус, то оно оскорбительно, если же это бытовая картина, то она не нужна. [*PSS* 24:84]

> [The episode in Cana of Galilee described in such detail is one of the most instructive passages in the Gospels, instructive of how harmful it is to regard the whole text of the so-called canonical Gospel as something holy. The episode in Cana of Galilee offers nothing remarkable, nothing in any respect significant. If it is a miracle, it is senseless, if it is a trick, it is insulting, if it is a picture of everyday life, it is not needed.]

The episode where Jesus forcibly drives the money-changers from the temple might have caused Tolstoy considerable difficulty, one would have thought, since Jesus's behavior in this instance seems quite violent and disruptive, not at all in accordance with the principles of непротивление злу [nonresistance to evil]. Without dealing with the basic implausibility of the whole episode (the Gospels say nothing of what would surely have been resistance by the tradespeople so abruptly expelled from their stations, nor of the likely intervention by the Temple authorities), Tolstoy gets around the problem by interpreting the "temple" as symbolic of the whole world. Jesus is therefore symbolically attacking all those, specifically the proponents of official Judaism, who concern themselves with technicalities of ritual and worship rather than with matters of the spirit. From this vantage point Tolstoy can then ridicule the ecclesiastical exegetes who assign Jesus the role of fulfilling "police responsibilities with regard to the cleanliness of the temple." [*PSS* 24:124] In connection with the money-changers episode, however, Tolstoy does evince considerable irritation with Jesus's boast, "Destroy this temple, and in three days I will raise it up" (John 2:19), which the evangelist then proceeds to interpret as a veiled reference to his prospective resurrection in the body. Tolstoy angrily exclaims: "Хорошо, он воскрес и предсказывал свою смерть. Неужели нельзя было предсказать яснее и, главное, уместнее?. . . Ведь стоит только снять очки церковные, чтобы видеть, что это не разговор, а бред сумасшедших." [*PSS* 24:124] [All right, he rose from the dead and predicted his own death. Couldn't he have found some way of predicting it more clearly and appropriately? . . . For you only need to take off ecclesiastical glasses to see that this is not a dialogue, but the raving of madmen.]

Usually, however, when he encounters passages that seem to reflect unfavorably on Jesus, Tolstoy blames the evangelists for misreporting or simply omits the passage altogether. Tolstoy says not a word, for example, about the cursing of the fig tree (Matthew 21:18–21), where Jesus, in a spirit of what seems to be mere petulant annoyance, surely abused his supernatural powers; and Jesus's upbraiding of whole cities—Chorazin, Bethsaida, and Capernaum—for failing to respond to his message (Matthew 11:20–24), is attributed by Tolstoy to a flaw in the Gospel text. Nevertheless, in this case some of Tolstoy's irritation still seems to spill over onto Jesus himself: "Стихи эти . . . не имеют не только ничего учительного, но даже никакого смысла. За что он упрекает города? Если они не поверили его чудесам, то значит незачем было делать чудеса или мало и плохо он их делал." [*PSS* 24:156] [These verses . . . have not only nothing instructive about them, but even make no sense. What is he reproaching the cities for? If they did not believe his miracles, that means there was no point in performing miracles or he performed too few of them or did them badly.]

Jesus's healing miracles Tolstoy interprets either as purely metaphorical, as in the case of the blind man whose sight was restored after washing in the pool of Siloam (John 9:1–41), or as a psychological rather than a physical event, as in the case of an impotent man healed at the pool of Bethesda (John 5:1–9). But some details of Jesus's medical practice, such as making a salve by spitting on the ground and mixing the saliva with clay (John 9:6), Tolstoy finds repulsive and omits as too realistic—"stupid, useless details." [*PSS* 24:468]

The greatest of the miracles, the raising of Lazarus, simply irritates Tolstoy. He makes nothing of the strong emotions attributed to Jesus in this episode (John 11:33–35), perhaps the strongest anywhere before the passion. And the miracle itself displeases him:

> Скажем, что воскресение есть проявление могущества Бога. Если так, то вместе с могуществом мы невольно думаем и о мудрости его и не можем не спросить себя: зачем он воскресил Лазаря, а не Ивана и Петра; а зачем он воскресил Лазаря, а не сделал того, чтобы у Лазаря выросли крылья или две головы? И мы должны признаться, что в этом действии Бога вместе с могужеством не выразилась его мудрость. [*PSS* 24:496]

> [Let us say that resurrection is a manifestation of the power of God. If so, then along with His power we involuntarily also think about His wisdom and cannot help asking ourselves: why did he resurrect Lazarus, and not Ivan or Peter; and why did He resurrect Lazarus and not cause Lazarus to grow wings or two heads? And we must admit that in this action by God along with His power His wisdom was not displayed.]

In fact the whole story must be rejected:

> Принять эту главу и подобные ей могли только люди церковные, те, которые никогда и не понимали учения Христа. Для всех же прочих, кто ищет учения, не может быть и вопроса о том, что значит рассказ о воскресении — он ничего не значит, как и все чудеса. Это надо очистить и отбросить. [*PSS* 24:498]

> [Only church people, those who never understood Christ's teaching, could accept this chapter and others like it. For all others who seek the teaching there can be no question of what the story of raising the dead means — it means nothing, like all miracles. It should be purged and discarded.]

But on the whole Tolstoy avoids even implied criticism of Jesus. When the Jews beg him at last to state clearly and unambiguously whether he is indeed the Christ, the Messiah (John 10:24), and Jesus again turns the question aside, Tolstoy at first seems indignant:

> Если он был Бог, то как же мог всемогущий, всеблагий Бог не знать всех тех страданий, которые примут и те евреи, и мы с миллиардом людей, мучимыми сомнениями и лишенными спасения... И ему стоило только сказать: да, я Бог, и евреи и мы были бы блаженны. [*PSS* 24:486]

> [If he was God, then how could an all-powerful, all-good God not know all the sufferings affecting the Jews and affecting us along with billions of people tormented by doubts and deprived of salvation... And all he had to do was say Yes, I am God, and the Jews and we would be blessed.]

And if he was only a man, Tolstoy goes on, even then he could have resolved people's doubts by a clear answer: "No, I am not the Messiah." Tolstoy justifies Jesus's "cruelty," however, on the grounds that, deeply believing in the truth of his teachings, he really did consider himself at one with God and therefore in some sense "God's anointed." But he knew that he was not the Messiah-king the Jews expected, and therefore he answered as fully and truthfully as he could, though metaphorically, with his image of the shepherd and the sheepfold.

Unlike Renan, Tolstoy tries to justify Jesus's evasiveness and hair-splitting disputatiousness in his arguments with the Pharisees and Sadducees. For example, with the prescription "Render therefore unto Caesar the things which are Caesar's and unto God the things which are God's" (Matthew 22:21), Jesus successfully avoids the trap, on the one hand, of making an explicitly seditious statement about Roman rule in Palestine, and, on the other, of offending orthodox Jewish beliefs by giving civic responsibilities precedence over religious ones. However, the statement is of no help in drawing a clear boundary between the two or adjudicating cases where the two may be in conflict. For his part, Tolstoy acknowledges no civic responsibilities at all. Therefore, despite the clearly parallel structure of the sentence, implying that both God and "Caesar" have legitimate claims on us, he interprets the first part as a denial by Jesus of any obligation at all toward "Caesar." Jesus simply examines the coin proffered him. Is that Caesar's image on it? Very well, if the coin is his, give it back to him. "Render unto Caesar" in no way means that a believing Christian should pay taxes: "потому что не из чего будет платить, да и незачем платить человеку, не признающему судов, государств и народностей." [*PSS* 24:599]. [Because there will be no money to pay with and no reason to pay for a person who does not acknowledge courts or states or nations.] However, earlier Tolstoy did admit that it might be permissible to pay taxes in order not to tempt the tax collectors to commit acts of violence, provided one states at the time that taxes cannot be obligatory or necessary for people living according to the will of God. [*PSS* 24:596]

Tolstoy does ascribe to Jesus some psychological tensions; to follow Christian teachings is not easy, even for their author himself. First, Jesus is beset all his life, according to Tolstoy, by the temptation of cowardice, the "renunciation of the teaching." The cowardice appears in some of his evasive answers to the Pharisees, when he "tries to contradict them as little as possible," and in his withdrawing or hiding when pursued. [*PSS* 24:704] Jesus's most dramatic—and successful—struggle with cowardice, Tolstoy believes, occurs when he is confronted in the Temple by pagan Greeks who are attracted by his teaching (John 12:20). At that moment he has to decide whether to turn away these Gentiles as uncircumcised and unworthy. He would thus remain, as it were, a critic of Judaism from within the fold. The alternative is to embrace the Greeks and thus alienate himself from Judaism altogether. However, to repudiate Judaism was to place himself in danger:

> Язычники, по понятиям иудеев, — это отверженцы, безбожники, подлежащие избиению, и вдруг он оказывается за одно с язычниками. То он, как будто, исправлял закон иудейский, был пророком иудейским, и вдруг одним сближением с язычниками оказывается явно, что он, по понятиям иудеев — язычник. А если он язычник, то он должен погибнуть и нет ему спасения. [PSS 24:673]

> [Pagans, according to the Jews' doctrine, were outcasts, godless people, subject to extermination, and suddenly he is at one with pagans. At one moment he was correcting the Jewish law, he was a Jewish prophet, and suddenly by joining with pagans it becomes clear that according to the Jews' perceptions he is a pagan. And if he is a pagan, he must perish, and there is no salvation for him.]

This was the decisive moment. Though Tolstoy points it out only retrospectively, not when discussing the passage itself, he ascribes to Jesus at this moment a tremor of fear. To identify with pagan Greeks meant to condemn himself to death at the hands of the Jews. But Jesus summons his resources of courage and resolves to proceed. As the omniscient Tolstoy reads his thoughts:

> И вот это-то сближение с язычниками вызывает в нем решительные слова, выражающие непреклонность его убеждения. Язычник — ну язычник, говорит он себе. Я то, что есмь. И вы, как хотите, понимайте меня. Я погибну, но зерно должно погибнуть, чтобы дать плод. [PSS 24:673–74]

> [And so this solidarity with the pagans evokes in him decisive words, expressive of the firmness of his conviction. A pagan — so a pagan, he says to himself. I am what I am. And you can understand me as you wish. I will perish, but the grain must perish in order to bear fruit.]

That moment of truth, according to Tolstoy, was a bold public acknowledgment of what had been implicit all along, that the teachings of Jesus were in no way a fulfillment or reform of Judaism, but a complete break with it.

Tolstoy's treatment of the passion story is reasonably straightforward, though with certain crucial emendations where his beliefs differ sharply from those of the churches. As before, he restrains his novelistic talent and makes no effort to expand the account of Jesus's last days. For instance, he does not elaborate on Christ's relationship with the disciple he particularly loved (John 13:23), nor does he elucidate or make more plausible the motives for Judas's betrayal. A major innovation is Tolstoy's insistence that in saying to Judas, "That thou doest, do quickly," Jesus was not at all referring to the betrayal itself; rather Jesus was warning Judas, by signals comprehensible only to the two of them, to leave in haste lest he be attacked by the other disciples. Jesus has just identified Judas as the future traitor by giving him the sop (John 13:26). If the other disciples had understood the message, they would have killed him:

> Иисусу незачем советовать предать его, но Иисус несколько раз уже намекал ученикам о том, что между ними есть предатель, и он видел, что Иуда тревожится и хочет бежать. Иуде нельзя не бояться. Если бы ученики узнали это, — не говоря про других, Симон Петр наверное бы задушил его. Теперь Иисус указал Иуду и указал Симону Петру. Если бы Иуда не ушел, его бы убили, и потому Иисус говорит ему: беги скорее, но говорит так, чтобы никто, кроме Иуды не мог понять. (*PSS* 24:699)

> [There was no reason for Jesus to advise someone to betray him, but Jesus had already several times hinted to his disciples that there was a traitor in their midst, and he saw that Judas was agitated and wanted to escape. Judas had good reason to be afraid. If the disciples had found it out, I don't speak of the others, but Simon Peter would surely have strangled him. Now Jesus pointed out Judas and did so to Simon Peter. If Judas had not gone, they would have killed him, and therefore Jesus tells him: go, as fast as you can, but he says it in such a way that no one except Judas could understand.]

In warning Judas, Jesus was simply following his fundamental principle of returning good for evil.

The major psychological drama Tolstoy attributes to Jesus as hero arises from a second temptation, the temptation to use violence in self-defense. In Tolstoy's version, there was a moment during the Last Supper when Jesus, foreseeing the consequences of Judas's betrayal and still surrounded by loyal disciples, seriously considered defending himself by force. First he sends his disciples out to buy swords, but then calls them back when it is discovered that they had two swords on hand (Luke 22:36, 38). As Tolstoy argues:

> Сколько ни бились толкователи над этим местом, нет никакой возможности придать ему другого значения, как то, что Иисус собирается защищаться. Перед этим он говорит ученикам о том, что они отрекутся от него, т. е. не защитят его, убегут от него. Потом он напоминает им то время, когда не было еще на них уголовного обвинения. Тогда он говорил: не нужно было бороться. Вы тогда были без сумы и ни в чем не нуждались, но теперь пришло время борьбы, надо запасаться пищей и ножами, чтобы защищаться. [*PSS* 24:703]

> [No matter how interpreters have struggled with this passage, there is no possibility of ascribing to it another meaning than that Jesus was preparing to defend himself. Before that he says to his disciples that they will deny him, i.e., not defend him, run away from him. Then he reminds them of a time when there was no criminal charge against them. At that time he had said, we do not need to fight. You were then without a purse and wanted for nothing, but now the time for struggle has come. We must have stores of food and knives to defend ourselves with.]

This is the most critical moment in Jesus's life, when he is sorely tempted to resist evil by evil. But again he summons his inner resources. He goes out into the Garden of Gethsemane and prays, and he overcomes the temptation. When he prays, "O my Father, if it be possible, let this cup pass from me," he is referring, according to Tolstoy, not at all to the crucifixion, but to the temptation to take up the sword in self-defense:

> Какая же эта чаша? По всем церковным толкованиям это—страдания и смерть. Но почему это значит страдания и смерть—не объяснено и не может быть объяснено. Сказано, что Иисус мучился и тревожился, но не сказано о том, что он ожидал смерти. И потом говорится, что он просил Отца о том, чтобы эта чаша отошла от него. Какая же эта чаша? Очевидно, чаша *peraismou, искушения,* так как я понимаю это место. [*PSS* 24:706]

> [What sort of cup? According to all the church interpreters, it means suffering and death. But why this means suffering and death is not explained and cannot be explained. It is said that Jesus was troubled and alarmed, but it is not said that he expected death. And then it is said that he asked the Father that this cup should pass from him. What sort of cup was it? It is apparent that it is the cup of *peraismou, temptation*, as I understand the passage.]

The disciples, however, overcome by sleep during this night of prayer, remain unaware of Jesus's moral struggle and its outcome. When the mob comes to arrest Jesus, therefore, Peter is still imbued with the violent spirit of the night before and cuts off Malchus's ear (John 18:10). Now he receives Jesus's admonition, "Put up again thy sword into his place: for all they that take the sword shall perish with the sword" (Matthew 26:52).

Tolstoy's account of the final tragedy follows closely the Gospel narrative; circumstantial and vivid as it is, it needs no elaboration or commentary. Like Strauss and Renan, Tolstoy ends the essential biography of Jesus with his death on the cross. He appends a brief excursus on the resurrection and Jesus's posthumous appearances, arguing as expected that these legends are unseemly and worthless. Miracle stories do attract some believers, but repel others; and in the long run the underlying truth is contaminated by lies. The first legends give birth to others, and those to still more, until the core truths of Jesus become more and more entangled in falsehood:

> Легенда содействует распространению учения, но легенда есть ложь, а учение — истина. И потому учение передается уже не во всей чистоте истины, но в смешении с ложью. Ложь вызывает ложь для своего подтверждения. Новые ложные легенды о чудесах рассказываются для подтверждения первой лживой легенды. Являются легенды о чудесах последователей Христа и о чудесах, предшествовавших ему: его зачатия, рождения, всей его жизни, и учение все перемешивается с ложью. Все изложение его жизни и учения покрывается грубым слоем краски чудесного, затемняющего учение. [*PSS* 24:794]

> [A legend helps the spread of the teaching, but a legend is a lie, and the teaching is truth. And therefore the teaching is not transmitted in all the purity of truth, but in a mixture with falsehood. Falsehood evokes falsehood in order to justify it. New false legends about miracles are told to justify the first false legend. Legends appear about the miracles of Christ's followers and about miracles that preceded him: his conception, birth, his entire life, and the teaching gets mixed up with falsehood. The entire exposition of his life and teaching is covered over with a crude layer of paint, the miraculous, which obscures the teaching.]

Tolstoy's effort has thus been to peel off this encrustation of legend and myth and restore the teachings of Jesus to their supposed original purity. After this process of purification, as we have seen, not much is left of the "hero," the personality of Jesus. As John Coleman Kenworthy puts it, the only hero to be found in the writings of the older Tolstoy is "the Jesus of *The Gospel in Brief*," and "even that Jesus is, with Tolstoy, little more than a body of divinest doctrine."[11] But perhaps enough remains for us to draw some conclusions about Tolstoy's attitude toward his hero. Was Gorky right?

Not entirely. To be sure, there was undoubtedly something cerebral and forced about Tolstoy's allegiance to Christian doctrine; it did not really come from the heart. Tolstoy was anything but a hero-worshipper or a mythmaker. As Isaiah Berlin has so vividly pointed out, the critical, destructive side of his intellect was infinitely more powerful than the positive, constructive side. Tolstoy could not abide idols on pedestals, and he tried to shoot down some of the loftiest literary ones, including Dante, Shakespeare, and Goethe. But Jesus is an exception. In the Gospels, despite their unsatisfactory literary qualities, there is a nucleus of ideas that struck Tolstoy as startlingly right and as applicable here and now. Though his personality is not important, the man who articulated those ideas must have had admirable qualities, and he did: born with common human weaknesses of flesh and spirit, he struggled with those weaknesses and at the most critical moments overcame them. Even Tolstoy could ask for no more. Whether Tolstoy felt love for him is, of course, another matter, and Gorky may be right: the emotion conveyed is not love, but rather admiration combined with pity, the two sometimes intersected by feelings of irritation at the contamination with myth and magic for which Jesus himself may have borne some share of responsibility.[12]

Gorky's remark about the village girls, however, suggests another dimension to Tolstoy's feelings about Jesus, a suspicion that Jesus was not irreproachably masculine. Tolstoy did in fact level a parallel accusation, as we have seen, against Renan. Did he secretly have the same suspicion about Jesus? Certainly nothing in Tolstoy's "Christian" writings could lead one to this conclusion. However, one could still perhaps argue the point by inference. Non-resistance to evil, непротивление злу, which Tolstoy makes the fundamental principle of Christian morality, is, after all, a principle of passivity, of physical submission, of refusal to defend oneself physically. Freudians would call it masochistic. It runs against the grain

---

[11] Kenworthy, 48.

[12] In discussion Richard Gustafson expressed doubt that in any case Tolstoy could have felt "love" for Jesus, who at best is nothing more than a tissue of words. I argued, however, that the example of Kutuzov shows that Tolstoy's creative powers were such that he could indeed contrive a "tissue of words" that *can* infect us with love, a love presumably also felt by the author. Could he not have done the same with Jesus had he chosen to do so?

of ideals of masculinity found in most cultures. Though Tolstoy officially espoused this ideal and preached it and at least consciously believed it, there may well have been a part of him that never fell in line with it, a part of him that wished Jesus and the disciples *had* defended themselves with the sword. Perhaps this Tolstoy longed for a more forceful, vigorous, red-blooded, macho hero than the pale Jesus of the Gospels, even the Gospel according to Saint Leo. It was this Tolstoy who, in his most officially Christian period, used to sneak upstairs to celebrate with his talent a non-Christian hero of a very different kind, Hadji Murat.

Rousseau's God and Tolstoy's God

The above title may strike readers as scandalously heretical: most of us, as heirs of the Judeo-Christian tradition, know that God is one.[1] My intent, however, is not to propagate a ditheistic or Manichaean heresy, but merely to symbolize a move from the (quasi-)objective realm of theology to the subjective one of psychology. My premise is simply this: all of us, Rousseau and Tolstoy included, use whatever God or gods we may have to serve our own intellectual and emotional needs. My aim is therefore to seek whatever illumination may emerge from a comparison of the ways each of these two great thinkers used his own private, internal God.

The comparison is not purely arbitrary; there is a strong genetic connection between the two. The importance of Rousseau as a formative influence on Tolstoy's ideas on many subjects, among them religion, has been clearly attested by Tolstoy himself:

> Rousseau has been my master since the age of fifteen [he wrote in 1905]. Rousseau and the Gospel have been the two great and beneficent influences of my life. Rousseau does not age. Quite recently I happened to reread several of his works, and I experienced the same

[1] An early version of this essay was presented at the AAASS convention in November, 1995, where excellent papers were presented by Liza Knapp, the organizer of the symposium, and by Donna Orwin. There was also an illuminating commentary by Robin Feuer Miller.

feeling of spiritual uplift and of admiration that I experienced reading him in my first youth.²

Earlier he told Paul Boyer:

> I read all of Rousseau, all twenty volumes, including the *Dictionary of Music*. I did more than venerate him; I formed a real Rousseau cult. I wore his portrait around my neck like a holy image.³

Such veneration is all the more surprising in that by temperament Tolstoy was anything but a hero-worshipper. He tended to regard all canonical lofty reputations with fierce skepticism and during his life shot down and contemptuously cast into his commodious cultural rubbish heap such seemingly sacrosanct master spirits of Western civilization as Shakespeare, Dante, Goethe, Bach, Beethoven, and Raphael.⁴ But Rousseau was the exception. Rousseau was even used as a personal measuring-rod. "I am reading Rousseau," Tolstoy wrote in 1852, "and I feel how much higher he stands than I do in education and talent, but lower in self-respect, firmness, and rationality" (diary 15 July 1852; *SS* 19:98–99).

To compare in full detail the religious views of Rousseau and Tolstoy, would be a vast topic, far beyond the scope of this essay.⁵ I will therefore

---

2   Tolstoy to Bernard Bouvier, president of the Societé Jean-Jacques Rousseau of Geneva, 20 March 1905 (*PSS* 75:234). Original in French, my translation. The letter was written in reply to an invitation to join the recently formed Rousseau Society. Tolstoy's favorable response to this invitation is most unusual: in general, he replied to all requests to lend his name to honorary societies, academies, public bodies of any kind with scornful silence.

3   Boyer, 40. In his biography of Tolstoy (p. 36) A. N. Wilson casts doubt on this statement, arguing that neither the locket nor anyone else's memory of it survived to corroborate Tolstoy's claim. Neither of these considerations seems to me weighty enough to impugn Tolstoy's unequivocal testimony. Moreover, Wilson's reference to *several* conversations, in *one* of which Tolstoy states only that he "wished he could have worn his [Rousseau's] portrait" seems to have no documentary basis at all.

4   In *What Is Art?* (1898) all of these eminences, along with all the great Greek dramatists, Tasso, Milton, and Michelangelo ("with his absurd *Last Judgment*") are cited as examples of art falsely and harmfully canonized by generations of elitist critics who copy one another's misassessments out of incompetence or cowardice (*PSS* 15:80). Shakespeare, of course, later got a special Tolstoyan roasting in "О Шекспире и о драме" (1906). Beethoven's early work is to some extent spared Tolstoy's blanket censure, but the music of his last period, when he had become deaf, was harmful, and it led directly to that very epitome of everything musically pernicious, Richard Wagner. See the illuminating study by Rischin.

5   The subject is quite well covered in the thorough, if somewhat dated book by Markovitch. A more literary, less ideological approach to the comparison is taken by Vladimir Zbožilek. I have also learned much from two books, one on each of my two protagonists: Weisbein

begin by simply highlighting a few crucial similarities and differences in the two men's religious *ideas*. My ultimate aim, however, is to try to elucidate the emotional relationship of each to the being they called God: what did God mean to each of them, why did they need Him, and to what uses did they put Him?

The religious evolution of both Rousseau and Tolstoy was marked by years of restless searching, with many twists, turns, and reversals of direction. Born in Geneva, Rousseau was brought up as a Calvinist Protestant. Formally converted to Roman Catholicism at age sixteen, largely for opportunistic reasons, he remained at least nominally a Catholic during his years of self-education under the cozy wing of his seductive sponsor, Mme. de Warens, his adored "Maman." But after his move to Paris and association with the *philosophes*, Rousseau's connection not only with the Church, but even with Christianity itself, at least as most believers would define it, was essentially sloughed off. To be sure, in one of his periods of conflict with the French establishment he did for a time proudly reclaim his Protestant Swiss birthright; but before long he found the Protestant clergy as dogmatic and intolerant as their Catholic confrères and renounced them in turn.[6]

Rousseau never embraced the complete atheism of his sometime friends Diderot, Helvétius, Holbach, and La Mettrie, nor did he share Voltaire's bitter animus against the Church as an institution. He also retained a deep admiration for the human personality of Jesus, who, he felt, had propagated lofty ideals in a debased milieu and had borne with dignity the sufferings of an ignominious death. But despite his differences with the *philosophes*, Rousseau remained very much a product of the rationalist Enlightenment. He emphatically repudiated *all* the central tenets of official—ecclesiastical—Christianity: Rousseau's Jesus was *not* an incarnate deity; he did *not* perform miracles; he did *not* rise from the dead; and his death was *not* a payment needed to redeem mankind from original sin.[7] In all these views Tolstoy was very much in accord with his Franco-Swiss mentor, except that the late Tolstoy placed much more emphasis

and Jacquet. On Rousseau, Grimsley is also to be recommended. Especially illuminating on Rousseau's relation to the intellectual history of the eighteenth century and on the later impact of his ideas is the fine essay by Melzer, "The Origin," recommended to me by Donna Orwin.

[6] In *Lettres écrites de la Montagne* (1763) he accused the Calvinists of having betrayed the chief principle of the Reformation, which he identifies, quite ahistorically, as the right of all Christians to interpret Scripture in the light of their own reason.

[7] My summary of Rousseau's religious views is derived primarily from the *Profession du foi du Vicaire Savoyard* from *Émile*, supplemented by other texts collected or extracted in *Religious Writings*.

than Rousseau did on the moral teachings of Jesus as set forth in the Sermon on the Mount.[8]

Rousseau retained a firm faith in the existence of God and in the immortality of the human soul—two basic tenets also fairly consistently shared by Tolstoy throughout his life, though Tolstoy suffered more agonizing doubts on both counts than Rousseau did, and Tolstoy's view of immortality, particularly in his later years, was of a more Buddhist-like, impersonal blending of the individual soul with the ultimate One than the complete survival of personality pictured by Rousseau.[9] Rousseau insisted that the existence of God is demonstrated by the universe He created, for it is impossible to explain the orderliness of the natural world without postulating an intelligent Being who formed it. Rousseau's God is good, and the universe He created is also good. The world is orderly and beautiful; all sin and disorder are of human making.

A good God must by definition be just; justice is one of the necessary attributes of an inherently orderly world. A just God could not favor certain peoples over others, hence Rousseau's rejection of Judaism, nor could He damn to perdition the millions of people in Africa, Asia, and the Americas whose only crime was that they had never heard of Jesus and His salvific sacrifice. The doctrine of original sin is likewise unjust: how can we be blamed for being born? Furthermore, Rousseau's conviction of the fundamental equality and goodness of all people bore the corollary belief that God has implanted in every human heart a basic understanding of right and wrong, good and evil, an innate conscience that lies at the foundation of the "natural" religion which could and should unite all men if only they would stop bickering over insoluble mysteries of theology or technicalities of ritual. This belief is very close to Tolstoy's *The Kingdom of God is Within You*: the moral principles preached by Jesus are already latent in every human being; we need only listen to the voice of God

---

[8] See "Tolstoy and Jesus" in this volume. In general, Tolstoy clung far more tenaciously than Rousseau did to the label "Christian." As Arthur Melzer argues, Rousseau essentially sought to replace institutional Christianity, a source of intolerance, strife, and war, with a "natural" religion based on each individual's "inner sentiment" or "sincerity," on "what, at the bottom of our hearts, we really *do* believe ("The Origin . . . , 352). Melzer pursues the question of "sincerity" further in another interesting essay, "Rousseau and the Modern Cult of Sincerity." Tolstoy, on the other hand, insisting that his Christianity was the true Christianity of Jesus, wanted to force all ecclesiastical Christians to recognize that their churches had falsified their Founder's central teachings.

[9] "Желать при смерти одержать свою личность, это значит желать лишения себя возможности новой, молодой жизни" (To wish to preserve one's personality after death means to wish to deprive oneself of the possibility of a new, young life), Tolstoy wrote in his diary on 20 September 1902 (*PSS* 54:136). It is not clear, however, in what sense the "young life" would be one's own if one had lost all personal identity.

within us. God does not care, Rousseau asserted, about what words are said by a priest before an altar, nor how many genuflections he makes. God cares only about what lies in our hearts.[10] These views were fully shared by Tolstoy, who in his later years was even more vehement in his fulminations against the sorcery and ritualism of the priests, culminating in the famous "defamiliarized" satirical representation of the Orthodox liturgy in *Resurrection*.

Unlike the late Tolstoy, Rousseau acknowledged a certain place for formal religion as an element of cultural unity in a particular country; he did not object to the notion that all a king's subjects should at least formally share his faith. Thus even late in his life Rousseau was willing to attend mass, just as his very unorthodox Vicaire Savoyard was willing to celebrate it, simply to mark his membership in French society. But of course Rousseau did not believe a word of what was said during that mass, including its central mystery, the transubstantiation of bread and wine into the body and blood of Christ.[11] Thus Rousseau in his mature period had only very loose and formal ties with Christianity. Though still living in a nominally Christian society and conforming to some of its traditional customs, he had essentially moved past Christianity to advocacy of a "natural" universal faith.

We can draw the obvious parallels with Tolstoy's religious biography, so vividly set forth for us in his *Исповедь* (A Confession, a title obviously inspired by Rousseau's *Confessions*).[12] Brought up as a child within the Orthodox Church, Tolstoy performed whatever religious observances were expected of him, but without deep involvement or conviction. By the age of fifteen, perhaps already under Rousseau's influence, Tolstoy had ceased to observe the fasts or go to church. In the *Confession* he claims that

---

[10] "The worship which God requires is that of the heart; and this, when it is sincere, is always the same. One must be vain to the point of madness to imagine that God takes such great interest in the form of a priest's garments, the order of the words he pronounces, the gestures he makes at the altar, and all his genuflections," says the Vicaire Savoyard (*Religious Writings* 169, my translation).

[11] "According to my new Principles," says the Vicaire, "I celebrate it [the mass] with more veneration," to which Voltaire, in his marginal comments, remarked sarcastically, "Ridicule, car tu ne crois pas à ta messe" (Ridiculous, for you don't believe in your mass). "With the thought that I am bringing to Him [God] the vows of the people in a prescribed form, I follow all the rituals with care; I recite scrupulously, I take care never to omit even the least word or the least ceremony," the Vicaire goes on, again provoking an angry comment from Voltaire: "Et pourquoi? Miserable!" (And why? Wretched one!) [*Religious Writings*, 191]. Voltaire's comments are cited in the footnotes.

[12] It appears that this title was not originally assigned by Tolstoy himself, but the evidence is clear that he later accepted and used it. See Gusev, *Материалы с 1881 по 1885 год*, 157–58.

all his middle years, up to the crisis of the late 1870s, were spent in this state of religious indifference, though his diaries do not entirely confirm this assertion. Like Rousseau, he retained a belief in the existence of God, though he was assailed by periods of doubt. For instance, his diary entry for 7/19 March 1857 laments, "Last night I was tormented by the sudden appearance of doubts about *everything*" (*PSS* 47:118). Earlier, in 1853, he had given the doubts logical underpinning:

> I cannot prove to myself the existence of God, I find no effective proof of it, and I find the concept unnecessary. It is easier and simpler to conceive of a world that has existed eternally with its unutterably splendid orderliness than of a Being who created it (diary 8 July 1853; *PSS* 46:167).

Just before writing this apparent apologia of atheism, incidentally, Tolstoy had again been reading the *Profession du foi du Vicaire Savoyard*. "As always after such reading," he adds modestly, "I conceived a mass of effective and noble thoughts. Yes, my largest misfortune is my big intellect (большой ум)" (diary 8 July 1853; *PSS* 46:167).[13] In 1857, sojourning in Rousseau's Switzerland, Tolstoy is affected, as he often was, by the beauty of the night.

> A marvel of a night . . . And not to believe in the immortality of the soul, when you feel in your soul such immeasurable greatness. I looked out the window. It was black, broken and light. What's the use of living? My God! My God! What am I? Where am I? And where am I going? (diary 7 July 1857; *PSS* 47:141).

But by 1860 Tolstoy had reasoned his way to belief in a rather impersonal, deistic God:

> To whom can one pray? What sort of God is it that one can represent to oneself clearly enough to supplicate Him, communicate with Him? If I do represent such a God to myself, he loses all greatness for me. A God who can be supplicated and served is an expression of weakness of mind. What makes Him God is that I cannot conceive of His whole being. And He is not a Being, He is law and power (diary 1 February 1860; *PSS*. 48:23).

---

[13] Donna Orwin, in a searching exposition of the impact on Tolstoy of the Savoyard Vicaire's *Profession du foi*, convincingly interprets this passage as an expression of doubt on Tolstoy's part in the capacity of human reason to penetrate the ultimate realities [Orwin, *Tolstoy's Art and Thought*, 41]. Such doubts were intermittent, manifestations of the lifelong warfare within Tolstoy of his "big intellect" and his yearning for faith.

Although, as we shall see, in his prayers Tolstoy addresses God as "Father" and seems to assume a personal relationship, in his moments of more severe rationalism he suspects himself—and others—of anthropomorphic projection. The only God we can be sure of is the law and will (закон, воля) to which we are called upon to submit (diary 30 March 1902; *PSS* 54:128).

Only after his crisis of the late 1870s did Tolstoy turn decisively back to Christianity. He first attempted to reembrace the Orthodox Church, but now on typically Tolstoyan "repentant nobleman," peasantophile grounds. The peasants must know best since they are peasants, and the peasants are Orthodox believers. (The plebeian Rousseau, incidentally, felt no such reverence for the superstitions of the *bas peuple*.) But when he actually examined systematically the theology of the Orthodox Church as taught to its clergy, Tolstoy's rationalist mind, perhaps shaped partly by his readings of Rousseau, revolted. Everything the Orthodox were supposed to believe was absurd, beginning with the Trinity: how could anything be one and three at the same time? He inveighs against this absurdity again and again.[14]

Yet as we have seen, Tolstoy still ranked the Gospels alongside Rousseau as his deepest spiritual influences. But the Gospels whose wisdom Tolstoy cherished were not the Gospels of the miracle cures, the marriage at Cana or the resurrection of Lazarus—violations of the natural order that Rousseau also found unacceptable, despite his admiration for the Gospels as a whole. Indeed, the resurrection miracles offended Tolstoy's very Rousseauistic sense of justice: why resurrect just Lazarus and not John or Joan? It was the Sermon on the Mount, with its crucial passage, *I say unto you, that ye resist not evil* (Matt 5:39), that Tolstoy

---

[14] Here, for instance, is a characteristic diary entry for 1 January 1900, lumping together the divinity of Jesus and the Trinity as irrational absurdities wrongfully instilled in children: "Если ребенку раз внушено, что он должен верить, что Бог—человек, что Б[ог] 1 и 3, одним словом, что 2 × 2 = 5, орудие его познания навеки исковеркано: подорвано доверие к разуму. А это самое делается над всеми детьми. Ужасно." (If it is once instilled in a child that he must believe that God is a man, that God is one and three, in a word, that 2 × 2 = 5, his instrument of cognition is forever spoiled; his confidence in reason is undermined. And this is done to all children. Terrible.) Similarly: "The person who believes in Christ the God, in the resurrection, the holy mysteries, etc., ceases to believe in reason. It is a direct statement: I do not believe in reason" (diary 9 November 1895; *PSS* 53:70). Texts like these seem to me to demonstrate that the influence on Tolstoy of Western rationalists like Rousseau was much more powerful than the latent effects on him, acquired simply by living in a Russian Orthodox culture, of "Eastern Christianity." The latter position is ably and exhaustively expounded in Richard F. Gustafson's splendid work, *Leo Tolstoy: Resident and Stranger: A Study in Fiction and Theology.* I argued my objection more fully in my review article, "Tolstoy Made Whole."

placed as the very keystone of his teaching. This was the deepest and most fundamental message Tolstoy wanted to preach to the world; and he insisted that it was, or should be, the essence of Christianity, since these were words uttered by Christ Himself in His most fully articulated statement of His teachings.

Thus Tolstoy's aim in the latter part of his life was quite different from any pursued by Rousseau. Tolstoy's purpose was to renovate Christianity, to purge it, to restore a pure "Jesus" Christianity, freed from all the lies and priestly encrustations of the ages, beginning with those imposed by that great traducer and distorter of the message of Jesus, St. Paul. Only very late in his life, after much reading in the scriptures of other faiths, did Tolstoy come around to a universalist position more like Rousseau's. He then found affinities between his Christian views and moral truths propagated by most of the great religions, especially Buddhism, Taoism, and Confucianism, and he hoped for a universal brotherhood that would transcend all religious labels.[15]

After this brief summary I turn to a more speculative attempt to assess the emotional underpinnings of these beliefs in both men.

One is struck at once by certain marked similarities in their life experiences. Each lost his mother at a very early age, too early to have any memory of her. Both fathers were a poor substitute for the lost mothers; in both cases relations between father and son were on the whole friendly and benign, but far from close. Tolstoy, whose father also died when he was only nine, was much better compensated for the loss of his parents than Rousseau—by his siblings, extended family, various aunts and mother-surrogates, and by his gentry status and inherited wealth. Rousseau's sense of isolation and abandonment remained acute, in his late years degenerating into real clinical paranoia. Of course, Rousseau did at times experience real persecution, but the atmosphere evoked in the late *Rêveries du promeneur solitaire* is a nightmarish one of a person beset from all sides by fiendish plots and diabolical intrigues. As Byron put it,

> His life was one long war with self-sought foes
> Or friends by him self-banished; for his mind
> Had grown Suspicion's sanctuary . . .
>   (*Childe Harold's Pilgrimage*, III, 18 [1816])

---

[15] See Pavel Biriukov, *Tolstoi und der Orient*. The subject of Tolstoy's connection with the Orient is also surveyed in Shifman, but unfortunately from a stridently "Leninist" point of view.

The God who serves Rousseau's emotional needs is more than the abstract principle of will, order, and virtue postulated in his philosophical works as permeating the universe. In his anguished isolation Rousseau longs for a more personal God, a paternal God of justice who will recognize his goodness and vindicate him. It is to this God he appeals in the famous opening paragraph of the *Confessions*:

> ... I shall ... with this work in my hand ... present myself before my Sovereign Judge ... I have displayed myself as I was, as vile and despicable when my behavior was such, as good, generous, and noble when I was so. I have bared my secret soul as Thou hast seen it, Eternal Being! So let the numberless legion of my fellow men gather around me, and hear my confessions ... Then let each of them in turn reveal, with the same frankness, the secrets of his heart at the foot of Thy throne and say if he dare, "I was better than that man."[16]

Rousseau puts his challenge in italics: *Je fus meilleur que cet homme-là.* Obviously, no one will dare.

What seems to me remarkable here is Rousseau's complete sureness: a sublime self-confidence that actually marked his entire life, making it possible for him to take on the world, as it were, with the full certainty that he was right and the world wrong. His fundamental, life-long existential stance was to place himself, his feelings, his *heart* as the most authentic reality, the ultimate source of truth and value. Thus standing before God at the Last Judgment, he is completely sure that he is not only no worse than any other person, but in fact better, since he has been more honest than they. He has confessed his sins, at least some of them.[17] However, I sense very little real contrition in Rousseau's *Confessions*. The confessed sins were errors of immaturity and growth, and he has corrected them by his

---

[16] *The Confessions of Jean-Jacques Rousseau*, 17. I have made some changes in the translation.

[17] Rousseau's most famous confessed sin was the theft of a ribbon in the household where he worked as a lackey. When the theft was discovered, he publicly blamed a young maidservant, who was then dismissed. Rousseau says that he was haunted all his life by this "cruel memory" (*Confessions*, Book II). For most readers, however, among them Voltaire, a far worse crime was the abandonment of the five children he had with his mistress Thérèse Levasseur, an act he blandly justifies by the thought that they were better off being brought up by the State to be workers and peasants "instead of adventurers and fortune-hunters." In fact, however, most of the babies left in the home for Enfants-Trouvés died in their first year, a fact Rousseau did not allow himself to face. He also seems to have given little or no consideration to Thérèse's feelings about the matter. The relevant passages are in the *Confessions*, Book VIII. Rousseau's fullest effort to justify his act is in his letter to Mme de Francueil of 20 April 1751, cited in the notes to *Les confessions* (*Oeuvres complètes*, I, 1431).

own efforts. He now stands before God proud of himself and his success. Perhaps surprisingly, Rousseau does not extend his scene of ultimate vindication to include a satisfying punishment imposed by God on his enemies. Apparently, his belief in the Lord's goodness and mercy was too strong to permit this bit of imaginative self-indulgence. He always insisted that a God "who condemns to eternal torments the majority of His creatures is not the good and peaceful God my reason has demonstrated to me."[18]

I discern much the same pattern in Tolstoy's Исповедь. Indeed, the similarity is more than literary, but stems from a profound similarity of these two men in personality, in basic attitude toward themselves and the world. Like Rousseau, Tolstoy was sublimely self-confident, insistent on thinking things through for himself, suspicious of all authorities and received opinions, willing to take on the whole world and set it right. Tolstoy's *Confession* also seems to me to lack any real contrition. He says he has committed all possible crimes, from adultery to murder, but he gives very little detail about them:

> I killed men in war, I challenged them to duels in order to kill them. I lost at cards and consumed the labor of peasants. I punished them, fornicated, deceived. Falsehood, robbery, adultery of all types, drunkenness, violence, murder. There was no crime I did not commit, and for all this I was praised. My coevals considered and consider me a comparatively moral person. (*SS* 16:98)

Even here the thrust of his discourse is to place the blame not on himself, but on the milieu, on the ubiquitous "they" (that wonderful, self-exonerating Russian third person plural verb without any subject!) who implanted false values in him and actively discouraged his striving for truth and goodness. Tolstoy, however, had none of Rousseau's paranoia. He does not look forward to a scene of triumphant vindication after death, and he issues no such bitter challenge to his fellow men as Rousseau's defiant dare to anyone who might venture to claim moral superiority over him. Indeed, Tolstoy does not seem much interested in any version of the Last Judgment, as some sort of reckoning performed by God with assignment of rewards and punishments.

The idea of metempsychosis, so charmingly articulated by Natasha Rostova in *War and Peace*, had been with Tolstoy for a long time. The idea of a "one-directional immortality" (from death onwards), as embraced by official Christianity and even by Rousseau's Vicaire Savoyard, seemed

---

[18] From *Émile*, cited from Markovitch, 120.

to him absurd: if our souls live eternally after death, they must have lived eternally before birth as well. As early as 1852, rereading the Vicaire's *Profession du foi*, Tolstoy found it

> full of contradictions, unclear and abstract passages along with ones of extraordinary beauty. All I got out of it was a conviction of the non-immortality of the soul. If the concept of immortality requires that we remember a previous life, then we are not immortal. But my mind refuses to comprehend immortality from one end (diary 29 June 1852; *PSS* 46:128).

In a diary entry of 24 January 1894 Tolstoy offers a diagram of the process of "double-ended immortality":

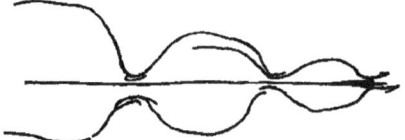

> The straight line is God [he explains]. The narrow places are the approach to death and birth. In those places God is closer. He is not hidden by anything. But in the middle of life he is obscured by the complexity of life. Lord, take me, teach me, enter into me. Be me. Or destroy me: without Thee it is not that I do not want to live, I cannot live. Father! (*PSS* 52:110)

Later Tolstoy overcomes the problem of our failure to remember our previous existence by postulating that the kind of consciousness we enjoy here on earth is specific to our animal nature here. Our life after death (and also, presumably, before birth) will lack (or lacked) personality, individuality. We were and will be fused with the deity in a state to which the earthly concepts of space and time are inapplicable:

> The essence of Christ's teaching [he wrote in 1895] is that man ... should understand that he, he himself, was never born and never died but always is and in this world passes through only one of the countless forms of life to fulfill the will of the One who sent him into this life (diary 7 December 1895; *PSS* 53:75).

Though prayer plays an important part in the relations with God of both our confessors, their prayers are never truly penitential, pleas for forgiveness. Clearly, they have already forgiven themselves, and God is given little choice in the matter. Their prayers serve other functions. Both also consistently reject the most common human prayer, the plea for some special benefit or concession. An omniscient and benevolent God, they insist, already knows what we require and will provide for us; He has no need of our instructions. It is presumptuous and childish to plead for favors, which if granted would disrupt the divine order. The Vicaire Savoyard prays simply in order to adore the wise Author of the universe. "I am moved by His benefactions and I bless Him for his gifts," he says.[19] And in the *Confessions* Rousseau recalls the delight of praying in the midst of nature's beauties, simply thanking God for the joy of being alive, a sentient part of His superb creation:

> I got up every morning before sunrise and climbed through a nearby orchard . . . As I walked up there I said my prayers, which did not consist of a vain motion of the lips but of a sincere raising of the heart towards the Creator of that beauteous Nature whose charms lay beneath my eyes. I have never liked to pray in a room; walls and all the little works of man come between myself and God. I love to contemplate Him in His works, while my heart uplifts to Him. I venture to say that my prayers were pure, and for that reason deserved to be heard. (*The Confessions*, 225)

Rousseau does, however, allow himself after all to make some modest requests, though none that demand any special intervention on God's part, let alone suspension of the laws of nature:

> For myself and for her whom I always remembered in them [i.e., Mme. de Warens], I asked no more than an innocent and peaceful life, free from all wickedness, grief, and distressing want, and that we should die the death of the just, and share their fate in the hereafter.

He does, to be sure, qualify the plea with the recognition that the best way of obtaining these benefits is not to ask for them, but to deserve them (*The Confessions*, 225).

In Rousseau's case almost our only data for speculating about his religious feelings come from his published writings.[20] With Tolstoy, on the other hand, we have the diaries, for our purposes a precious source of insight into their author's feelings about God, especially since he often

---

[19] Cited from Jacquet 154. "Je m'attendris à ses bienfaits, je le bénis de ses dons."

[20] An early prayer composed by Rousseau in the Chambéry period was found among his papers and published (*Oeuvres complètes*, 4:1036–39). After the expected effusion of awe and admiration before God's infinite power and benefactions, Rousseau does confess, in very general terms, to a plethora of sins brought on by his "passions." He promises to amend his life. "In a word, O my sovereign Master, I will dedicate my life to serving Thee, to obeying Thy laws, and to fulfilling my duties." Quoted form *Religious Writings*, 6.

incorporates into it actual prayers. What were these feelings? One is reminded of a famous image evoked in Gorky's memoir on Tolstoy: "With God he has ill-defined relations, but sometimes they remind me of the relations of two bears in one den" (*GSS* 14:261). After the evidence of Tolstoy's diaries, early and late, however, I conclude that Gorky's image is misleading. The two bears metaphor, however picturesque, does not seem to me at all to convey the nature of Tolstoy's relationship with the deity. Tolstoy was not a богоборец, a God-fighter, like several of Dostoevsky's characters. He does not argue with God or threaten Him, like Kirillov in *The Devils* nor blame Him for the moral disorder in the universe, like Ivan Karamazov.

There was, to be sure, at least one moment in his life when Tolstoy did shake his fist at the heavens, a burst of cosmic rage after the death of his beloved brother Nikolai in 1860.

> What's the use of anything [he exclaimed in a letter to Fet] when tomorrow the torments of death may begin . . . What a funny joke! Be useful, be virtuous, be happy while you live, we and other people have been saying to one another for centuries; and happiness and virtue and usefulness lie in truth, and the truth which I have extracted from my 32 years is that the situation in which someone has placed us is the most terrible deception and crime, one for which we (we liberals) would not find words if a human being had placed another in such a situation. Praise Allah, God, Brahma! What a benefactor! (17/29 October 1860; *PSS* 60:357–58)

One would have thought that the death in 1895 from scarlet fever of his seven-year-old son Vanichka might have provoked outrage in Tolstoy similar to what he had felt at his brother's passing thirty-five years earlier. Vanichka was the adored child of his and Sofya Andreevna's old age, evidently an exceptionally loving and promising boy. The loss was devastating to both of them. But though he himself connected the two events, the late Tolstoy cannot allow himself to blame God:

> We buried Vanichka. It was terrible—no, not terrible, but a great spiritual event. I thank Thee, Father, I thank Thee . . . Vanichka's death was for me like Nikolenka's, no, to a much greater degree a manifestation of God, an approach to Him. And therefore I not only cannot say that it was a sad, melancholy event, but I say straight out that it was (joyous) [радостное]—not joyous, that is a bad word, but an act of God's mercy, which dispels the falseness of life, an event which draws one to Him. (26 February and 12 March 1895; *PSS* 53:10)

In general, Tolstoy's most frequent attitude in prayer seems genuinely humble. One might have thought that a man as proud and self-assured as Tolstoy would be unable to assume an attitude of humility even before God. Certainly his model Rousseau could hardly be described as humble: Rousseau as it were smiles at God and expects God to smile back, a mutual admiration society.

But in the privacy of his diary Tolstoy repeatedly confesses to weakness, inadequacy. Feeling awkward and unattractive in the presence of women of his own class, Tolstoy in his youth even violated the Rousseauistic prohibition against asking God for favors. In one of his nocturnal moments of intense awareness, he begs the Lord to make him better looking: "I just looked at the sky. A glorious night. God have mercy on me. I am ugly. Let me be good-looking and happy. God have mercy" (25 August 1855; PSS 47:60). Later, after a repeated failure of nerve he begged God to help him screw up his courage to propose to his future wife, Sofya Bers: "Lord, help me, teach me," he pleads twice, for reinforcement even turning to the Mother of God, a personal, anthropomorphic deity he later emphatically repudiated (10 September 1862; *PSS* 48:44). By far the most frequent prayerful note in the diary is: Help me, give me strength. "Do not abandon me, Lord," he writes in 1853. "Teach me. Give me strength, decisiveness, and intelligence" (4 January 1853; *PSS* 46:156). It is a plea repeated again and again over the years. "Father, help me," he begs in 1888, troubled by his failure to win over his wife and family by love (25 January 1889; *PSS* 50:29). "I am sad, sad," he writes in 1892, appalled at the greed and strife displayed by his children when he undertook to renounce all his property rights. "Heavy-hearted. Father, help me. Have pity on me. I do not know what I should do. Help me. Teach me to love" (5 July 1892; *PSS* 52:68)."Lord, help me," he writes in 1894, tormented by the ever-present contradiction he felt he had to live with: while advocating for others voluntary simplification of life to its basest fundamentals, Tolstoy himself continues to lead the comfortable life of a Russian gentleman, surrounded by a wife and family who share few of his spiritual aspirations. He would like to right the moral balance with some dramatic display of sacrifice, but voluntary self-abnegation, self-repudiation in the name of family love, was much more difficult. He had to endure the mockery of his critics and often the reproaches of his followers. "Teach me how to bear this cross. I keep preparing myself for the cross I know, for prison, the gallows, and this is quite different, a new one, and I don't know how to bear it" (24 January 1894; *PSS* 52:110).

In his moments of need Tolstoy obviously perceived God as a loving father who will hold out a hand, pull him out of his difficulties, and instill strength in him. But all too often his rationalist mind keeps undermining his belief. He knows that God cannot be conceived as a personality: that is the root of anthropomorphism.

> One of the chief causes of the evil of our life is the belief, taught in our Christian world, in a crude, Jewish, personal God; whereas the chief feature (if one can use this expression) of God is that He is in no way limited and therefore is *not* personal. (18 December 1899; *PSS* 53:232)

Maybe God as the addressee of prayer does not even exist.

> I love to address myself to God [he writes]. If there were no God, even so it would be good to address an impersonal void. In such address there is none of the weakness, vanity, desire to accommodate others and calculation almost inescapable when one addresses people. (25 November 1888; *PSS* 50:5)

And elsewhere Tolstoy suggests that in praying to God one is in fact simply addressing what is holy within oneself:

> You pray to God. They say, to what God. How can you know that He hears you?
> That God who is in me hears me, of that there can be no doubt.
> Then you are praying to yourself?
> Yes, only not to my lower self, not to my whole self, but to that part of me that is divine, eternal, loving. And it hears me and answers.
> I thank Thee and love Thee, O Lord, who dwellest in me. (19 March 1900; *PSS* 53:15)

Year after year the tragic struggle goes on. Both demands of the public persona, as the prophet of a new religion, and the private yearning to see himself as a loving, self-abnegating human being who will blissfully blend in death with the principle of love that pervades the universe—this need and this hope are continually undercut by assaults from his relentless reasoning intellect.

Always there lurked in the shadows the all-purpose nihilistic weapon he had once aimed at a critical article by Aleksandr Druzhinin: "It never occurs to him to wonder whether it's all nonsense" (не вздор ли это все)[21] (7 December 1856; PSS 47:104). If zapped by this fearful weapon, perhaps the whole edifice of Tolstoyan Christianity might also be deemed "all nonsense"—indeed, a shattering thought.

---

[21] In teaching Tolstoy, I used to advise students to make for themselves and carry a pocket copy of this marvelous weapon, не вздор ли это все—very useful when reading newspapers, listening to political speeches, or reading articles by learned professors.

But back in his youth the tragic contradiction was still only latent, the optimism he found in Rousseau was still accessible. Perhaps the most purely Rousseauistic prayer recorded in Tolstoy's diaries occurs very early, on 12 June 1851, at age 23, in the Caucasus:

> Yesterday I almost didn't sleep all night and after writing my diary began to pray to God. The sweetness of the feeling I experienced in prayer is inexpressible. I recited the prayers I ordinarily say, to the Father, the Mother of God, the Trinity, the Gates of Mercy, to my guardian angel, and then I went on praying. If prayer is defined as begging or gratitude, then I did not pray. I wanted something lofty and good; but what, I cannot express, although I clearly understood what it was. I wanted to merge with an all-embracing Being. I asked It to forgive my transgressions, but no, I did not ask that, for I felt that if It [Оно] had given me this blessed moment, It had forgiven me. I asked and at the same time felt that there was nothing for me to ask for, that I could not and did not know how to ask. I gave thanks, yes, but not in words and not in thoughts. In that one feeling I combined everything, both plea and gratitude [crossed out: and submission to Its will]. Any feeling of fear completely disappeared . . . No, the feeling I experienced yesterday was love of God, a sublime love, combining in itself everything good and excluding everything bad . . . I did not feel the flesh, I was all spirit.

To be sure, Tolstoy goes on to admit that the flesh soon reasserted itself. He went to sleep and dreamt about glory and women. But even to that he adds a disclaimer of responsibility: Я не виноват, я не мог (I'm not to blame, I couldn't help it) (*PSS* 46:61–62).

There is no evidence, alas, that such a sublime moment in Tolstoy's life was ever repeated. Far more typical, I fear, is the cry "Father, help me!"—the cry of a man who, like Dostoevsky's Shatov, is desperately trying to defend his belief against the unremitting assaults of his "big intellect."

Claws on the Behind
Tolstoy and Darwin

In his diary for 28 October 1900 Tolstoy reports his ruminations during a walk taken that day. His mind, as it often did, dwelt on the distance between the "religion of true Christianity," of which he felt himself almost the sole living spokesman, and false religion, the superstition of the "cultured mob," propagated by such unjustly celebrated eminences as Hegel, Darwin, Spencer, Shakespeare, Dante, Ibsen, the Decadents, Raphael, Bach, Beethoven, and (perhaps worst of all) Wagner. Tolstoy's thoughts then turned to his growing fingernail. Why should the fleshy end of the finger be covered with a nail? According to Darwin, Tolstoy (questionably) argues, the nails originally "grew everywhere, but except on the extremities the nails were useless and were not retained. Animals that had claws produced a race with claws. But the formed embryos [зародыши] of claws, even on the extremities, provided no advantages, and animals with the rudiments [зачатки] of claws on their extremities had no reason to leave more descendants than those which had claws on their behinds." Sic! Perhaps we should simply regard this garbled statement as a slip of the pen and credit Tolstoy with intending to write a more credible version of the evolution of claws. Surely claws on the extremities would prove more useful than claws on the behind and therefore survived, while the latter, if they ever existed, were discarded. But at least Tolstoy had assimilated the basic notion of evolution, perhaps Lamarckian rather than Darwinian.

"Darwinism," Tolstoy goes on, "has all that is needed for a philosophy of the mob. It is not simple and can be puzzling, and the fact that it is stupid is not immediately perceptible, because it is curly [курчав].

Refinement, impressiveness, stupidity and curliness are the hallmarks of the religion and philosophy and poetry and art of the mob. Such are Dante, Shakespeare, Beethoven and Raphael" (*PSS* 54:50–52). I gratefully leave aside Tolstoy's aspersions on such literary or artistic luminaries as Dante et al., which have been well studied by eminent scholars, to focus on the contemptuous dismissal of Darwin and Darwinism. How did this antagonism evolve?

The first mention of Darwin in Tolstoy's literary *Nachlass* is found in one of the drafts to *War and Peace*. There Darwin is listed, apparently quite favorably, among leading thinkers "working toward new truth": zoology (Darwin), physiology (Sechenov), psychology (Wundt), philosophy [name illegible to the editors, but Schopenhauer seems a likely candidate for this slot], history (Buckle)" (*PSS* 15:233).[1] Thus by the late 1860s the name of Darwin as a leading scientist was already familiar to Tolstoy and duly respected.

The name Darwin had of course been in the news for some time. Despite its heavy technical baggage, *The Origin of Species* had been an instant best-seller in England on its first publication in 1859, and its ideas were quickly disseminated abroad, including Russia. The first Russian translation, by Sergei Rachinsky, did not come out until 1864, but Russian scientists, including Rachinsky (at that time a professor of botany at Moscow University) had assimilated its ideas earlier and were excited by them. In 1863 Rachinsky published a beautifully written article entitled "Flowers and Insects," subtly and delicately illustrating Darwin's discoveries. This essay is the best type of *haute vulgarisation*. The author gently leads his readers out into the fields to look closely at the grasses that grow there. Eventually, to help explain how these grasses became what they are through a process of adaptation to environmental conditions and fierce competition among rival species, he tells of the appearance of "one of the most brilliant books ever written in the natural sciences," Darwin's *Origin*. Rachinsky concludes with the announcement that a Russian translation of this great work is being prepared, but modestly refrains from identifying himself as the translator. Whether Tolstoy read this article we do not know, but he might well have done so: his own story, "The Cossacks," marking

---

[1] Ivan Mikhailovich Sechenov (1829–1905) was a distinguished scientist, active in introducing the methods of physics and chemistry into physiology. He was strongly pro-Darwin and translated *The Descent of Man* into Russian. Wilhelm Max Wundt (1832–1920), a professor at Leipzig, founded the first laboratory for experimental psychology. Henry Thomas Buckle (1821–1862) wrote *A History of Civilization in England* that attempted to apply the methods of science to history. He had an enormous vogue in Russia in the 1860s.

his reemergence as a writer of fiction after a four-year hiatus, appeared in the very same issue of *Russkii Vestnik* (January, 1863).

A noteworthy feature of this early article by Rachinsky is its stress on the mutual dependence of organisms, for instance, flowers' dependence on insects for pollination. This kind of "mutual aid" was later celebrated by Petr Kropotkin as a counterbalance to the grim picture put forward by other evolutionists of a pitiless and lethal struggle for existence, pitting all against all.[2] However, Rachinsky also makes clear the overwhelming importance of death in the biological world, noting especially (as Darwin also did), how disastrous it would be if all the individuals produced by the stupendous reproductive powers of all species were to survive. He calculates, for instance, that if all the 2,500 to 3,000 seeds produced by each poppy were to mature and produce seeds which then continued to do the same, in six generations all the land on the globe would be completely covered by poppies.

I wish to pause briefly on the matter of Tolstoy's relations with Rachinsky, since they seem culturally illustrative. Back in 1858, the same Rachinsky had proposed to translate Tolstoy's military stories—into what language is not clear[3]—and Tolstoy wanted him to understand that in "Sevastopol in May" certain patriotic sentences denying Russian responsibility for the Crimean War had been inserted by Ivan Panaev, then an editor of *Sovremennik*, and were not his.[4] (No such translation ever appeared.) There was yet another, more lasting strand of connection between Tolstoy and Rachinsky, schools. Sergei Rachinsky (1833–1902) and his brother Konstantin (1838–1909) together with their sister Varvara (1836–1910), both in the 1860s and 1870s were following Tolstoy's example and sponsoring schools for peasant children on their estates. Sergei Rachinsky read Tolstoy's short-lived pedagogical journal *Yasnaya Polyana*, and Tolstoy seems to have asked him to contribute to it.[5] On 7 August 1862 Tolstoy wrote to Rachinsky, warning him against hiring ex-seminarians as

---

[2] See Kropotkin. Todes (*passim*) shows in detail that the idea of mutual aid among organisms had been popular in Russia long before Kropotkin's book and was evoked as an alternative to natural selection as a determinant in evolution.

[3] Probably German: Rachinsky published a German translation of Sergei Aksakov's Семейная хроника in Leipzig in 1858. See *PSS* 60:435.

[4] Tolstoy did not write directly to Rachinsky about this, but asked his friend Evgeny Korsh to tell Rachinsky about Panaev's untoward interpolation. Tolstoy to E. F. Korsh, 12 May 1858. *PSS* 60:269.

[5] Once again Tolstoy used an intermediary. On 28 October 1861 he wrote to his then friend B. N. Chicherin, asking him to "pass on my request" to Rachinsky. The letter was damaged, and the nature of the request is missing, but it has been surmised that Tolstoy hoped Rachinsky could be persuaded to contribute to his journal. See *PSS* 60:408.

teachers, since they invariably prove too "ideological," regarding it as their mission to eradicate the peasants' "superstition" (*PSS* 60:433–34).[6] Tolstoy and Rachinsky seem to have been acquainted, since at the end of the letter Tolstoy sends warm greetings to "all your family."

In the late 1870s Tolstoy and Rachinsky again corresponded about schools. Their letters were not only cordial, but one of Tolstoy's contains an actual declaration of love ("Я вас очень люблю").[7] However, the love does not seem to have drawn Tolstoy to any recognition of Rachinsky's professional standing as a scientist. The Tolstoy-Rachinsky dialogue veered from pedagogy into literature, and it was in a letter to Rachinsky (27 January 1878), in reply to a question about the structure of *Anna Karenina*, that Tolstoy made the famous statement that Tolstoy scholars know by heart ("I am proud of the architecture—the arches are joined in such a way that you cannot discover where the keystone is" [*PSS* 62:377]). But how many of us have bothered to find out who Rachinsky was?

What seems to me significant in this relationship is that despite personal acquaintance and some very cordial exchanges about peasant schools, at no time did Tolstoy appear to take cognizance of the fact that Rachinsky was a person of some distinction in his own right, a professional scientist and a university professor. (Actually, in 1866, along with four other Moscow University professors, including Tolstoy's sometime friend, B. N. Chicherin, Rachinsky resigned his position in protest against highhanded behavior by the university administration.) Tolstoy's obliviousness reminds one of the famous "two cultures" of C. P. Snow. The sciences and the humanities are two distinct spheres, and the twain meet not. But in fact they do meet, but only from one side: the scientist is quite well informed about Tolstoy's literary accomplishments and discusses them intelligently with him, whereas Tolstoy draws a complete blank on Rachinsky's science.

Like many humanists, Tolstoy never showed much interest in science. In 1859 he wrote to Chicherin that he had "begun to study the natural sciences" (*PSS* 60:316)[8] and earlier that year his diary mysteriously reports that "on August 6 I went to Moscow and began to dream of botany. Of course, it was a dream and childish" (*PSS* 48:21).[9] Whatever they were, these studies do not seem to have gotten very far. Later, when he was

---

[6] Rachinsky hardly needed the warning. In the 1870s and later he strongly advocated basing his pupils' literacy on readings of Scripture in both Church Slavic and Russian. He also favored using village priests as teachers. Tolstoy does not seem to have known about these latter-day developments.

[7] Tolstoy to Rachinsky, 5 April 1877. *PSS* 62:318.

[8] Tolstoy to Chicherin, end of October or beginning of November, 1859.

[9] Diary entry of 9 October 1859.

organizing and running a school, Tolstoy did consider science a necessary part of the curriculum and spent some effort reviewing science textbooks used in British schools (*PSS* 8:397). In Weimar in 1860 Tolstoy had met a young graduate of the Jena Polytechnic Institute named Gustav Keller and engaged him as a teacher for the Yasnaya Polyana school, especially to "conduct experiments in physics and chemistry."[10] However, in a later account of the actual school, Keller is listed as a teacher of *drawing*.[11] There seems to be no record of Keller's experiments, but a teacher's diary does report experiments carried out by students themselves and also that Tolstoy himself performed physics demonstrations.[12]

Later in life Tolstoy developed a marked antagonism to science, regarding as especially invalid its prestige among intellectuals and its claims to offer general truths about the world and about life. His aversion was expressed most vehemently in his preface to a Russian translation of an article entitled "Modern Science" by the English essayist Edward Carpenter.[13] Scientists, Tolstoy proclaims, study the wrong problems and evade the right ones. Ordinary people, whose toil actually supports the scientists, naturally look to them for answers to the basic existential questions: what is life for, why am I here, how should I live. But the scientists assiduously avoid such questions. Symbolizing their elitism and distance, they answer in French, "Vous êtes hors la question, cela n'est pas du domaine de la science" (*PSS* 17:140)[14] (You are off the question, that is not in the domain of science). Instead, mainly for their own amusement, they occupy themselves with problems as remote as possible from the concerns of ordinary folk.

> When the ordinary person asks, how should I live, how relate to my family, to my neighbors, and to foreigners, how can I control my passions, what should I believe and not believe, and much else, what does our science answer him? It triumphantly tells him how many miles separate the earth from the sun, how many millions of vibrations per second in the ether constitute light, how many vibrations in the air make sound. It will tell about the chemical composition of the Milky Way,

---

[10] Gusev, *Материалы с 1855 по 1869 год*, 426.
[11] After the school was closed Keller served for a time as tutor to Tolstoy's nephew Grigory, son of his brother Sergei, and later taught German in the Tula gymnasium. The writer V. V. Veresaev remembered him there. See N. M. Mendel'son and V. F. Savodnik, *PSS* 8:489–520.
[12] Gusev, Материалы, 479.
[13] Tolstoy, "Предисловие." The translation was by Tolstoy's son Sergei, but Sergei did not want his name to appear as the translator.
[14] Tolstoy, "Разговор о науке."

about a new element called helium, about microorganisms and their excreta [. . .] about X-rays and so forth. "But I don't need any of that," says the ordinary man. "I need to know how to live" (*PSS* 31:89–90).

That question, say the scientists, belongs to sociology. But before we can answer a sociological question, we must first answer zoological, botanical, physiological—in general biological questions; and to answer those questions we must answer questions of physics and chemistry, and we must agree about the about the form of infinitesimally small atoms and about how the weightless and inelastic ether conveys motion. (*PSS* 31:90)

Tolstoy was equally unwilling to see any benefit in applied science or the remarkable technological advances of his time. At least in his later, post-conversion years, and to some extent earlier, his basic yardstick for measuring value was the Russian muzhik. Self-sufficient peasant agriculture—a man, a woman, and a farm—was the right life, he believed, the way we are all meant to live, in close harmony with the earth and her seasons. Everything else, all urban culture, was an excrescence, harmful, exploitative and often murderous. Tolstoy's article "Progress and a Definition of Education," published in his own magazine in 1862, shows that his views on this point were then already well established. He does not, he asserts, "hold to the religion of progress." The "progress" that historians like Buckle boast of, Tolstoy notes scornfully, consists of improved means of communication, printing, gas-lit streets, and . . . the gunpowder and shells with which "we" are introducing the idea of progress into China. Political progress is likewise an illusion. (*PSS* 8:333) "In ancient Greece and Rome there were more freedom and equality than in the new England, with its Chinese and Indian wars, the new France, with its two Bonapartes, or the new America, with its fierce war over the right of slavery" (*PSS* 8:334). Only the upper classes benefit from technological advances. Peasants do not send telegrams to one another, but a Russian lady vacationing in Florence wires her husband to send her more money. Do steamships, locomotives, and machines make life better for peasants? Tolstoy answers with an unqualified No, a persistent nihilism that later exasperated Dr. Chekhov, already annoyed by Tolstoy's hostile treatment of doctors in his fiction. "Something in me protests . . . ," Chekhov retorted, "that in electricity and steam there is more love for humanity than in chastity and abstention from meat."[15] But Tolstoy's absolutism would concede nothing, not even admitting the value to peasants of such vital tools as steel plows, scythes, spades, knives, hammers, nails, and their

---

[15] Chekhov to A. S. Suvorin, 27 March 1894. Переписка 1:248.

beloved samovars—all manufactured goods made in cities, not to mention factory-made cloth, which liberated peasant women from the spinning wheel and loom. Tolstoy could argue, of course, that the most ruinous factor in peasant life, vodka, also came to them from cities.[16]

Tolstoy even refuses to credit any of the advances in medicine as improvements in the lot of mankind. To cure one child of diphtheria under current social conditions, he asserts, is of no value, when

> not only children, but the majority of people, because of poor food, unbearably heavy work, poor habitations and clothing, and because of their poverty do not live half as many years as they should. Our way of life is such that children's diseases, syphilis, tuberculosis, and alcoholism affect more and more people, and a great part of human labor is extracted from the population to prepare for war, and every ten or twenty years millions of people are destroyed by war.

Tolstoy thinks that all these evils would disappear if science would devote itself to "propagating among people correct religious, moral and social concepts" (*PSS* 31:94).

To return to Darwin, Rachinskii's translation of *Origin* evoked a lively reaction in the Russian intellectual world, including many articles addressed to a lay public in the "thick" journals. Perhaps the liveliest of these was a lengthy celebration written by Dmitry Pisarev from his cell in the Peter and Paul Fortress, "Progress in the World of Animals and Plants."[17] Tolstoy very likely did not read this drawn-out, but animated effusion; he was not a fan of Pisarev's, despite two very favorable early reviews of his works by the young critic.[18] Tolstoy probably also eschewed the parallel article by Pisarev's rival radical, M. A. Antonovich, "A Theory of the Origin of Species in the Animal Kingdom."[19] The same may well be true of other articles on Darwin, reviews of the Rachinsky translation, addressed to non-specialists.[20] Scientifically the best grounded of these was by the

---

[16] There were occasionally some breaks in Tolstoy's total abhorrence of urban products. In 1885, during an excursion to the Crimea, he visited a glass factory and iron foundry belonging to a rich tycoon named S. I. Maltsov. He was appropriately horrified by the child labor in the glass factory—twelve-year-old girls working twelve-hour shifts—but of the iron foundry he wrote that it was "terrible and *very necessary* [*необходимейшая*]." Tolstoy to S. A. Tolstaya, 9 March 1885 *PSS* 83:490. My italics.

[17] "Прогресс в мире животных и растений" (1864).

[18] "Три смерти" (1859); "Промахи незрелой мысли" (1864).

[19] "Теория происхождения видов в царстве животных" (1864).

[20] These are well studied in A. B. Georgievskii; S. R. Mikulinskii and Iu. I. Polianskii; Kline; a series of articles by James Allen Rogers; Alexander Vucinich, "Russia: Biological Sciences" and *Darwin in Russian Thought*; Todes.

youthful Kliment Timiriazev (1843–1920), then a student at St. Petersburg University, later a professor of botany at Moscow University, commended in Soviet times for enthusiastically joining the Communist Party in 1918 at the age of seventy-five. Timiriazev's article, "Darwin's Book, Its Critics and Commentators," originally published in *Otechestvennye Zapiski*,[21] was signed only "K.T." It was later expanded and issued as a separate brochure that went through several editions.[22] We will encounter Timiriazev again as a leading combatant in the Darwinian debates of the 1880s.

For our Tolstoyan purposes a particularly important response to Darwin's *Origin* was published as early as 1862 in the Dostoevskys' magazine, *Vremia*. It was written by Nikolai Strakhov, who a decade later was to form with Tolstoy a close intellectual and personal friendship that lasted until Strakhov's death in 1896. Strakhov had better credentials for evaluating Darwin's theory than any of the other popular commentators except perhaps Timiriazev—he was a trained scientist, held a master's degree in biology (with a thesis on the ankle bones of mammals) and was well informed about the scientific issues of the day. A brochure by Strakhov on the place of science in education appeared in 1865,[23] and his 1872 book *The World as a Whole*[24] reprints a variety of articles on scientific topics published over the preceding decade. The 1862 article on Darwin was ominously entitled "Bad Signs," but the bad signs refer not to Darwin's book itself, for which—surprisingly, in view of his later attitude—Strakhov at this early stage had words of unqualified praise, crediting Darwin with having taken "an enormous step [forward] in the movement of the natural sciences."[25] The "bad signs" Strakhov used for his title referred to the introductory essay accompanying the French translation, written by the translator, Clémence Royer. Royer was more a social than a natural scientist—she published a prize-winning book on taxation simultaneously with the Darwin translation[26]—and Darwin's book appealed to her as much for the philosophical conclusions she could draw from it as for its scientific theories. With remarkable chutzpah—latterly she has been celebrated by French feminists as "l'intrépide"[27]—Royer qua militant atheist used Darwin's book as the basis for a general assault on the whole history of Christianity, stressing its stupefying effects on man's

---

[21] "Книга Дарвина, ее критики и комментаторы" (1864).
[22] *Краткий очерк теории Дарвина*.
[23] *О методе естественных наук и значении их в общем образовании* (1865).
[24] *Мир как целое*.
[25] *Критические статьи*, 2:391.
[26] Royer, *Théorie*.
[27] In the title to the book by Demars, *Clémence Royer l'intrépide*.

intellectual development and in particular its systematic and often brutal efforts to inhibit the growth of science.[28]

Not too sure of his own Christianity, ex-seminarian Strakhov glides over Royer's atheism (perhaps with an eye to the censors of his own article), but finds the "bad signs" in the latter part of her preface, where she voices in an extreme form ideas that later became well known under the name "Social Darwinism." Christianity and the laws derived from it, she asserts, have interfered with and impeded the operation of the basically benign natural law of the struggle for existence and natural selection, which is the guarantee of progress. Christianity has led us

> always and in everything to sacrifice what is strong to what is weak, the good to the bad, beings well endowed in mind and body to beings deformed and sickly. What is the result of this exceptional and foolish protection accorded to the weak, the infirm, and the depraved themselves, indeed to all those disfigured by nature? It is that the evils that have affected them tend to be perpetuated indefinitely [by reproduction].[29]

Shocked by this statement, Strakhov recognizes its connection with Malthusian calculations and reduces it for effect to familial terms:

> When there are many children in a family and nothing to eat, Malthus simplemindedly takes this as a misfortune. Now [from Royer] we see that the more children the better, the more powerfully will operate the beneficent law of competition. The weak will perish, and only the *naturally selected*, most privileged members will win the struggle, so that as a result progress will ensue, the betterment of the whole tribe.[30]

Such a formulation is appalling. "Such opinions are monstrous, incredible," Strakhov exclaims. He believes that mankind, to deserve the name of human, should set itself a different, higher ideal than the one

---

[28] Darwin himself was rather amused by this preface. In June 1862 he wrote to his American friend Asa Gray, " "I received 2 or 3 days ago a French Translation of the Origin by a Mlle. Royer, who must be one of the cleverest and oddest women in Europe: is ardent Deist & hates Christianity & declares that natural selection and the struggle for life will explain all morality, nature of man, politicks, &c., &c.!!! She makes some very curious & good hits, & says she shall publish a book on these subjects, & a strange production it will be." Darwin, *Correspondence*, 10:241.

[29] I cite in my translation the original 1862 preface as reprinted in Dorothée, 403. In the 1866 and 1870 editions Royer made changes in the original preface as well as adding new prefaces.

[30] *Критические статьи*, 2:393.

imposed by nature. Finally, Strakhov inveighs against Royer's assertion that both races and individuals within each race are inherently unequal. He counters with the claim that in a puzzling, mysterious sense people *are* equal as people, if not as animals. "We cease to understand human life, we lose its meaning, as soon as we do not separate man from nature [. . .] and begin to judge mankind as we judge animals and plants" (396).

Again we do not know whether Tolstoy read this Strakhov article, either when published or later. But the ideas it expressed, the horror aroused by the application of Darwinian principles to human life, became the dominant feature in Tolstoy's rejection of Darwinism and remained such all the rest of his life. After 1870 there was to be no more recognition of Darwin as a great zoologist. In Tolstoy's eyes he had been permanently transmuted into an over-praised, intellectually sloppy mediocrity, on a par with Wagner.

The first scientific article by Strakhov we know Tolstoy read was "Revolution in Science," which appeared in 1872.[31] This article was written as a review of a new and equally sensational book by Darwin, *The Descent of Man* (1871), of which no less than three Russian translations appeared within a year. In this new work Darwin crossed the border he had carefully avoided in *Origin* and applied his theories to the human species, explicitly asserting man's kinship with the apes and opening the door to moral and philosophical speculations (which of course had already begun) about the application within human society of natural selection and the struggle for existence. The 1870s began an era of increasing polarization in Russia over "Darwinism," with the two camps, pro- and anti-Darwin, engaged in increasingly acrimonious dispute, culminating in the bitter and verbose polemic that marked the late 1880s.

In his 1872 article Strakhov already took a firm stand with the anti-Darwinists. He does not revert to Clémence Royer's incipient Social Darwinism, but now attacks Darwin himself on scientific/philosophical grounds. No longer crediting Darwin with having moved science an "enormous step" forward, Strakhov's tone is uniformly hostile. What Darwin did, he maintains, is to attribute changes in species to sheer accident, with favorable changes providing organisms with advantages in the struggle for existence and unfavorable ones the reverse, leading to their eventual demise. But Darwin does not explain the causes of these variations; therefore his title, *The Origin of Species*, is inaccurate, because their origin is never explained. Likewise, to classify man as an animal related to monkeys does nothing to explain the uniqueness and complexity of human beings. The stampede to

---

[31] "Переворот в науке."

celebrate Darwin and his theories only illustrates the unfortunate tendency among scientists and others to succumb to fads.

Originally published in the neo-Slavophile journal *Zaria*, of which he was serving as the de facto editor, this article was later reprinted in a collection significantly entitled *The Struggle with the West*. Strakhov had now assumed a permanent stance of suspicion and hostility toward all intellectual emanations from Western Europe, even in science. It was no longer as if all human beings were engaged in a common search for truth; now every intellectual product came marked with its national origin and was judged accordingly. Russia had its own unique voice, its own contribution to make, and it need not join the cheering squad for each new Western fad. To be sure, it was important to keep abreast of the intellectual life of "Europe," and Strakhov assiduously did so by massive readings in German, French, and (occasionally) English. But the underlying impetus behind all this effort was to belittle, downgrade, and deflate the West's unjustified claims to embody the highest and most valuable attainments of human civilization. Russia had its own, independent path to pursue; there was no need to be in thrall to the false gods of the West.

In this article Strakhov cites a programmatic book by his friend Nikolai Danilevsky, *Russia and Europe*, a work that was to become famous only later, in the 1880s, which provided a world-historical, theoretical foundation for the position Strakhov essentially maintained for the rest of his life, a "struggle with the West."[32] Danilevsky later also became one of the leading Russian anti-Darwinists, publishing a massive treatise, *Darwinism: A Critical Investigation* in 1885. Apparently he began work on this project soon after finishing *Russia and Europe*.

As for Tolstoy, in his letter to Strakhov of 3 March 1872 he describes this article, "Revolution in Science," as "splendid" (прекрасная), but unfortunately he does not discuss its contents.[33] By that time he and Strakhov were already friends. The previous summer Strakhov had paid his first visit to Yasnaya Polyana, visits that were to be repeated almost every year until Strakhov's death. Strakhov in many ways served as a conduit through which Tolstoy "kept up," after a fashion, with current ideas and intellectual trends both in Russia and the West. Tolstoy was never so thoroughly "Slavophile" as Strakhov in orientation, and he was never pan-Slavic at all; but he did share with Strakhov an attitude of suspicion and hostility toward voguish ideas (like spiritualism) emanating from the West.

---

[32] *Россия и Европа* (1869–1870). On Danilevsky see MacMaster.
[33] Donskov, 1:19.

In 1874 a new scientific article by Strakhov, "On the Development of Organisms,"[34] evoked a more considered, but notably pessimistic response from Tolstoy.

> Thank you, dear Nikolai Nikolaevich, for sending me your article on Darwin; I devoured it and felt it was good and satisfying food. For me it was a confirmation of my vague dreams on the same subject, and an expression of what I had seemed to want to express. One thing is surprising. The article is published, people will read it. It is impossible to regard it with contempt and impossible not to agree with it. But will it change even by a hair's breadth the current opinion about some sort of new word uttered by Darwin? Not at all.[35]

Tolstoy goes on to lament the alleged and doubtless discouraging "fact" that a critical article affects public opinion only when it purveys nonsense (мелет околесную); a serious and sincere one like Strakhov's has no effect. Strakhov did not respond to this mournful prophecy; versatile journalist that he was, he had already moved on to another topic altogether, an article on Pushkin.

Later in the 1870s reverberations of the debate over Darwinism even found their way onto the hallowed pages of *Anna Karenina*. The novel's alter ego hero, Konstantin Levin, (unlike his author) was a *estestvennik*, a university graduate in the sciences. "The origin of man as an animal" is listed among the current scientific topics that interested him, despite the fact that like all academic ratiocination, in his view it cravenly dodged the basic existential question, which alone should be its pressing subject, what is the meaning of life (One: vii). Levin's half-brother Koznyshev and his friend, the professor from Kharkov, are thus typical "scientists" in their evasions.[36] Later we learn that Levin's friend, the nominally liberal Sviyazhsky, "considered the Russian peasant in his state of development to stand in a transitional stage between the monkey and man" (Three: xxvi)—clearly an echo of Darwin reverberating in the Russian provinces. Most importantly, at the end of the novel Levin, like his author, is engaged in an agonized effort to find some "meaning" that could justify his continuing to live. Darwinism, or more properly Social Darwinism, though never named, enters into these ruminations. "Reason,"

---

[34] "О развитии организмов.". This article unfortunately proved inaccessible to me. The editors of the Jubilee edition (*PSS* 62:66) tell us only that it "criticizes Darwin from idealist positions."

[35] Tolstoy to Strakhov, 13 February 1874. Donskov 1:151.

[36] This conversation is very similar to the one in the fragment "Разговор о науке." See note 14 above.

Levin argues, "has discovered the struggle for existence and the law that demands that I suffocate all those who hinder the gratification of my desires." But happily, he continues, man is governed not only by reason. He also experiences love, "and reason could not discover how to love another person, because it is irrational" (Eight: xii).[37]

K. A. Timiriazev rightly argued that Levin has not read his Darwin very carefully, because in fact Darwin himself maintained that "as applied to humans the struggle for existence signifies not hatred and extermination, but on the contrary, love and protection."[38] Doubtless for tactical reasons, Timiriazev made Darwin's views sound more benign than they really were, but Darwin did indeed recognize the value of love, notably parental love, as a factor in survival, and he also saw man's moral capacity as a product of evolution, observing that rudiments of morality are found among many animals, especially those that band together in packs or herds, where social cohesion enhances the likelihood of survival. These same tendencies have only been expanded and intensified in man, likewise very much a "social animal."[39] Tolstoy, however, never recognized or made use of this potential support from Darwin for his doctrines of love.

The next major reverberation from Darwinism to affect Tolstoy came from an article in the *Revue des deux mondes*, a magazine to which he subscribed for many years. Entitled "La démocratie devant la morale de l'avenir" (Democracy before the Morality of the Future), it was written by a prominent Catholic philosopher and moralist named Elme-Marie Caro (1826–1887). Ostensibly judicious and evenhanded, Caro spelled out what he felt were the terrible moral conclusions to be drawn from Darwin's theories, conclusions already partly articulated by Herbert Spencer. (They had already in fact been voiced by Clémence Royer, but Caro does

---

[37] My friend Brett Cooke has kindly called my attention to two additional passages in *Anna Karenina* containing echoes of Darwinism. As early as One: iii, as part of an enumeration of Stiva Oblonsky's fashionable views, he jokes about people who take excessive pride in their aristocratic ancestry, saying that they should not stop with Riurik, but go back to our true forefather, the monkey. And at the very end of the novel, in Konstantin Levin's anguished effort to find meaning in his life, he seems to be troubled by Darwinian thoughts: "In all of us, along with the aspens, and the clouds, and spots of fog, development is going on. Development out of what and to what? Endless development and struggle?.. As if there could be any development and struggle in infinity!"

[38] Cited from Todes, 162 and 208.

[39] Darwin, *Origin*, p. 310. "As man is a social animal, it is also probable that he would inherit a tendency to be faithful to his comrades, for this quality is common to most social animals. He would in like manner possess some capacity for self-command, and perhaps obedience to the leader of his community. He would from an inherited tendency still be willing to defend, in concert with others, his fellow-man and would be ready to aid them in any way which did not too greatly interfere with his own welfare or his own strong desires."

not mention her.) The basis for the (Darwinian) "morality of the future" is this: the measure of good is what is good for the species. The good of the species demands that the strongest and most intelligent individuals should reproduce themselves; the weak and stupid should not. Caro gleefully points out how undemocratic such ideas are; they deny anything like equality before the law. In fact, what the Darwinists advocate is "scientific despotism," which would not hesitate to sacrifice one or more individuals if the "common interest" required it. Recoiling before this prospect, Caro ends with a celebration of pan-human solidarity and extols the charity that succors the weak ones whom nature had condemned to die, seeing in them the "seeds of beautiful souls" (53).

Tolstoy essentially agrees with Caro, in fact appearing to derive from Caro his basic notions of what Spencer and Darwin said. "Spencer and Darwin," he wrote, "demand the killing of the weak and the prohibition of their marriages, because human progress is retarded [by their reproducing themselves]. This is indubitable for people who do not see any aim of human life beyond earthly life. But this is contrary to love, the basic emotion of human nature, and this very fact proves that the aim of life cannot lie in earthly life alone."[40]

The Darwinian theme seems to fade from Tolstoy's field of vision in the early 1880s. The great scientist's death, on 19 April 1882, and the flurry of Russian writing it evoked, does not seem to have aroused Tolstoy's interest. Again via Strakhov, he once more became somewhat engaged only in 1885, when Strakhov's friend Danilevsky at last completed his massive *Darwinism: A Critical Investigation*.[41] On hand in Petersburg, Strakhov saw this monumental work through the press and was available to defend it when his friend suddenly died (7 November 1885).[42]

The appearance of Danilevsky's book triggered the beginning of a long and bitter journalistic war in which Strakhov took a very active part. Since Tolstoy only watched it from the sidelines without much *engagement*, it can be summarized here briefly.[43] Though he had been in effect editor of Danilevsky's book, Strakhov nevertheless published a laudatory review of it in 1887, under the inflammatory title, "A Complete Refutation

---

[40] "О значении христианской религии," a title given by the editors to a series of disconnected notes probably written in 1875.
[41] "Volume One" was issued in two voluminous "parts" in 1885. "Volume Two," consisting of one additional chapter culled by Strakhov from Danilevsky's papers and a long article by Strakhov himself, did not appear until 1889.
[42] In March of that year Tolstoy had become personally acquainted with Danilevsky, visiting him at his Crimean estate, Mshatka. Gusev, *Материалы с 1881 по 1885 год*, 396–97.
[43] An excellent and full account can be found in Vucinich, *Darwin in Russian Thought*.

of Darwinism."[44] Strakhov now saw Darwinism as an offshoot of the materialism and "nihilism" he had dedicated his life to oppose, and Danilevsky's book, "one of most extraordinary phenomena in world literature," was a powerful salvo aiming at their destruction. The Darwinists were not slow to fire their own guns in reply. K. A. Timiriazev responded with a strong affirmation of Darwinian doctrine, "Has Darwinism Been Refuted?" originally delivered as a public lecture at the Petersburg Technological Museum and published soon after.[45] Strakhov lost no time in counter-attacking with a new article, "The Perpetual Mistake of the Darwinists," devoted mainly to exposing flaws in Timiriazev's logic and deploring the crudely disrespectful tone in which he spoke of the late Danilevsky.[46] With that the war subsided for a year. Then in 1889 a new combatant entered the fray, Andrei Famintsyn, professor of plant physiology at St. Petersburg University. Famintsyn was basically on Darwin's and Timiriazev's side, but he tried to assume a more conciliatory tone in relation to Danilevskii's attack.[47] He agreed that there were flaws in Darwin's theory, great as its achievement was, and that later research would undoubtedly add to or supplant many of his ideas.

Strakhov would have none of such concessions and attacked Famintsyn as a vacillating Darwinist insufficiently respectful of Danilevsky.[48] Meantime Timiriazev launched two new attacks, one on Famintsyn, for his lack of full allegiance to Darwinism, and yet another on Strakhov.[49] Strakhov of course had to respond. In his final article in the series, "An Argument over N. Ia. Danilevskii's books," still another figure is found wandering in the battlefield, a bit like Pierre Bezukhov at Borodino: the philosopher Vladimir Solovyov. Solovyov had nothing to do with the Darwin dispute, but had attacked Danilevsky's other controversial opus, *Russia and Europe*. That traitorous deed showed Strakhov that Solovyov, formerly considered an ally, had gone over to the Westernizers. Therefore, in one concentrated blast Strakhov sought to deliver the coup de grace to both Solovyov and Timiriazev. Showing off his erudition, he reduced the essence of the whole Darwin polemic to the ancient dispute between Epicurus, who held that the order of the world rose by itself out of chaos, and Anaxagoras, who believed in an intelligence forming the cosmos.[50]

---

[44] "Полное опровержение дарвинизма" (1887).
[45] "Отвергнут ли дарвинизм?" (1887).
[46] "Всегдашняя ошибка дарвинистов" (1887).
[47] "Н. Я. Данилевский."
[48] "А. С. Фаминцын."
[49] "Странный образчик" and "Бессильная злоба антидарвиниста" (1889).
[50] "Спор из-за книг" (1889).

At the conclusion of the war, in April, 1889, Strakhov expresses himself to Tolstoy as "in general very satisfied." He enjoys the fact that the Darwinists Timiriazev and Famintsyn are themselves at odds. There will be other, more substantial responses to Danilevsky's book, he concludes, but they will end with "Danilevsky's triumph and therefore mine."[51] And Strakhov was shrewd enough to see that the value of this "victory" lay not so much in the success of his arguments as in the publicity generated for Danilevsky's book.[52]

Strakhov kept Tolstoy informed about the progress of the war, sending him copies of his articles along with his letters. On hearing of Timiriazev's public lecture, for instance, he wrote Tolstoy, "Finally they are speaking, but—what a weapon—a public lecture! I have no choice but to get ready for a fight and plant my feet wide apart."[53] Tolstoy thanked Strakhov for one of these articles, probably "The Perpetual Mistake of the Darwinists," saying that he had "derived much from it,"[54] and he seems to have been generally convinced by Strakhov's arguments and claims on behalf of Danilevskii. In 1886 he told the American journalist George Kennan that the Russian scientist Danilevsky was said to have "written a book that will completely demolish the Darwinian theory." The notes of Ivan Ivakin, who lived with the Tolstoys in the 1880s as tutor to their sons, reports the same verdict from Tolstoy: "Danilevsky . . . wrote a book, and according to Strakhov after his objections nothing will be left of Darwin's theory."[55]

Thus by and large Tolstoy tended to go along with his friend. He even thought Strakhov's attack on Famintsyn "too weak": Famintsyn had deserved "total annihilation for proclaiming without proofs that Darwin was a great man and Darwin's theory a great theory." But then in the same letter Tolstoy abruptly dismisses and even condemns the whole controversy. "Enough of him [Famintsyn] and of Darwin. I hope you will not be offended if I say . . . that what we think about how species originated is not only not important, but that old men like us, preparing to appear before Him, should even be ashamed, that it is disgraceful and sinful to talk and think about that."[56]

Strakhov tried weakly to justify himself after this drastically deflationary reproof, arguing that to demolish such a false idol as Darwin in the defense of his friend Danilevsky was a worthy effort, part of his ongoing

---

[51] Strakhov to Tolstoy, 13 April 1889. Donskov 2:785.
[52] Strakhov to Tolstoy, 18 May 1889. Donskov 2:789.
[53] Strakhov to Tolstoy, 25 April 1887. Donskov 2:737.
[54] Tolstoy to Strakhov, 23/24 January 1888. Donskov 2:767
[55] Ivakin 59.
[56] Tolstoy to Strakhov, 21 April 1889. Donskov 2:788.

war against "materialism and nihilism."⁵⁷ Tolstoy does not seem to have been mollified; a year later he was still shocked that people as civilized and decent as Strakhov and Timiriazev could engage in such vicious verbal fisticuffs. "Why? From science, like peasants from alcohol. Conclusion: their science is bad."⁵⁸

Even before the conclusion of the war Tolstoy, independently of Strakhov, had discovered an unexpected anti-Darwinian ally, none other than his old nemesis Nikolai Chernyshevsky, after twenty years in Siberia at last returned to civilization (though only as far as Astrakhan) and allowed to publish (although not under his own name). In December, 1888, under the name of "An Old Transformist," Chernyshevsky published an article entitled "The Origin of the Theory of a Beneficent Struggle for Life."⁵⁹ By signing it as he did, Chernyshevsky seemed to proclaim that he was no creationist nor even a follower of Cuvier, who had insisted that species were fixed forever. He believed in evolution, just not Darwinian evolution. Chernyshevsky concludes that the transformation of species must have taken place by some less murderous process than natural selection. Future transformationists will discover the answer.

Tolstoy read this article and commented in his diary, "Chernyshevsky's article on Darwin is splendid [прекрасна]. Strength and clarity" (*PSS* 50:16). It is hard to discern just what Tolstoy liked so much about the article other than the denial of natural selection. A large part of it is given over to a biographical and bibliographical account of Darwin's career, filled with many highly laudatory assessments of Darwin's character and achievements. As a research scientist and writer on particular topics, Chernyshevsky says, Darwin was superb: conscientious, gifted, industrious, and learned.⁶⁰ In view of his many later disparaging comments about Darwin, one can hardly believe that Tolstoy found agreeable such praise of the man. Where Darwin failed, according to Chernyshevsky, was in extracting large generalizations from his research, in particular his theory of natural selection. The idea that a horribly cruel struggle for existence could lead to *progress*, to improvement of the species, seemed to Chernyshevsky clearly wrong. It would lead rather to degradation and extinction. Tolstoy may have liked that idea; he had never believed in progress anyway, at least material progress. Further, Chernyshevsky maintained that Darwin's reliance on Malthus was suspicious. Malthus was a political reactionary, believing that political reforms were useless in view

---

57   Strakhov to Tolstoy, 18 May 1889. Donskov 2:789.
58   Diary entry of 20 August 1890. *PSS* 51:79.
59   "Происхождение теории" (1888).
60   Н. Г. Чернышевский, *Полное собрание сочинений*, 10:750.

of the overwhelming threat of overpopulation. Tolstoy was also strongly anti-Malthusian. He had taken a swipe at Malthus as early as "Progress and a Definition of Education" (1862), but his most withering denunciation is found in *What Then Must We Do?* (1886):

> A very bad English journalist, whose works were all forgotten and adjudged the most worthless of the worthless, writes a treatise on population in which he invents a supposed law that the growth of population is incommensurate with the food supply. This writer pads this supposed law with mathematical formulas with no basis and publishes it [. . .] The journalist who wrote this work suddenly becomes a scientific authority and has been kept at this level almost half a century. (*PSS* 25:333)

One of Malthus's deluded admirers was Darwin, who applied his theory to animals and plants. This aspect of Darwinism had never found favor in Russia, and in this respect for once Tolstoy found himself in the mainstream.[61]

In general, after 1890 Tolstoy's views of Darwin and Darwinism solidified into a permanent pattern. The purely scientific part, the origin of species and the descent of man from ape-like creatures, though perhaps true, was of no significance, irrelevant to the problems of here and now. It was a typically useless intellectual game played by idle, upper-class people to amuse themselves. We live now, and the important thing is to decide how to live, what then must we do, not to ponder over rocks and fossils and try to figure out what was the state of the earth millions of years ago. On the other hand, what was dangerous about Darwinism were the *moral* conclusions some people drew from it, i.e., Social Darwinism.

Of course, many Darwinists had also been troubled by the apparent moral implications of their theories, and such conclusions as those drawn by Clémence Royer seemed just as appalling to them as they did to Strakhov. One of the most thoughtful responses to this problem was an essay by one of Darwin's most loyal and energetic disciples, Thomas Huxley, once known as "Darwin's bulldog," a response especially important to us because Tolstoy read it and argued with it.[62] By late September, 1893, Tolstoy had read the Russian translation and wrote to Strakhov,

---

[61] Todes's informative book is centrally devoted to this topic, the Russian effort to embrace their Darwin without the contamination of Malthus.

[62] The response time was unusually fast. Huxley's essay was first delivered as the Romanes Lecture at Oxford on 18 May 1893 and published as a pamphlet immediately after delivery. The alert Timiriazev obtained a copy at once, had it translated into Russian, and published it with his notes in *Русская мысль*, No. 9 (1893).

asking him to obtain a copy of the English original. Of Huxley's article he said only, "How stupid."[63]

In the meantime Tolstoy had received a letter from one Georg von Gizycki, a professor of philosophy at Berlin, who had founded an Ethical Society which in turn published a journal, *Für Etische Kultur*. Von Gizycki asked Tolstoy to answer two vital questions: what he understood by the word "religion" and whether he considered possible the existence of morality independent of religion. Huxley, of course, had attempted to do just that, construct a morality without religion; so Tolstoy's reply to von Gizycki, which grew into a substantial article entitled "Religion and Morality," was at the same time a direct confrontation with the views of the English scientist.[64]

Huxley began his essay with a long and learned excursus, designed to engage his erudite Oxford audience — the article was originally delivered there as the Romanes lecture — into the earliest formulations of morality found in ancient religions, notably Hinduism, Buddhism and the ancient Greek philosophers. This section only irritated Tolstoy, a useless display of irrelevant learning. Huxley carefully avoids Christianity. His basic idea is that man as a conscious, rational being can set himself moral principles or laws different from the crude imperatives of the struggle for existence. Some of these, as Darwin had noted, stem from the fact that man is a social animal, and that even within the struggle for existence the good of the social unit may take precedence over the desires, interests, and will of the individual. Some of these principles may be enforced as "laws" and violations punished; others may be internalized as shared values. The example of the perfectly functioning societies of ants and bees is telling, but man is different, for unlike the ant or bee the individual man retains independent desires and will, sometimes leading to conflict with his own society. Many of the competitive and aggressive qualities that enabled human beings to win "the headship of the sentient world" become harmful and destructive under conditions of civilization. To apply the doctrine of the "survival of the fittest" to civilized man is a "fallacy."[65] "Social progress

---

[63] Tolstoy to Strakhov, 25 September 1893. Donskov 2:931.

[64] "Религия и нравственность." In October Strakhov did send Tolstoy the English text of "Evolution and Ethics" (Strakhov to Tolstoy, 20 October 1893; Donskov 2:933), but Tolstoy had already finished his article; he sent it to von Gizycki on 4 October. It was translated into German and appeared in four numbers of *Für Etische Kultur* (December 1893–January 1894) and as a separate brochure (Berlin, 1894). In Russia it was drastically mutilated by the censors and appeared in *Северный Вестник* (no. 1, 1894) under the title "Противоречия эмпирической нравственности." I draw these details from V. S. Mishin's commentary in *PSS* 39:225–29 and from L. D. Opul'skaia, 64–65.

[65] I cite the edition edited, with excellent accompanying essays, by James Paradis and George C. Williams, 138.

means a checking of the cosmic process at every step and the substitution for it of another, which may be called the ethical process, the end of which is not the survival of those who happen to be the fittest, [. . .] but of those who are ethically the best" (139). Man has tamed nature; he can tame himself, restrain "the instinct of savagery in civilized man." Oddly, in setting the human quest for morality in opposition to man's instinctual nature, Huxley does not invoke Darwin's observation that loving and altruistic behaviors are also observable products of evolution.

In any case, like his fellow Christian moralist Dostoevsky, from whom he differed in so many respects, Tolstoy cannot accept Huxley's idea of a morality designed by man for man. Nature, Tolstoy argues (sounding almost like a Darwinian), offers only

> the law of evolution, which lies at the base of all the science of our time and rests on a general, eternal, and unchanging law—the law of the struggle for existence and the survival of the most capable (the fittest)[66] and that therefore each man, to obtain his own good and the good of his society, must be this fittest and make such his society, so that the one to perish will be not him or his society, but the other, the less fit. (PSS 39:21)

This law governs the whole organic world. Some naturalists like Huxley have taken fright at the application of this law to the human species and have tried to think up ways around it. Huxley invents something called the "ethical process," which is embodied both in self-denial by individuals and in laws enforced on those who do not practice self-denial.

So far Tolstoy has given a pretty fair exposition of Huxley's ideas. Then, however, he unjustifiably ascribes to Huxley the claim that contemporary English society, with all its faults—"its Ireland, poverty, insane luxury of the rich, trade in opium and vodka, executions, wars, destruction of people for profit and politics, secret vice and hypocrisy"—embodies the "ethical process" fully realized. Huxley, of course, made no such claim. But the essence of Tolstoy's objection is the lack of any foundation for the "ethical process." The cosmic law of the struggle for existence applies only to man as an animal. It is a cruel and immoral process. Even if all men were included in a single state, the struggle would still go on. Man must indeed govern and change himself, but this can never happen as a result of social "progress." Using his favorite device of metaphorical analogies, Tolstoy argues that to try to base morality on non-religious prescriptions is like having a person totally ignorant of music try to conduct an orchestra.

---

[66] Tolstoy inserts the English word here.

Morality can only be founded on religion. It would indeed be desirable, Tolstoy goes on, to have a religion-based moral doctrine with no admixture of ecclesiastical superstition. But the fact remains that "moral doctrine is only the consequence of a definite, established relationship of man to the world and to God. By applying reason we can free this doctrine from superstition, but in no way can we substitute for it an unfounded, so-called secular, non-religious morality. (*PSS* 39:26)

Such remained Tolstoy's moral doctrine for the rest of his life. The basic principles of morality, though enunciated in the writings of the great religious thinkers, especially Jesus, are fundamentally not learned or inculcated. They are implanted by God in every human heart. We have only to look within to find them. Tolstoy in his writings merely shows us what we should find there and will find if we persevere. It may take much time for most men to accomplish this process — Tolstoy is not a millenarian. But eventually people, perhaps helped by reading his treatises, will understand "what then must we do."

As for Darwin and evolution, in his late years, as several of the above citations demonstrate, Tolstoy basically accepted a great deal of what Darwin said: the origin of species by natural selection, the struggle for existence and the survival of the fittest, and even the simian kinship of man. All this applied, however, only to man as an animal. But man is also a spiritual being, a child of God, from whom he receives directly moral imperatives quite different from those that affect him as an animal.

Since Darwin and the Darwinists do not recognize this fundamental principle, Tolstoy gives them no credit for their discoveries, which have proved morally pernicious. Therefore, in all Tolstoy's pronouncements of his old age, Darwin is invariably classed as a moral enemy and included among all those over-hyped, meretricious, fake eminences, idols of the educated mob, such as Dante and Shakespeare. Tolstoy even seems to take malicious pleasure in the perception that by 1903 in the minds of the educated "mob" Darwin was beginning to be superseded by a figure even more evil and immoral, Nietzsche. (*PSS* 35:261)[67]

Yet there is hope. Hope comes from the common folk of the world, who more and more, Tolstoy claims, recognize the God within them. The educated classes must do the same. They must cast aside "the complex code of unnecessary knowledge called science." Tolstoy makes use of another favorite rhetorical device, pluralizing the names of thinkers he disagrees with, thus depriving them of individual identity and casting them into a common pool of derogation. He proclaims: mankind will find

---

[67] "О Шекспире и о драме" (1903–04).

answers "not from the Darwins, the Haeckels, the Marxes, the Avenariuses, but from the greatest religious thinkers of all times and peoples" (*PSS* 38:290).[68] Perhaps secretly he would have liked to include his own name among the latter luminaries, the lights that shine in darkness.

Yet the demon of Darwinism haunted Tolstoy to the very end. After his celebrated уход (departure) from Yasnaya Polyana, lying mortally ill in the stationmaster's house at Astapovo, Tolstoy dictated a letter to his two oldest children, Sergei and Tatyana. In the letter he singles out Sergei as the especially contaminated one who needed one last admonition. "Darwinism," it would appear, had come to encapsulate for Tolstoy much that he hated in the modern world: its urbanism, its secularism, its God-denying "science":

> I still wanted to add for you, Seryozha, some advice that you should take thought about your life, about who you are and what you are, what is the meaning of human life and how every rational man must live it. The views you have assimilated of Darwinism, evolution, and the struggle for existence will not explain to you the meaning of your life and will not provide guidance in your actions; and life without explanation of its meaning and significance, and without the immutable guidance that stems from that meaning, is a pathetic existence. Think about that. I say this loving you, probably on the eve of my death.[69]

---

[68] "O 'Bexax'" (1909). *PSS* 38:290. Ernst Heinrich Haeckel (1834–1919) was a distinguished German biologist, an early follower of Darwin. Richard Avenarius (1843–96) was a German philosopher and positivist, originator of the "empiriocriticism" attacked by Lenin.

[69] Tolstoy to S. L. Tolstoy and T. L. Sukhotina, 1 November 1910. *PSS* 82:222–223. The letter was dictated to Aleksandra Tolstaya and signed by Tolstoy "in weakened handwriting." Later Sergei Tolstoy wrote: "Father attributed to me views of Darwinism, evolution and the struggle for existence, recalling the distant past—my conversations and arguments with him in my student days. In 1910, when I was already 47 years old, my views had greatly changed. They were little known to him, because to avoid arguments I rarely spoke with him about matters of principle." S. L. Tolstoy, 259.

A Clash of Utopias
Tolstoy and Gorky[1]

> Such is the ideal of Christ—the establishment of the kingdom of God on earth, an ideal foretold already by the prophets, that there will come a time when all people will be taught by God, will forge their swords into plowshares and their spears into sickles, the lion will lie down with the lamb, and all beings will be united in love.
>
> Tolstoy, *Afterword to "The Kreutzer Sonata"*

Like most nineteenth-century Russian intellectuals, Tolstoy and Gorky were utopians. They looked around them and saw a deeply flawed society, a society obviously irrational, inefficient, and unjust, presided over by an inept and outmoded government, still dedicated to the absurd principle of autocracy, with all legislative, executive, and judicial authority theoretically concentrated in the hands of one person, and that person selected not by any demonstration of wisdom or capacity to rule, but by sheer accident of birth. It was a society deeply divided, between a small class of "haves"— landed gentry, capitalists, merchants, professionals, and civil servants on one side, and on the other a huge, benighted mass of "have-nots," consisting mostly of impoverished agricultural peasants, but with an increasing segment of these being transformed into an industrial working class, the latter toiling under the harsh conditions characteristic of the early phases of industrialization.

The country's system for educating this population was inadequate and grossly discriminatory. Opportunities for women to emerge from their traditional domestic roles were severely limited. (It must be admitted, however, that feminine emancipation was not very high on Gorky's agenda and was not on Tolstoy's at all.) Both Great Russians, Tolstoy and Gorky

---

[1] An early version of this paper was presented at the annual meeting of the American Association for the Advancement of Slavic Studies, November, 2001. I greatly benefited from the discussion there and especially from the astute comments of the official discussant, Donna Orwin. Subsequently I was helped to improve the article by generous suggestions from anonymous reviewers for the *Tolstoy Studies Journal*.

concerned themselves mainly with Russian social ills, but both were nevertheless outraged by the oppression and discrimination visited by the Imperial government on ethnic and religious minorities, thinking especially of Jews and Poles. In short, Russian society was an appalling mess. Surely intelligent human beings could devise and implement a better way of organizing their common existence than Russia's ramshackle agglomeration of worn-out relics of its medieval past. Concerning the evils of their contemporary world Tolstoy and Gorky were in virtually total accord: it had to be changed, profoundly changed. But changed into what and how—on these questions there was ample room for disagreement.

The Tolstoyan utopia is not easy to reproduce. As Isaiah Berlin has argued so eloquently, Tolstoy's critical powers, his capacity for discerning flaws in the reasoning of others, were infinitely greater than his ability to construct positive systems of his own. We know much better what he disliked in his world than what he hoped would replace it. But let us try to piece together Tolstoy's image of mankind's ideal future.

The keystone of Tolstoy's doctrine is the formula "non-resistance to evil by violence," непротивление злу насилием, the wording derived from the well-known turn-the-other-cheek passage in the Sermon on the Mount (Matthew 5:39). This rule Tolstoy regarded as an absolute categorical imperative. Although Tolstoy did not acknowledge the divinity of Jesus or consider the Gospels as anything more than error-prone human artifacts (which he undertook to correct[2]), he nevertheless believed "resist not evil" (by violent means) to be divine law, implanted by God in every human heart.[3] The epistemological basis for this belief is not entirely clear to me. It was apparently derived from introspection: Tolstoy found the law inscribed

---

[2] In his *Соединение и перевод четырех Евангелий* [Union and Translation of the Four Gospels], written 1880–84, published 1892–94. Tolstoy also wrote his own "Gospel," a condensation and purgation of the other four: *Краткое изложение Евангелия* [A Brief Exposition of the Gospel]. Though it could not be published in Russian until 1899 (in Geneva), Tolstoy's Gospel was circulated widely in manuscript and lithographed copies as early as 1883 (*PSS* 26:1002). An English translation under the title "The Spirit of Christ's Teaching (A Commentary of the Essence of the Gospel)" appeared in 1885 in a volume of Tolstoy's writings entitled *Christ's Christianity*.

[3] This belief is spelled out in many of Tolstoy's treatises and essays written after his "conversion" of the late 1870s, must fully in *В чем моя вера* [What I Believe], written 1883–84, publication forbidden in Russia. French, German, and English translations appeared in 1885, but the full Russian text was not published until 1902, in England. The doctrine is also central in *Царство Божие внутри Вас* [The Kingdom of God is Within You, written 1890–93, published in 1894, in Germany]. It may be of interest to note that *The Kingdom of God is Within You* was originally undertaken as a preface by Tolstoy to a Russian translation of *Christian Non-Resistance* (1846) by the American pacifist Akim Ballou. On Tolstoy's indebtedness to American pacifists see Sokolov and Roosevelt.

in his own heart and therefore concluded that it must be there in all of us. People for centuries and centuries had been deterred from observance of this innate divine law by contrary sinful impulses and by false doctrines propagated by various vested interests, notably the churches; but he, Tolstoy, had now stripped away the thick tissue of lies laid over the law by such traducers as St. Paul.[4] He had set forth his findings in a series of treatises that he apparently considered so reasonable and so persuasive that eventually humankind could not fail to be convinced by them. People would then abandon their irrational and violent ways, and utopia would ensue. Tolstoy insisted that persuasion was the only means permitted for bringing about this happy result; any use of coercion or force would only evoke counterforce, bloodshed, and evil. The most important work to be done was private and personal. People one after the other must change themselves, by hard and constant introspective labor, as Tolstoy himself had been trying to do all his life.[5]

There has always seemed to me to be a Manichaean element in Tolstoy's image of the human psyche. God has implanted a correct, non-violent moral core in every human heart, but there seems to be a plethora of other forces there, many of them evil, and it is hard to see how St. Paul and his successors can be blamed for all of them. Though Tolstoy would never admit it, it is hard to avoid seeing the hand of Satan also at work in us. What about the sex drive—does it not also come built into us? Yet Tolstoy wants us to spend our entire lives, at least after puberty, trying to root it out.[6]

---

[4] In the preface to his *Short Exposition of the Gospel* Tolstoy dates the long sequence of false or corrupted interpretations of Christ's message from St. Paul, who, "not fully comprehending Christ's teaching and not knowing it as it was later set forth in the Gospel of Matthew, connected it with doctrines in the Pharisaic tradition and with all the doctrines of the Old Testament. [. . .] This teaching concerning tradition, the connection of the Old Testament with the New, was introduced into Christianity by Paul, and it was this doctrine concerning tradition, the principle of tradition, that was the chief cause of the distortion of Christian teaching and the misunderstanding of it. From Paul's time begins the Christian Talmud called the church" (*PSS* 26:808).

[5] To be sure, besides being "persuaded" by Tolstoy's eloquent treatises (and other pacifist writings), people could, as Tolstoy asserts in *What Is Art?*, be "infected" by "good" art with kind, generous, non-violent feelings. Tolstoy's own efforts to "perfect" himself go back to the 1850s, when his diaries record, often in overwhelming daily detail, the multitude of his failings and sins and his plans for self-reform.

[6] Of course, Tolstoy would never acknowledge any belief in a supernatural source of evil. However, one cannot help concluding from his writings that God's creation was fundamentally flawed. Humankind, Tolstoy believed, is in the process of evolving from a primitive, "animal" state into his non-violent utopia, true Christianity being a powerful progressive force propelling this development. The sex drive would seem to be a component of that "animal" state which we must outgrow. In one of the versions of his "Afterword" to *The Kreutzer Sonata* Tolstoy wrote, "Christ's teaching, expressed simply, says only that a Christian in order to fulfill the will of God must suppress in himself

In any case, what would happen if people really obeyed the divine law inscribed in their hearts and stopped resisting evil by violence? First of all, the entire apparatus of the state would vanish, "wither away" in the parallel Marxist utopian formulation, as unwanted and unnecessary.

No armed forces would be needed, because the country would not defend itself by force. If a foreign army were to invade it and met no resistance, the foreign soldiers would be morally overwhelmed by the spirit of brotherhood they encountered and would lay down their arms. At least this would seem to be the hoped-for result. In such works as "Не убий" ([Kill Not], 1900) and "Одумайтесь!" ([BethinkYourselves!], 1904), Tolstoy as usual concentrates on negative formulations: war is murder, those who participate in it are murderers, those who pay taxes to support armies are guilty of complicity in murder. People are "hypnotized" by governments and patriotic propaganda. Tolstoy's—and every Christian's—job is to bring people to their senses, repudiating the state's instruments of violence. But he never explicitly spells out what would happen if his prescriptions were actually followed and there were a foreign invasion. However, in a diary entry of 13 January 1910 Tolstoy says that he does not care whether the practice of his doctrines leads to anarchism or to [Russian] slavery under the yoke of the Germans or the Japanese. (*PSS* 58:295) Virtuous, non-violent slavery is far better than bloody resistance.

No law courts would be required in Tolstoy's utopia, because they too are ultimately based on coercion and violence. With regard to criminals, people have no right to judge and punish one another. "Vengeance is mine"—and mine alone—saith the Lord.[7] Civil disputes could be settled easily by negotiation, especially since there would be no private ownership of land—on this point Tolstoy drew heavily on the American reformer Henry George—and people's holdings of other property would be about equal.[8]

[Tolstoy always takes the male point of view] lust for a woman and enamoration (влюбленье). It is better not to marry, but if you cannot suppress your lust, then gratify it with one woman, and if you are married, do not part from your wife. [. . .] Marriage is not and never was a Christian institution" (*PSS* 27:423–24).

[7] This is at least a plausible interpretation of the famous epigraph to *Anna Karenina*, based on the citation in Romans 12:19 of the original text in Deuteronomy 32:35, where St. Paul urges the faithful to "avenge not" themselves, but to leave that task to God. Tolstoy's repudiation of law and law courts is explicitly spelled out in *The Kingdom of God is Within You* and elsewhere; it provides the satirical force in "The Death of Ivan Ilyich" and also *Resurrection*.

[8] Tolstoy wrote that George's *Progress and Poverty* had made a "tremendous" impression on him (letter to V. G. Chertkov of 24 February 1885 [*PSS* 35:144]), and in a letter to his wife described it as "an important book. It is that important stage on the path of common life, like the liberation of the peasants—liberation from private property in land" (letter of 22 February 1885 [*PSS* 83:480]).

Such necessary communal enterprises as operation of schools and building of roads would be arranged communally and locally. "Taxes" would be given voluntarily as people saw the value and necessity of communal projects; no coercion would be needed. It would be a stateless society, the "Kingdom of God on earth," as Tolstoy said in his 1906 article, "What Shall We Do?"[9]

The economics of Tolstoy's utopia are less clear. Essentially he advocated a return to a society of subsistence agriculture, where people would all live on the land and raise their own food. He acknowledged the need for some specialists such as blacksmiths, but he firmly rejected the idea that there should be some who worked only with their brains and others with their muscles.[10] All should do their share of farming: it is joyful, healthy work, good for body and soul. Cities would eventually disappear. Tolstoy viewed cities from the perspective of a "repentant nobleman" and former serf owner: cities are places where useless government officials and equally useless, idle gentlefolk expend wealth extracted from the countryside on such excrescences as large houses staffed with multitudes of servants (former peasants) and on such expensive and pernicious amusements as fancy restaurants and Wagnerian operas. In Tolstoy's utopia all these parasitic people — voluntarily, of course — will return to the land, get out their spades, and joyfully begin to dig. Their capacity for intellectual work will even be enhanced by the exercise.

What about the cities as centers of commerce and industry? Here Tolstoy seems genuinely puzzled and out of his depth. He would argue, I think, that with a greatly simplified economy there will be much less need for exchange of goods, and money may not be needed at all.[11] And as for manufacturing, Tolstoy seems to regard most factories as expendable. When listing their products, he always makes it appear as if most of what they turn out consists of luxury goods for the well-to-do, like the silk and satin produced in a sweatshop factory near Tolstoy's house at Khamovniki in Moscow. Peasants don't need satin ("Рабство нашего времени" [The Slavery of Our Time], Chapter 11). If there is need for

---

[9] "Что же делать?" (*PSS* 36:371). Tolstoy sometimes resisted the tainted word "anarchism," associated with bomb-throwing terrorists, but chapter after chapter of the major treatise *Так что же нам делать?* ([What Then Must We Do?], written 1882–85, Russian text not published in full until 1906) is devoted to demonstrating the harmfulness and immorality of all state activities. There is a trenchant analysis of Tolstoy's anarchism in Kline.

[10] Tolstoy's rejection of the notion that people who do intellectual work should therefore be freed from the necessity of doing physical labor is set forth in *What Then Must We Do?*, Chapter xxvi and especially chapter xxxii. The blacksmiths are discussed in chapter xxxi.

[11] Tolstoy's ideas on money are set forth in *What Then Must We Do?*, Chapters xvii, xviii and xix.

something to be made cooperatively, by many people working together, workers will organize such "factories" ad hoc. How such matters as capital, credit, distribution, and pricing would be organized in Tolstoy's ideal world is not clear to me. Though he regularly traveled by train between Tula and Moscow, Tolstoy—as far as I can see—simply refused to deal with the question of how such major enterprises as the railroad would in the future be financed, maintained, equipped, and managed. Despite all its convenience, the railroad remained for him the symbol of urban evil as he had depicted it in *Anna Karenina*, spreading its iron and death-dealing tentacles through the countryside. Tolstoy lived into the age of the electric light, telegraph, telephone, automobile, airplane, phonograph, and radio, but the advance of technology does not seem to have affected his economic thinking at all. For Tolstoy these were nothing but toys, and while playing with them human beings continue to evade their moral duties, fulfillment of which would solve their social problems.

How was the Tolstoyan idyll to be attained? Here too its author is a bit hard to fathom. Tolstoy never tired of repeating that only persuasion was to be allowed; no one would be forced to join this ideal world. Surely people would eventually see the light and carry out the program he had set forth so compellingly in his treatises. It might take some time—he never provided anything like a timetable—but it would happen. An added impetus would be the example of virtuous people living self-sufficient, non-violent lives. A nucleus of such people already existed in the form of the Tolstoyans and such peasant allies as the Dukhobors.

If large numbers of young men would simply refuse to serve in the tsar's armies, as the Dukhobors did, how could there be wars?[12] Nevertheless, Tolstoy never seems to have had much interest, or to have expended much effort, in organizing Tolstoyan missionaries. The work of persuasion should apparently be more spontaneous, the effect of living examples of people "witnessing." Somewhat incidentally, the novel *Resurrection* strikes me as a powerful artistic refutation of the author's own theories. In that novel only one upper-class gentleman, the hero, Prince Nekhliudov, shows any signs of self-improvement to the point of divesting himself of his land holdings, and even he does not give up all of them, apparently retaining enough to provide him with a comfortable private income. Furthermore, he suffers from unique sexual guilt, added to the universal social guilt of the gentry, to motivate his self-denial. No other member of his class shows the

---

[12] Chapter ix of *The Kingdom of God is Within You* sets forth in detail Tolstoy's view that ultimately governments are helpless to deal with those whose non-violent resistance, including refusal to serve in armed forces or to pay taxes to support them, rests on a firm moral and religious foundation.

slightest inclination toward repentance or self-impoverishment.[13] It would seem from Tolstoy's own evidence that realization of his utopia is a long, long way off.

*

Gorky never produced a reasoned critique of Tolstoy's utopia, but it is clear from many passing remarks that he regarded it with deep skepticism; moreover, the requirement that it could be attained only by persuasion he considered actually harmful, since Tolstoyan non-resistance was hard to distinguish in practice from supine passivity in the face of evil. Russians, he thought, had been passive long enough; it was time for more direct and more promising forms of action. The most forthright statement of his criticisms we have is an "open letter" he wrote (but never sent) to Tolstoy in March 1905, still furious and indignant over the senseless bloodshed he had witnessed in Petersburg on "Bloody Sunday," only a month before. Gorky's letter was written in response to Tolstoy's article "On the Social Movement in Russia" [Об общественном движении в России], which had itself been written as a response to inquiries from foreign journalists about his reaction to the political situation in Russia.[14] Most of all Gorky takes issue with Tolstoy's doctrine that the only avenue of real progress is for people to devote themselves to self-improvement.

"Can a man engage in perfecting morally his own personality on days when on the streets of our cities men and women are being shot and after the shooting for some time were not allowed to gather their wounded?" (*GSS* 28:360).[15] Tolstoy, Gorky insisted, had no right to speak even for the peasants, let alone the workers, whom he did not know at all. The pacifistic

---

[13] To be sure, in *Resurrection* Tolstoy does represent with considerable sympathy revolutionary socialists of various stripes who are mostly of upper class origin. However, since they are shown only as prisoners, victims of tsarist cruelty and oppression, he does not have to deal in any detail with the pernicious, violent aspect of their programs. He does, however, provide an example of the "Lenin" type of violence-prone, power-hungry, self-important socialist revolutionary in the character of Novodvorov, who says casually that the people always worship power. "Now the government has power, and the people worship it. Tomorrow we will have power, and they will worship us" (*Resurrection*, iii, 14).

[14] Tolstoy's article appeared in the London *Times* in February, 1905, and was later widely summarized in the Russian press, though the censorship would not allow it to be published in full.

[15] The letter was dated 5 (18) March 1905, but never sent to Tolstoy and apparently not published until 1954. The doctrine Gorky deplored is even more vividly and succinctly expressed in a telegram Tolstoy sent to the *Philadelphia North American Newspaper* on 18 November 1904; "True social amelioration can be attained only by the religious moral perfectionment [*sic*] of all individuals. Political agitation putting before individuals illusion of social improvement by change of forms habitually stops the real progress as can be observed in constitutional countries France, England, America" (*PSS* 36:635).

peasants he idolized were anything but typical. (In the end Gorky decided that the tone of the letter was too harsh; moreover, he did not want to add his voice to attacks on Tolstoy from the Right.[16]) In the article "The Destruction of Personality" (Разрушение личности, 1909) Gorky put his criticism even more strongly, lumping Tolstoy and Dostoevsky together as "the greatest geniuses of a land of slaves . . . With one voice they cry out 'Endure' . . . 'Resist not evil by violence.' I do not know in Russian history a more painful moment than this, I do not know a slogan more offensive to a person who has already proclaimed his capacity to resist evil and to fight for his goal". (*GSS* 24:53)

Though he was far from a lover of violence or warfare — Gorky was especially eloquent about the idiocy of World War I, when millions of Europe's ablest young men spent four years busily slaughtering each other[17] — Gorky was convinced that the tsarist regime could never be brought down by peaceful means, certainly not by masses of people trying to extirpate the aggressiveness from their own souls. As early as November 1904 he had proclaimed, "[W]e will not let ourselves be whipped or trampled on. We will have to use our revolvers, daggers and even our teeth in the struggle" (cited from Yedlin 47).

Gorky did not, of course, share Tolstoy's negation of cities and industry, nor did he condone Tolstoy's repudiation (in which Tolstoy included his own great novels) of the "elitist" culture built up over centuries by the intelligentsias of Russia and the world. On the contrary, Gorky regarded the intelligentsia as Russia's main bulwark against peasant, "Asiatic" mindlessness and superstition. Perhaps these anti-Tolstoy views will be better explicated in the more positive form of an exposition of Gorky's own utopia.

Another strong anti-Tolstoyan impulse in Gorky stemmed from his personal encounters, not with Tolstoy himself, for whom Gorky continued

---

[16] From the unfinished letter to Korolenko that forms part of the great memoir, *Лев Толстой* (1919; *GSS* 14:279). The reasons for not sending or publishing the letter are also adumbrated in a letter to his ex-wife, E. P. Peshkova, of 12/13 March 1905 and in comments to the French writer Claude Anet. See the notes in *GSS* 28:554. The unsent letter to Tolstoy is in the same volume, 357–61.

[17] Unlike such Marxists as Plekhanov, Gorky opposed World War I from the beginning, in 1914 anathematizing the "mad dogs of worldwide slaughter" who have plunged the world into war ("Несвоевременное" [Untimely], *GSS* 24:158). In June 1917 he wrote that "Three years of bloody nightmare have annihilated the flower of Europe's population, for three years all Europe, in bloody intoxication, has been destroying its healthiest and strongest sons" (*Untimely Thoughts*, 58). By the end of the war Gorky had adopted the official Leninist line, that the war had been fought entirely as a struggle for markets by capitalists, "Now," he wrote in November 1918, "when this accursed and most shameful war has revealed to the ultimate all the vileness and inhumanity, all the cynicism of the old order, showing its senselessness, its rottenness, — now the death sentence on capitalism has been confirmed" (*GSS* 24:188).

to feel boundless admiration and fascination, despite their disagreements, but with certain Tolstoyans. As a young man Gorky had been snubbed and patronized by a sanctimonious Tolstoyan named Klobsky, and the image of this hypocrite haunted him for years, surfacing again as late as *My Universities* (Мои университеты, 1923).[18] Gorky's disdain for Tolstoyans extended to the disciple-in-chief, Vladimir Chertkov. In response to Chertkov's book, *Уход Толстого* (Tolstoy's Departure, 1922), which celebrated as a spiritual victory the eighty-two-year old author's nocturnal flight from his wife, home, and ancestral estate, Gorky wrote a vigorous defense of Countess Tolstaya, who for years had been Chertkov's rival in the struggle for Tolstoy's soul ("О С. А. Толстой" (On S. A. Tolstaya)).[19]

Officially, Gorky's own utopia was the standard socialist one espoused by so many intellectuals in Russia and indeed all over the world. After all, Gorky was the author of *Мать* (The Mother, 1906), the very model, the progenitor of what was much later dubbed "socialist realism," a socialist classic if there ever was one. But in fact socialisms came in many shapes and sizes, and Gorky's variant was very much his own. First of all, Gorky never shared the narrow factionalism and sectarian antagonisms that so beset the socialist camp. He was essentially a reconciler, an includer, not a purist. He tended to look benignly and fraternally on the whole spectrum of radicals and reformers who were trying to pull the country out of its slough, and his reverence for culture and its all too sparse bearers was so great that he hated to see any intellectuals at bitter odds with one another. The Russian veneer of high culture was far too thin to be squandered on squabbles.

However, Gorky had been radicalized by his experience on Bloody Sunday and subsequent brief imprisonment.[20] Though soon released, he now wanted to fight tsarism as furiously as possible. He participated actively in the December 1905 armed uprising in Moscow, his apartment

---

[18] It is a curious fact that this same Klobsky or Klopsky (Ivan Mikhailovich, 1852–98) emigrated to the United States, but within two years was killed, like Berlioz in Bulgakov's *Master and Margarita*, by being run over by a streetcar. See *PSS* 50:261.

[19] Gorky felt particularly qualified to defend the Countess because he actually had never liked her and felt that she did not like him. But he recognized that Tolstoy was "the most complicated person among the biggest [крупнейших] people of the nineteenth century," and that to be the only intimate friend of such a person, his wife, mother of his numerous children, and mistress of his household, had been no easy task. She had performed it well until the last years, when fatigue, old age, and jealousy had sometimes pushed her over the edge. In any case, she deserved far more credit and sympathy than she had received.

[20] See, e.g., Yedlin 49–52. The fiery declaration, "To All Russian Citizens and to the Public Opinion of European States," which after his arrest Gorky acknowledged writing, is in *GSS* 23:333–36. It concludes by accusing Nicholas II of the "murder of innocent people" and calls for "an immediate, determined, and collaborative struggle with the autocracy" (p. 336).

being used as an arms depot and bomb factory. After the collapse of the revolution he was forced to emigrate to prevent renewed arrest, and he was to remain abroad for eight years, until the amnesty of 1913.

Though by his own admission he was never a very good Marxist,[21] Gorky found the Bolshevik wing of the Russian Social Democratic Labor Party most congenial to his mood and hopes, and he supported the party generously, both by substantial financial contributions and by organizing, at his home on Capri, a school for educating and training worker revolutionaries. It was during this period that Gorky formed with Lenin a relationship that by some definitions could be called a friendship.[22] However, Gorky's Bolshevism was from the beginning tainted by heresy, some overt, some more hidden. Overtly, Gorky for several years associated himself with the "God-building" enterprise within the party, led by Lunacharsky and Bogdanov and anathematized by Lenin. For Gorky, at least, God-building was little more than an effort to generate for the secular cause of socialism the same kind of passion and dedication that supernatural religions have aroused (see Sesterhenn). He connected it with his own celebration of Man, with a capital M, i.e., our human species, which with no help from nature has accomplished such amazing feats in its journey from the jungle to the heights of European civilization.[23] The word "European" is of some significance here. At least consciously, Gorky vehemently insisted on "Europe" as the model of civilization and progress for Russia; "Asia" represented its bad, backward, stagnant, slothful side. In any case, the human species itself deserved to be an object of worship, but within it

---

[21] Lenin quotes Gorky as saying to him on Capri, "with an inimitable and disarming smile, 'I know that I am a poor Marxist'" (Cited from Yedlin, 115).

[22] The complex, up-and-down relationship between Gorky and Lenin has been the subject of several studies which refute the official Soviet myth of an unbroken friendship marred only by occasional ошибки (mistakes) committed by Gorky, such as "God-building" or disapproval of the coup d'état of October 1917, mistakes which had to be corrected by the all-wise Lenin, who never made mistakes. See, e.g., Wolfe. Gorky's own memoir on Lenin, originally published in Русский современник (Russian Contemporary, 1924), was later revised more than once under pressure from Soviet censors. The final version, stripped of the original's "mistakes," such as references to Kamenev and Trotsky and citation of Lenin's expression of nostalgic affection for the late Menshevik leader L. O. Martov, appeared in 1931. Perhaps the phrase that best sums up Gorky's feelings about Lenin is found in his letter to Romain Rolland of 3 March 1924: "I loved him with anger" (cited from Yedlin, 163).

[23] Gorky argues the Europe vs. Asia case most forcefully in "Две души" [Two Souls, 1915], a work considered heretical in Soviet times and not reprinted until 1997 (Burlaka, 95–106). The "two souls" of Russia are European and Asiatic. Gorky is of course passionately on the side of Europe—rational creative, progressive. Later Kornei Chukovsky played effectively with Gorky's antithetical title, arguing that Gorky's own atavistic heart, from whence he drew his most vivid representations, lay firmly on the side of "Asia"; his "European" allegiance was cerebral and sterile. See Chukovskii 1924.

most venerable of all were those individuals who embodied its best qualities, its creative potential. And one of these Men, despite all their disagreements, was Lev Tolstoy.

Gorky's less overt heresy against Bolshevism became fully apparent only after 1917: it was his fear and even abhorrence of the Russian peasantry. Here Gorky was not only off the official Leninist line, which regarded the peasants as worthy junior partners of the workers, but even further from the peasantophile Tolstoy. Gorky just did not like peasants. Ever since his experience, related so vividly in *My Universities*, when peasants in a village where he was living with a Ukrainian populist named Romas deliberately set fire to Romas's house and store, putting Gorky's life at risk, Gorky's view of peasants remained jaundiced.

Peasants were backward, ignorant, superstitious, anarchic, and potentially violent.[24] His aversion to the peasants was one reason why Gorky allied himself with the Social Democrats rather than the Socialist Revolutionaries: the Marxist SD's saw the industrial workers as the main revolutionary force, one which would pull the laggard peasants after them. The chief reason Gorky, in his *Несвоевременные мысли* (Untimely Thoughts), written serially in 1917–18, took issue with the Bolshevik coup d'état was his conviction that the industrial working class and their Bolshevik leaders were too weak to hold onto power for long. They would be engulfed in the anarchic mass of the peasantry, and the country would descend into barbarism.[25] Much later, one of Gorky's most questionable accommodations to Stalinism was again partly motivated by his antagonism to the peasantry. The collectivization and de-kulakization campaign of 1929–32, brutal and murderous as it actually was, nevertheless evoked Gorky's enthusiastic approbation. It seemed to him a heroic effort to drag the benighted peasants forward into the modern world, a happily speeded-up process he had thought would require generations.[26]

---

[24] "О русском крестьянстве" (On the Russian Peasantry). This heretical essay also could never be reprinted in Soviet times.

[25] Inveighing against the Bolsheviks' destruction of civil liberties, Gorky in January 1918 prophesied that "we shall have a lengthy and extremely cruel struggle of all democratic forces and the best part of the working class against that animal [or "zoological"] anarchy which the leaders from Smolny [the Bolsheviks] are actively fostering" (*Untimely Thoughts, 132–32*).

[26] Gorky accepted and supported with enthusiasm the whole collectivization project, including the bloody "liquidation" of the so-called "kulaks." From time immemorial, he wrote, the only ambition of a poor peasant has been to become a rich peasant, a kulak, until now, when the poor peasant has grasped the "great, simple truth of Lenin": abolish private property in land and collectivize yourselves. See "Письмо селькору-колхознику" [A Letter to a Village Journalist] (*GSS* 25:269).

Gorky was not really very strongly anti-capitalist. He admired the vigor and creativity of the capitalist entrepreneurs, the primary accumulators, the organizers and builders of factories and industrial empires, and he portrayed them not unsympathetically in a number of novels and plays.[27] It was their children who tended to degenerate into feckless futility. Even stronger was his dedication to culture, whatever its source. People able to contribute to culture, as creators or students or performers, in science, art, music, or literature—such people were for Gorky heroes, to be cherished and nurtured. He never liked the Bolsheviks' harsh and punitive politicization of culture, and during the Civil War he used all his prestige and direct access to Lenin to save countless intellectuals and Kulturträger from arrest or starvation.[28]

To sum up: Gorky's utopia was an egalitarian society in which people, working cooperatively, would pursue in both agriculture and industry the basic task of exploiting the resources offered by nature to meet the fundamental human needs for food, clothing, shelter, transportation and communication. Enough time and energy should be left so that all could pursue intellectual and cultural interests. The technicalities of economics—investment, resource allocation, central planning vs. local initiative—such questions interested Gorky very little. But of one principle he was sure: the ideal society should invest heavily in education and culture. Everyone should be enabled to absorb and enjoy as much of mankind's accumulated cultural heritage as possible. How this society was to be governed also did not seem to concern Gorky very much. It is striking that neither he nor Tolstoy showed the slightest satisfaction in the establishment of constitutional government in Russia after 1905 or showed any interest in the subsequent activities of the Duma and its struggles with the tsar. For both of them all that was irrelevant, не то, not what was really needed. Utopia required much more profound changes.

*

Tolstoy of course never specifically criticized Gorky's utopia as such; he hardly knew what it was. But Tolstoy in his late years was much concerned with the general topic of socialism. In fact, the very last article that Tolstoy

---

[27] E.g., Ignat Gordeev in *Фома Гордеев* [Foma Gordeev, 1899], Antipa Zykov in *Зыковы* [The Zykovs, 1912–13], or Ilya Artamonov in *Дело Артамоновых* [The Artamonov Business, 1924–25].

[28] Gorky's indefatigable efforts both to rescue intellectuals from the clutches of the Cheka (secret police) and to feed and house them afterward are amply attested in the memoirs of those close to him at that time. See., e.g., Khodasevich. Khodasevich himself benefited by Gorky's intervention to escape being drafted into the Red Army. The whole period is vividly described in Scherr.

produced, whose manuscript he asked for after his celebrated departure from Yasnaya Polyana, was entitled "О социализме" (On Socialism).[29] In this final statement, nominally addressed to Czech youth, Tolstoy with regard to economics reverts to the same epistemological nihilism he had applied to history in *War and Peace*. No one can predict the economic future of mankind, because to do so one would have to know and predict the economic behavior of every human individual. All those who claim to have discovered the "laws" of such behavior, among them such socialists as Marx, Engels, and Bernstein, along with their predecessors Saint-Simon, Fourier, and Owen, are simply deluded. Unlike the heavenly bodies or biological organisms like plants, laws for whose behavior human beings have really discovered, human economic behavior is inherently unpredictable, because we are creatures endowed with reason and free will. Moreover, the fact that the socialists cannot agree concerning these "laws" and are themselves divided into so many quarreling factions is sufficient evidence that the "laws" they claim to have discovered are not laws at all. The only valid law governing human life is the moral law articulated by the great religious thinkers of the past and implanted in every human heart: do not unto others what you would not have them do unto you. If people would observe *that* law, all economic, political, and social problems would be solved.

The socialist utopia is a mirage, and the effort to attain it, involving prescriptions about how other people should live, requires violation of the fundamental moral law against coercion. If socialists were to gain power, they would require and use the same instruments of coercion which the capitalists now use against them: prisons, executions, police, armies. The participants in this coercive force will have to be deceived and brainwashed, just as the participants in present-day armies and police forces are deceived. The only remedy is for each individual to refuse to take part in any form of coercion, or to pay taxes to support those who do. Governments and capitalists are far more afraid of this awakening moral consciousness than they are of all the schemes of the socialists. One person who refuses to participate in state-sponsored violence, Tolstoy asserts, is incomparably more powerful than the millions of people who will engage in torturing, imprisoning, and executing him.

Such was Tolstoy's parting shot against the socialists. But in the debate with Gorky we have tried to reconstruct here, Gorky had a supreme

---

[29] "О социализме," written in reply to an invitation from the Prague newspaper *Mladé Proudy* to participate in a symposium on socialism. The article was not found until after Tolstoy's death and not published until the Jubilee Edition in 1936 (*PSS* 38:426–35).

advantage: he lived for twenty-six years after Tolstoy lay silent in his grave. During that time, among many other works, Gorky produced his remarkable memoir of Tolstoy, based on notes he had taken during their brief acquaintance back in 1901–1902 in the Crimea, to which he added an unfinished letter to Korolenko written after he received the news of Tolstoy's departure from Yasnaya Polyana and then death. That memoir is a generally acknowledged literary masterpiece. But in terms of the debate sketched here, Gorky carried out in the memoir a most insidious maneuver: he turned Tolstoy against Tolstoy. He pitted *his* Tolstoy, a magnificent, primeval creative giant, against the self-muzzled, doctrinaire Tolstoy of the treatises.

Gorky's Tolstoy is not a Tolstoyan at all. He has a difficult, contentious relationship with God (the famous "two bears in one den") and has to feign admiration for an evasive, often deluded and unmasculine Jesus. This Tolstoy is sublimely distant from such unworkable principles as nonresistance to evil by violence. The Tolstoy of Gorky's memoir is a much bigger, more contradictory, elusive, creative, and powerful figure, a sort of primordial pagan deity and at the same time an exemplar of Man at his very best. He is, perhaps, not a utopian at all . . .

For Gorky himself, those twenty-six years of survival were a moral catastrophe. In him eventually the craving for utopia proved stronger than the quest for truth and even the capacity for empathy with human suffering. As Pushkin once said, in a very different, fictional context: "Тьмы низких истин мне дороже / Нас возвышающий обман" ("Герои," 1830) [Dearer to me than a multitude of base truths is the illusion that elevates us, "Heroes"]. For Gorky the illusion that "elevated" him was the desperately clung-to belief that Stalin's Russia of the 1930s, with all its abominable cruelties, its atmosphere of rampant paranoia, its midnight arrests, rigged trials, wholesale executions, and immense concentration camps, including the one on Solovki, which Gorky visited and praised, was the embodiment of the socialist dream of his youth. So perhaps Tolstoy won the argument after all.

III

TOLSTOY
beyond TOLSTOY

Hemingway and Tolstoy
A Pugilistic Encounter

"Am a man without any ambition," Ernest Hemingway wrote to his publisher in 1949, "except to be champion of the world. [. . .] Know this sounds like bragging but Jeezo Chrise you have to have confidence to be a champion and that is the only thing I ever wished to be."[1] "Writing whether you want it or not is competitive," Hemingway had written twenty years earlier, no doubt sensing that some of his own creative energy, his striving toward excellence, was derived from his strong sense of rivalry. "Most of the time you compete against time and dead men."[2] One of the "dead men" Hemingway felt impelled to challenge on his road to the world championship was Lev Tolstoy, on whom he persistently bestowed the title "Dr." or "Mr.," occasionally "the great Count." A trained and powerful boxer himself, Hemingway liked to imagine these encounters in the form of boxing matches:

---

[1] Hemingway to Charles Scribner, 6/7 September 1949. Baker 1981, 673.
[2] Hemingway to Maxwell Perkins, 20 August 1928. Bruccoli, 76. As early as 1935 Hemingway had articulated this same idea of competition with "dead men" as an important motivating force for a writer with serious ambitions. "There is no use writing anything that has been written before unless you can beat it. What a writer in our time has to do is write what hasn't been written before or beat dead men at what they have done. The only way he can tell how he is going is to compete with dead men. Most live writers do not exist." "Monologue to the Maestro: A High Seas Letter," in White, 218. Originally in *Esquire*, October, 1935.

> I wouldn't fight Dr. Tolstoi in a 20-round bout because I know he would knock my ears off. The Dr. had terrific wind and could go on forever and then some. But I would take him on for six and he would never hit me and [I] would knock the shit out of him and maybe knock him out. He is easy to hit. But boy can he hit. If I live to 60 I can beat him (MAYBE).³

That belated, but capitalized MAYBE is no doubt a sign of Hemingway's deep admiration for the Russian master and a crack in the façade of superconfident superiority he affected toward great writers of the past. Except for Shakespeare, one of the "guys nobody could ever beat," Hemingway in 1949 claimed that he would have no difficulty in out-boxing Turgenev, Maupassant, Henry James, and even Cervantes. But Tolstoy still inspires fear of defeat. "I can write good and I would not get into the ring with Mr. Tolstoi over the long distance unless I and my family were not eating."⁴

This same boxing imagery is repeated almost verbatim in Hemingway's famous interview with Lillian Ross, with the same awe of Tolstoy following imagined victories over other distinguished forebears:

> I started out very quiet and I beat Mr. Turgenev. Then I trained hard and I beat Mr. de Maupassant. I've fought two draws with Mr. Stendhal, and I think I had an edge in the last one. But nobody's going to get me in any ring with Mr. Tolstoi unless I'm crazy or I keep getting better.⁵

Curiously, twenty-four years earlier, during his first excited ventures into Russian literature, Hemingway had rated Turgenev above Tolstoy:

> Turgenieff to me is the greatest writer there ever was. Didn't write the greatest books, but was the greatest writer. [. . .] *War and Peace* is the best book I know, but imagine what a book it would have been if Turgenieff had written it.⁶

Fascinating as it might be to speculate on what Hemingway's image was of a *War and Peace* by Turgenev (or perhaps alternatively a *Rudin* by Tolstoy!), Hemingway's letter unfortunately provides no grounds for doing

---

³ Baker 1981, 673.
⁴ *Ibid.*
⁵ Lillian Ross, cited from Lynn, 549.
⁶ Hemingway to Archibald MacLeish, 20 December 1925. Baker, 179. The subject of Hemingway's indebtedness to Turgenev has been ably explored by Wilkinson. Wilkinson also makes some very cogent observations about Hemingway's attitude toward Tolstoy (especially pp. 81–84).

so, nor does he ever invoke this possibility again. In any case, Tolstoy seems to have remained more formidable on Hemingway's list of potential dead antagonists than any other writer except Shakespeare.

May I observe here parenthetically that Tolstoy too was by no means immune to the same spirit of competition with dead predecessors. Though he disguised the contest more adroitly, perhaps even from himself, and certainly would never have visualized the rivalry in the crude form of a boxing match, one cannot help wondering why the old Tolstoy, laden with honors and world-wide recognition, nevertheless felt it necessary to launch a vehement attack on Shakespeare, or why he made so many disparaging remarks about such other sacrosanct idols of literature as the ancient Greek dramatists, Dante, Tasso, and Milton, all of whose reputations he considered entirely undeserved.[7]

To return to Hemingway, the image of the great Russian novelist, and especially of his overwhelming *War and Peace*, had been an imposing presence in the American writer's mind ever since his first ventures into Russian literature in the mid-1920s, even, for a time, to the point of feeling crowded by Tolstoy out of treating the subject of war at all. "After I read *War and Peace*," he wrote to Maxwell Perkins on 24 April 1926, "I decided there wasn't any need to write a war book and I'm still sticking to that."[8] Fortunately, this resolution proved exceedingly brief: by March 1928 Hemingway had already climbed back into the ring with the author of *War and Peace* and was hard at work on *Farewell to Arms*.

Our knowledge of Hemingway's later readings of Tolstoy, as of Russian literature generally, is regrettably fragmentary. Michael S. Reynolds has meticulously assembled the evidence of his readings up to 1940, using such data as borrowings and purchases from Sylvia Beach's bookstore and lending library in Paris, Hemingway's inventory of books shipped or discarded when he moved from Key West to Cuba in 1940, as well as references in his writings. Besides *War and Peace*, for which Hemingway's high regard never waned, he owned two copies of *Anna Karenina*[9],

---

[7] Tolstoi 1965, 15:154, from Что такое искусство?.

[8] Bruccoli, 37.

[9] There are no extended comments about *Anna Karenina* in Hemingway's published correspondence or other writings, but in 1935 he did list it among those books he would rather read again for the first time than have an assured income of a million dollars. Among the others were *War and Peace*, *A Hunter's Notes*, and *The Brothers Karamazov*. "Remembering Shooting-Flying: A Key West Letter," White, 186–87. Originally in *Esquire*, February 1935. In "Monologue to the Maestro: A High Seas Letter" *Anna Karenina* was also included among the books any aspiring writer should have read, along with *War and Peace*, *The Brothers Karamazov* "any two other Dostoevskis," and "all of Turgenev," plus, of course, many other non-Russian books. White, 218.

a volume containing *The Cossacks* and the *Sevastopol Sketches*, and *The Journal of Leo Tolstoi*, the last a selection from Tolstoy's diaries. It was published in 1917, but doubtless acquired much later.[10]

Hemingway may, of course, have read a great deal more of Tolstoy than is contained in these volumes or is mentioned in his correspondence or other writings. But it is striking that the Tolstoy he does mention is the Tolstoy most like Hemingway, Tolstoy the writer on hunting and war, the masterful conveyer of direct, palpable experience of life. Though he undoubtedly knew about other Tolstoys, Hemingway seems to have had little interest in them: Tolstoy the explorer and moralizer on human sexual relations, Tolstoy the commentator on social issues, Tolstoy the seeker after religious truth. In fact, not only was Hemingway not interested in these other Tolstoys, he actively disapproved of them, as we shall see, at least when they intruded into the novels. Of course, it could be argued that Hemingway's disparagement of these other Tolstoys was a defensive maneuver, an effort to compensate for his own neglect of such issues and the resulting sense of inferiority.

On one of his hunting expeditions to Africa in the 1930s Hemingway took along a volume containing *The Cossacks* and the *Sevastopol Sketches*.[11] He had interesting things to say about both these texts. *The Cossacks* impressed him by the sense of immediacy it conveys, with its evocation of Hemingway's own favorite themes of hunting, nature, and warfare among simple, unsophisticated people, so vividly realized that he felt he was there among them:

---

[10] Reynolds, 192. Maiants notes that beginning in the early 1920s Hemingway voraciously read the classics of Russian literature, "Gogol, Dostoevsky, Tolstoy, Turgenev, and Chekhov" (p. 285). Though Maiants credits Hemingway with many affinities with Tolstoy, she maintains that he had more "inner community" (внутренняя общность) with Chekhov (p. 286). Actually, however, Hemingway was quite disparaging in some early comments on Chekhov: "Chekov [sic] wrote about 6 good stories. But he was an amateur writer" (Hemingway to MacLeish, 20 December 1925, Baker, 179). By the end of his life, however, Hemingway had come to rate Chekhov somewhat higher. In *A Moveable Feast*, calling Chekhov "a good and simple writer," he compares Katherine Mansfield unfavorably to him, as near-beer to water. "It was better to drink water. But Chekov was not water except for the clarity. There were some stories that seemed to be only journalism. But there were wonderful ones too." Hemingway 1992, 133. But whether there was "inner community" is open to question. Chekhov, for instance, had a strong sense of social engagement and responsibility largely lacking in Hemingway, and he did not share Hemingway's obsession with muscular maleness.

[11] The volume had probably been supplied to him gratis by his publishers from their own list: Tolstoy 1913. This was by no means the best translation then available, but the writing impressed Hemingway nonetheless.

> In it [*The Cossacks*] were the summer heat, the mosquitoes, the feel of the forest in the different seasons, and that river that the Tartars crossed, raiding, and I was living in that Russia again.[12]

The *Sevastopol Sketches* interested Hemingway as evidence of Tolstoy's own direct experience of war and prompted speculation on the relation between a writer's experience and his imagination. War seemed to be an experience you could not invent, and Tolstoy had known it at first hand:

> Tolstoi's *Sevastopol* [. . .] was a very young book and had one fine description of fighting in it, where the French take the redoubt and I thought about Tolstoi and about what a great advantage an experience of war was to a writer. It was one of the major subjects and certainly one of the hardest to write truly of and those writers who had not seen it were always very jealous and tried to make it seem unimportant, or abnormal, or a disease as a subject, while, really, it was just something quite irreplaceable that they had missed.[13]

The topic of the relation between experience and imagination, "truth" and "invention," was one that troubled Hemingway, as indeed it did Tolstoy. Both writers set great store by the "truthfulness" of their writing, but they could not help asking, how could fiction be truth? In any case, Hemingway concluded that one cannot write "truthfully" about war without having directly experienced all its chaos and horror, and like Hemingway, Tolstoy had known war at first hand. But there was a further paradox: Tolstoy's best war scenes were about battles that had taken place before he was born:

> Dr. Tolstoi was at Sevastopol. But not at Borodino. He wasn't in business in those days. But he could invent from knowledge. We were all at some damned Sevastopol.[14]

"True" fiction thus draws on experience, but the imagination must recreate, revise, reshape that experience to give it the vividness and immediacy that both writers especially prized. Yet that core of experience was vital:

> Tolstoi made the writing of Stephen Crane on the Civil War seem like the brilliant imagining of a sick boy who had never seen war but had only read the battles and chronicles and seen the Brady photographs that I had read and seen at my grandparents' home. Until I read the

---

[12] Hemingway 1935, 108.
[13] *Ibid.*, 70.
[14] Hemingway to Charles Poore, 23 January 1953. Baker 1981, 800.

> *Chartreuse de Parme* by Stendhal I had never read of war as it was except in Tolstoi and the wonderful Waterloo account by Stendhal was an accidental piece in a book that had much dullness.[15]

In the early part of World War II, as America's leading writer with extensive experience both in fighting and in writing about war, Hemingway was asked to edit a huge, thousand-page volume of literary selections entitled *Men at War*. From Tolstoy he included three excerpts, all from *War and Peace*: "Bagration's Rearguard Action," "Borodino," and "The People's War," the last referring to the section describing partisan warfare behind the French lines, including the account of the death of Petya Rostov.[16] All these selections had in fact been suggested to Hemingway by Maxwell Perkins. Perkins first wrote Hemingway on 12 March 1942 about a conversation he had had with the prospective publisher of the anthology:

> I told him about that magnificent episode from *War and Peace* where the boy Petya joins Denisov's band of partisans and then goes into the French camp with Dolokov [sic], and then, the next morning in the attack gets himself killed.[17]

Then in a letter of 8 June 1942 Perkins recommended the same three *War and Peace* excerpts later chosen by Hemingway:

> The rear guard action in the early part of *War and Peace*, where Andrei joins Bagration and acts as an aide, is one of the finest "battle pieces" in the world, partly because it gives you a complete little battle that anyone can comprehend, and then partly because of the way the battery commander fought his guns, and then the way it all turned out to be so different from what Andrei thought it was going to be, his first battle. Then there is the episode of the Russian partisan band's pursuit

---

[15] Hemingway 1992, 133–34. Of course, Hemingway could not guess how much Tolstoy himself had learned from Stendhal. Earlier, Hemingway had given high praise to *The Red Badge of Courage* despite Crane's lack of direct experience of war, including it entire in the anthology *Men at War*. ". . .[H]e wrote that great boy's dream of war that was to be truer to how war is than any war the boy who wrote it would ever live to see." Hemingway 1942, xvii.

[16] Abrosimova has discerningly analyzed the changes Hemingway made in Tolstoy's texts when preparing them for the anthology, mostly to give each of them a "short story" completeness, eliminating what in that context seemed extraneous matter. She also offers interesting speculations about what Hemingway may have learned from Tolstoy, especially as manifested in his early collection, *In Our Time* (1924). My thanks to Valery Aleksandrov of the Institute of World Literature in Moscow for calling my attention to Abrosimova's article.

[17] Bruccoli, 317.

of the French in the rain, and their attack the next day. The boy Petya beings a message to the band from a German general and then when he finds there is going to be an attack on the French, he persuades the leader to let him stay and be in it, and then of course gets himself killed through recklessness. These two Tolstoi pieces have almost perfect unity, and Borodino, grand as it is, hasn't the same completeness and is rather confusing, I should think—taken all by itself. I did also suggest a short story called "The Thistle" by Tolstoi [i.e., *Hadji Murat*], but I don't really think it should be in because it is perhaps about war on too small a scale.[18]

In his "Introduction" Hemingway had high praise for all these selections, in fact drawing heavily on Perkins in formulating his own comments:

> The account of Bagration's rearguard action [. . .] is the finest and best understood relation of such an action that I have ever read and it gives an understanding, by presenting things on a small enough scale to be completely understood, of what a battle is that no one has ever bettered. I prefer it to the account of Borodino, magnificent though that is. Then, too, from Tolstoi is the wonderful account of young Petya's first action and his death. [. . .] It has all the happiness, and freshness and nobility of a boy's first encounter with the business of war.[19]

Just to keep the score even, as it were, Hemingway likewise included three selections from his own works: "The Fight on the Hilltop," i.e., the account, in *For Whom the Bell Tolls*, of "El Sordo's" last-ditch battle against overwhelmingly superior Fascist forces, including air power; "The Retreat from Caporetto," from *Farewell to Arms*, one of Hemingway's most vivid pieces of writing, conveying the utter confusion, desperation, fear and rage that prevailed as the Italian army was pushed back on itself by superior German/Austrian forces; and "The Chauffeurs of Madrid," a brief, semi-humorous memoir of Hemingway's experiences in the Spanish civil war.[20]

One of the main points Hemingway makes in his "Introduction" resembles the discovery made by Nikolai Rostov after Schön Graben, how hard it is to tell the truth about war:

---

[18] *Ibid.*, 321. I have no evidence that Hemingway ever read *Hadji Murat*. A pity: he would surely have liked it.

[19] Hemingway 1942, xviii. Russian translations of some of the comments on Tolstoy in Hemingway's "Introduction" and elsewhere were published in *Literaturnoe nasledstvo*, 157–61.

[20] "The Chauffeurs of Madrid" seems to have been published in *Men at War* for the first time. No previous edition is cited; a note (p. 993) says "By permission of the Author."

> Rostov was a truthful young man and would on no account have told a deliberate lie. He began his story meaning to tell everything just as it had happened, but imperceptibly, involuntarily and inescapably he lapsed into falsehood. [. . .] He could not tell them simply that everyone had started off at a trot, that he had fallen off his horse, sprained his arm and then run as hard as he could from a Frenchman into the woods. [. . .Tolstoy then concludes with one of his famous "absolute" obiter dicta]: To tell the truth is very difficult, and young people are rarely capable of it.[21]

What is true of the oral accounts of participants in the immediate aftermath of a battle is even more true, according to Hemingway, of professional writers treating war from a historical perspective. The First World War, for example, was in Hemingway's words "the most colossal, murderous, mismanaged butchery that has ever taken place on earth. Any writer who said otherwise lied."[22] Yet "a writer's job," Hemingway insisted, "is to tell the truth,"[23] and few writers have lived up to that standard when dealing with war. One who did, at least some of the time, was Tolstoy:

> There is no better writing on war than there is in Tolstoy, but it is so huge and overwhelming that any amount of fights and battles can be chopped out of it and maintain all their truth and vigor and you feel no crime in the cutting.[24]

But even Tolstoy has his flaws; even Tolstoy sometimes deviates from the criterion of absolute truth. First of all, according to Hemingway, Tolstoy goes much too far with his idea that generals do not really lead: "Tolstoy carries the contempt of the man of common sense who has been a soldier for most generalship to such a length that it reaches true absurdity."[25] He does not do justice to Napoleon. Most generals, Hemingway agrees, are indeed incompetent, but Napoleon was an exception, "one of the few really great generals of the world."

> [I]nspired by a mystic nationalism [Tolstoy] tried to show that this general, Napoleon, did not truly intervene in the direction of his battles but was simply a puppet at the mercy of forces completely beyond

---

[21] Tolstoy 1942, 259–60. I have made some small changes in the translation. Gary Saul Morson has discerningly analyzed Tolstoy's use of "absolute" language in narrative sequences with otherwise limited points of view. Morson 9–36 and *passim*.
[22] Hemingway 1942, xiv–xv.
[23] *Ibid.*, xv.
[24] *Ibid.*, xvii.
[25] *Ibid.*

his control.[. . .]His hatred and contempt for Napoleon makes the only weakness in that great book of men at war.[26]

Hemingway credits Tolstoy, when writing of the Russians, with showing "in the greatest and truest detail how the operations were directed,"[27] seemingly forgetting that the generals on the Russian side (to be sure, several of them, e.g., Barclay de Tolly, Pfuel, and Bennigsen were not truly "Russian") also cannot "direct operations" in battles, because, according to Tolstoy, no one can do that. In Tolstoy's view the true greatness of Kutuzov lay in his acceptance of the fact that generals—at least most of the time—do not and cannot really lead; hence it is perfectly appropriate for him to go to sleep during the council of war before Austerlitz, when his fellow generals display their long-windedness and vanity. Kutuzov understands that the only sure function of a general is to serve as a human symbol of the unified will of the army and the nation against the invader. (However, it could be argued that Tolstoy's position is not so absolute as Hemingway and others have made it. During the council of war at Fili, after Borodino, Kutuzov is very much awake, and after listening to other generals insisting that to abandon Moscow without fighting another battle would be unthinkable, Kutuzov issues what sounds very much like a real decision, invoking his power as commander-in-chief: to preserve the Russian army as a fighting force they will retreat through Moscow without fighting again.)

In any case, Hemingway has far more confidence than Tolstoy in what generals do, or should do. In *Across the River and Into the Trees* Hemingway tried to create a polemical counter-image, an (ex-)general, now demoted to colonel, who had truly and ably led his troops during World War II. But Cantwell's post-war demotion symbolized the hatred of the "political generals," who always remain safely in the rear, for a real fighting leader whose many wounds testify to his closeness to his men and to the front.

Actually, even the underestimation of Napoleon turns out not to be the "only weakness" in Hemingway's estimation of *War and Peace*. Perhaps even more irritating to him was Tolstoy's tendency to load the

---

[26] *Ibid.*, xvii–xviii. The Russian Hemingway scholar and correspondent I. A. Kashkin defends Tolstoy against this criticism, arguing that Tolstoy's portrait of Napoleon, even in the final text of *War and Peace*, was more complex than the memorable caricature at Borodino of a fat, self-important little man suffering from a cold. After all, both Pierre and Andrei were enamored of Napoleon early in the novel. Kashkin believed that Hemingway may have been influenced by the aureole surrounding Napoleon in France, where he lived for so long. He also may have been affected, Kashkin asserts, by myths prevalent in the West about the inscrutable Slavic soul possessed by "mystic nationalism." *Literaturnoe nasledstvo*, 160–61.

[27] Hemingway 1942, xviii.

book with "big ideas" of his own manufacture. For Hemingway this was stepping outside the proper territory of the novelist. The only valid function of fiction, he believed, was to create the illusion of life, to tell it "the way it was."[28] The reader should feel as he, Hemingway, had felt when reading *The Cossacks*, that he or she was really there, experiencing the summer heat and mosquitoes. Tolstoy could do that superbly, as well as any writer ever did. But at times Tolstoy could not resist injecting himself into the narrative, pontificating and arguing:

> I love *War and Peace* for the wonderful, penetrating and true descriptions of war and of people but I have never believed in the great Count's thinking. I wish there could have been someone in his confidence with authority to remove his heaviest and worst thinking and keep him simply inventing truly. He could invent more with more insight and truth than anyone who ever lived. But his ponderous and Messianic thinking was no better than many another evangelical professor of history and I learned from him to distrust my own Thinking with a capital T and to try to write as truly, as straightly, as objectively and humbly as possible.[29]

Hemingway's objection to Tolstoy's use of novels as vehicles for intellectual discourse stemmed from deep conviction about the nature and purpose of fiction. Too much intellectual talk, too much literariness interfered with its fundamental function, to render experience "the way it was." When writing *For Whom the Bell Tolls* Hemingway invoked the same comparison, again insisting on "humble" abstention from excessive intellectualizing: "I can write it like Tolstoi," he wrote to Perkins on 26 August 1940, "and make the book seem larger, wiser, and all the rest of it. But then I remember that was what I always skipped in Tolstoi."[30]

To summarize: apart from all the macho boasting and vulgarity, Hemingway does pose some interesting and valid questions in his comments both about *War and Peace* and about Tolstoy generally. These questions had of course been raised earlier in Tolstoy criticism, some of

---

[28] Cited from Baker 1972, 48.

[29] Hemingway 1942, xviii. Hemingway had voiced this same criticism as early as 1934. "Then when you have more time read another book called War and Peace by Tolstoi and see how you will have to skip the big Political Thought passages, that he undoubtedly thought were the best things in the book when he wrote it, because they are no longer either true or important, if they ever were more than topical, and see how true and lasting and important the people and the action are." "An Old Newsman Writes: A Letter from Cuba" (1934). White, 184. As noted earlier, the argument may have its defensive side. In general, one wonders what Hemingway's Thinking might have been.

[30] Bruccoli, 291.

it dating back to the writer's own time; but it is striking that Hemingway's own artistic intuition enabled him to single them out so unerringly. Several of them have implications that go beyond Hemingway's formulations. The question of whether generals really lead and whether Napoleon was so pompously useless as Tolstoy depicts him points to the much debated larger question of historicity in historical fiction: is Tolstoy's representation of the whole Napoleonic era historically valid, and if not, does it matter? Are our criteria for judging historical novels the same as those for judging history proper? If Tolstoy's Borodino "works" artistically within the novel, is it important whether this Borodino coincides with the "real" Borodino as reconstructed by military historians (assuming the historians can agree about what "really happened")?[31]

Further, was it an artistic mistake, as Hemingway believed, for Tolstoy to include within the fabric of his novels so many "big ideas" — not just the anguished ratiocinations of such characters as Pierre Bezukhov, Andrei Bolkonsky, or Konstantin Levin concerning the famous проклятые вопросы (accursed questions) — the meaning of life, the existence of God, the reality of death — (which might be justified artistically as part of their characterizations), but also the many pages of the author's own eccentric theorizing about historical causality? This question in turn leads on to an even larger one, that of artistic truth vs. simple or literal truth, as suggested by Hemingway's contradictory exploration of the issue of the balance between experience and imagination in the depiction of war.

By way of conclusion for this Hemingway-Tolstoy confrontation, it seemed interesting to attempt actually to stage the imaginary boxing match Hemingway envisioned between himself and "the great count." Hemingway thought he could win if the match were held to six rounds. I have allowed him exactly that number. Casting myself, no doubt hubristically, in the Olympian role of referee, I conclude that he failed, but I hope that I gave him a fair trial.

Round One: Birth and Death. Both Hemingway and Tolstoy might be classified as "biological" writers, since both strive to portray human life in terms of its most fundamental physical realities, the life of the body, beneath any veneer of culture or civilization. Obviously birth and death are the most basic biological events we must all experience, and their representation in literature should be a critical test for such "whole truth" writers.

---

[31] Of course, in recent years doubts have been raised about the very capacity of historians themselves to "tell the truth" about what "really happened." All sources are limited and biased in one way or another and no historian can ever be fully "objective."

The happy birth in *Anna Karenina* of Kitty's and Levin's son is surely one of the greatest celebrations in literature of joyful, "normal," biological human reproduction, despite the woman's travail and groans and the father's desperate, guilt-ridden anxiety.[32] It is pointedly contrasted with the death-threatening birth of Anna's and Vronsky's illegitimate daughter, where the mother's adultery is evidently being symbolically punished by the puerperal fever which nearly causes her death. Both these births, however, are presented from the point of view not of the parturient women, but of male observers, who must confront their own irrelevance at this moment of biological truth. A new life enters the world from a woman's body, and the woman herself is in danger of leaving it forever—a danger still not at all unlikely in the nineteenth century, as demonstrated in *War and Peace* by the demise of the poor "little princess," Lise Bolkonskaya, despite (or perhaps because of?) the ministrations of a touted Moscow doctor.

In contrast, Hemingway would seem greatly to exceed the bounds of twentieth-century probability in sentencing to death in *Farewell to Arms* both the mother, Catherine Barkley, and her and Frederic Henry's child. The resulting tragic emptiness and aloneness of the stoic hero are no doubt vividly rendered and provide satisfying artistic closure; but the hero's feelings are essentially a response to death, first in anticipation and then in fact, rather than to birth. There are no "normal" birth scenes in Hemingway.

Both Tolstoy and Hemingway were obsessed with death, though in different ways. For Tolstoy, death was first of all a moral and metaphysical conundrum: how can there be any meaning at all to life if it must end? After his beloved older brother Nikolai died in his arms in 1860, Tolstoy angrily shook his fist at God for imposing on us all such a cruel and unjust sentence.[33] Treating death in fiction early in his career, Tolstoy could still celebrate as a model the peasant's calm, "natural" acceptance of death, the not unwelcome termination of a life of toil, hardship, and finally illness. This typical response of Uncle Fyodor in "Three Deaths" contrasts with the useless, querulous whining of a dying gentlewoman, who keeps grasping at straws and blaming those around her. After Tolstoy's "conversion," approaching death is shown as a moral lever of immense power, forcing

---

[32] Vladimir Nabokov considered this scene one of Tolstoy's triumphs, an example of how successive generations of writers keep probing deeper into human experience. "It is quite impossible to imagine Homer in the ninth century B.C. or Cervantes in the seventeenth century of our era—it is quite impossible to imagine them describing in such wonderful detail childbirth." Nabokov, 164–65.

[33] I comment in more detail on this episode, and its reflection in *Anna Karenina*, in "Truth in Dying."

the shallow and self-satisfied Ivan Ilyich to confront the reality that his entire past life, at least since childhood, had been a waste, a moral desert. He is thus enabled to achieve transcendence and "rebirth" in his final moments. In the meantime, in the great novels, there had been astonishingly potent demonstrations of human mortality. The death of Andrei Bolkonsky in *War and Peace* is in my view the most powerful representation in literature of the experience of dying, rendered not only, as is much more usual, from the point of view of the bereaved observers, his sister and fiancée, but from that of the dying man himself. In *Anna Karenina* Tolstoy created equally vivid renditions, first of Nikolai Levin's death from tuberculosis, and finally the suicide of the great heroine.

Hemingway, like Tolstoy, had seen how easy it is for bullets and shells to transform a vigorous young man into mangled, lifeless flesh. He had also seen what happens to the human corpse when left for some time unburied. A long description of the changing shapes and colors caused by putrefaction of the human body is inserted as a somewhat gratuitous digression in *Death in the Afternoon*. Thus the physical aftermath of death is hideous and not at all heroic, a fact a twentieth-century writer could demonstrate more starkly and naturalistically than was possible in the more decorous and taboo-ridden nineteenth, although both Tolstoy and Dostoevsky had achieved the same effect by invoking the odor of decay that invades the nostrils of mourners approaching a corpse. In compensation, perhaps, the deaths of major male characters in Hemingway are all heroic: Harry Morgan in *To Have and Have Not*, Robert Jordan in *For Whom the Bell Tolls*, Santiago in *The Old Man and the Sea*, Thomas Hudson in *Islands in the Stream*. In all these cases the dying itself, caused by violent external forces, is not deeply internalized. The heroes struggle for life as long as they can, lose the fight, and the light goes out. Only Colonel Cantwell, in *Across the River and Into the Trees*, is ill, of heart disease, but even this sickness seems more like a delayed battle wound, of which he has many others.

Hemingway's fascination with bull fighting seems to fit this same pattern: a highly ritualized death scene, dramatizing and encapsulating the eternal conflict of man vs. beast, acted out under very rigid rules, where the beast must always die, and the man risks death, titillating the spectators by narrowing to the minimum the distance between the bull's charging horns and his own vulnerable body. Death for Hemingway is rarely an occasion for philosophizing, but there are exceptions. In perhaps the greatest of his death stories, "The Snows of Kilimanjaro," the death is notably unheroic. Indeed the story exactly echoes the formula of "The Death of Ivan Ilyich": in the face of impending death Harry is forced to recognize the emptiness and corruption of his past life. In his case the recognition, however, does not bring transcendence or redemption, but bitterness and aggression against his wife and finally a wonderfully poetic fantasy of rescue, the effect of which is rendered even grimmer by our awareness that the rescue is entirely illusory. Harry will soon be as much a lifeless corpse as that of the leopard which had mysteriously climbed the mountain and died near the summit.

Verdict: despite Hemingway's often vigorous and successful death scenes, they are scarcely equal to Tolstoy's, and on birth he misses altogether. The round is Tolstoy's, by a wide margin.

Round Two: War. Both writers get very high marks. Both render war with extraordinary vividness, with all its excitement, its boredom, its absurdity, its horror. Sufficient examples have been presented above. A draw.

Round Three: Love. Though he handles the theme with intensity and power, Hemingway never gets beyond love's first, romantic phase. Like Turgenev, he never attempts to show the mature, fulfilled, biologically fruitful love in marriage rendered so powerfully in both Tolstoy's great novels—not only sex, but the babies that sex engenders, in short, family life. There are no real families in Hemingway. Adultery as a moral issue interests Hemingway much less than it did Tolstoy. Divorce, twentieth-century style, is always a ready possibility, marriage not nearly so ironclad a bond. Human sexuality is in general more fluid and unstable. Even homosexuality is invoked, most vividly the Lesbianism of *The Garden of Eden*.[34] The round clearly goes to Tolstoy on points, though perhaps if one takes his entire oeuvre into consideration, he should receive a substantial deduction for such late works as "Father Sergius," "The Devil," and especially "The Kreutzer Sonata," which represent human sexuality itself as intrinsically evil.

Round Four: Nature. Both writers superbly convey the look and feel of nature—mountain, forest, field, and stream. Both are excellent on hunting, though of different kinds (of course, late in life Tolstoy repudiated hunting on moral grounds, something that would have been quite out of character for Hemingway, who in *Death in the Afternoon* even claimed that man assumes "Godlike attributes" in administering death to animals[35]).

---

[34] An excellent, much more searching study of the love theme in Hemingway than can be attempted here is to be found in Lewis.
[35] Hemingway 1932, 233.

Tolstoy is far superior on agriculture, sowing and mowing and harvesting, in which Hemingway has no interest, but Hemingway is ahead on everything connected with the sea, fish, and boats, themes which the landlocked Tolstoy never attempted. A draw.

Round Five: Culture. Both writers affect in varying degrees a kind of anti-cultural primitivism—back-to basics, life stripped of any elitist cultural veneer. Yet paradoxically both were deeply embedded in culture. Tolstoy knew French and German from childhood, later learned English, ancient Greek and Hebrew, and read widely in all these literatures except Hebrew. He was a competent pianist, attended concerts (and even, on occasion, operas!), was moved by music even to tears, though he disliked and disapproved of most musical developments of the nineteenth century, especially Wagner and his imitators. His experience with the visual arts was much less extensive. At least late in his life he seemed to judge paintings by the standards of the Russian *Peredvizhniki* (Itinerants), as vehicles for moral or social lessons; thus he angrily repudiated even such sacrosanct masters as Raphael and Michelangelo, the latter "with his absurd Last Judgment," presumably because they represented the Christian mythology in its traditional, church-sanctioned forms.[36] In contrast, he extolled as works of genius "realistic" treatments of the same themes by his disciple Nikolai Ge. Earlier, however, he seems to have faulted Raphael on purely artistic grounds, for his "lumpy, potato-like forms," preferring to him an obscure contemporary French artist named Grenier.[37] As for the use of the visual arts in literature, in *Anna Karenina* Tolstoy uses the painter Mikhailov as a vehicle for expressing his own

---

[36] SS 15:154. Tolstoy was in Rome in January 1861, when he presumably visited the Sistine Chapel, though there is no record of his doing so. He may also have seen engravings of Michelangelo's "Last Judgment." Eulogies of Ge are to be found in Tolstoy's correspondence, e.g., Tolstoy to P. M. Tret'iakov, 30 June 1890 and 14 July 1894, and to V. V. Stasov, 4 September 1894. Tolstoi *PSS*:65:124–25; 67:175; 67:216. See also "Tolstoy and Jesus."

[37] The authenticity of this eccentric judgment, however, is somewhat suspect. It is found in a no longer extant letter of 1862 from Tolstoy to his sometime friend Boris Chicherin, who cites it from memory in his memoirs, which are partly designed to show up Tolstoy as an arrogant cultural ignoramus. "It did not enter his head that his taste might be unsure, that he could be mistaken, and that to pronounce judgments one must first do some studying." Pirozhkova, 192. The identity of "Grenier" remains obscure. Pirozhkova, the editor of Chicherin's memoirs, helpfully identifies "Raphael" for us, but is silent about Grenier. The most likely candidate seems to be François Grenier de Saint-Martin (1793–1867), a painter and lithographer, first of antique mythological and Christian themes, later genre scenes and portraits. His genre pictures showed "the small joys and sufferings of a poor family," which may have appealed to Tolstoy. See *Allgemeines Lexicon*, 14:597–98.

deep convictions about artistic talent and its capacity for revealing levels of truth inaccessible to ordinary mortals. Mikhailov's portrait of Anna, with whom he was only superficially acquainted, showed depths of her character that even Vronsky, who loved her, had never perceived, let alone been able to represent pictorially.

Like Tolstoy, Hemingway was mostly self-educated, reading widely all his life. He learned French well enough to read Stendhal in the original and knew at least some Spanish and Italian.[38] Hemingway's immersion in Russian literature, including Tolstoy, was a sign of his voracious cultural appetite. He seems to have had little interest in music, perhaps repudiating it as associated with Oak Park and his mother. He makes Thomas Hudson, the autobiographical hero of *Islands in the Stream*, a painter rather than a writer, but the disguise is rather thin, and little is said about his actual paintings. His oldest son, who had a Parisian childhood similar to that of Hemingway's son John ("Bumby"), boasts of his acquaintance with a whole series of cultural celebrities—writers like Joyce, Ford, and Pound, and such painters as Picasso, Braque, Miro, Masson, and Pascin. But the novel never really engages with painting as an art, and Thomas Hudson never comes alive as a painter.

In short, both Tolstoy and Hemingway absorb and contribute to culture while at the same time resisting and denying it. I again give the round to Tolstoy on points, on the grounds that his cultural immersion was deeper and more serious than Hemingway's. He made the immense effort of formulating and arguing his anti-cultural biases in a massive treatise, *What Is Art?*, something Hemingway would have been quite incapable of doing.

Round Six: Man in Society. Tolstoy all his life remained deeply, if idiosyncratically, engaged with Russia and its life, its problems—moral, social, political, economic, all vividly rendered in artistic form. Serfdom, class conflict, the Emancipation, legal reforms, industrialization, urbanization, revolutionary movements, stagnation and corruption of the bureaucracy, foreign policy—it is all there, even if most "progressive" change is regarded with disdain and vilified. Tolstoy's engagement contrasts with Hemingway's striking weakness, his avoidance of his own country. Though a great American writer, Hemingway seems strangely allergic to America as a subject, as he was to living in American cities. All his major works are situated elsewhere—France, Italy, Africa, Spain, the Caribbean, Cuba—with American characters, to be sure, but rootless,

---

[38] Josephs has shown that Hemingway's Spanish was far from faultless. Josephs 205–24.

disengaged, out of touch with realities at home. In this he contrasts markedly not only with Tolstoy, but with such American contemporaries as Faulkner, Fitzgerald, and Dos Passos. The round again goes to Tolstoy, perhaps a knockdown.

Overall score: a clear victory for Tolstoy, at least by the measure of the criteria applied here, where I have attempted to assess the range and depth of each writer's treatment of the selected themes. However, the very term "range and depth" may subsume dimensions of Tolstoy as "thinker" that Hemingway specifically repudiated, as we have seen. Likewise, my "deduction" for Tolstoy's late anti-love stories no doubt reflects non-aesthetic values of my own. Other criteria of judgment could be invoked, such as style, where Hemingway perhaps has the lead, and impact on other writers. In short, the overall judgment of Tolstoy's victory must be acknowledged as conditional and subjective. Objectively we can say only that both writers seem clearly established as classics: their books are in print and widely read all over the world. That achievement makes possible the unthinkable ultimate verdict: both writers win in a knockout.

Foxes into Hedgehogs
Berlin and Tolstoy

One of the most celebrated essays by the late Sir Isaiah Berlin is "The Hedgehog and the Fox," in which Berlin explores the philosophy of history expounded by Tolstoy in *War and Peace* and beyond that analyzes the tortured, but supremely creative mind that produced the great novel and the philosophical disquisitions it contains.[1] Berlin's essay is of course especially celebrated among Slavists and historians of Russia, but the contrast Berlin evokes between "hedgehogs" and "foxes" as two fundamental intellectual modalities or prototypes has proved popular in other disciplines as well, to the extent that the image has virtually entered the language as a standard phrase, almost a cliché.

We learn from the Ignatieff biography that Berlin claimed to have read both *War and Peace* and *Anna Karenina* at the age of ten,[2] "much too early," as Berlin said toward the end of his life.[3] "He loved the former, but could not make head or tail of the latter," Ignatieff tells us.[4] *War and Peace* was thus embedded in Berlin's consciousness very early, adored for the extraordinary vitality of its characters, the vividness and concreteness

---

[1] I wish to express here my thanks to several colleagues who offered valuable suggestions for improvements to this article: Brian Horowitz, Liza Knapp, Robert P. Hughes, and Nicholas V. Riasanovsky.
[2] Michael Ignatieff, *Isaiah Berlin: A Life* (New York: Henry Holt, 1998), 22.
[3] "The Pursuit of the Ideal" (1988), in Isaiah Berlin, *The Proper Study of Mankind: An Anthology of Essays*, ed. Henry Hardy and Roger Hausheer (New York: Farrar, Straus and Giroux, 1998), 2.
[4] Ignatieff, 22.

of their human experiences, and the sweep of its historical vision. On the other hand, with its focus on the permutations of adult sexuality, good and bad, *Anna Karenina* might well baffle a ten-year-old. But even in later life *Anna Karenina* seems never to have engaged Berlin's intellect and imagination to the same extent as its great predecessor. During his famous conversation with Anna Akhmatova the poet attacked the Tolstoy of *Anna Karenina* for its conventional moralizing. "The morality of *Anna Karenina*," she said, "is the morality of Tolstoy's wife, of his Moscow aunts; he knew the truth, yet he forced himself, shamefully, to conform to philistine convention."[5] Even writing about this encounter decades later, Berlin chose not to defend Tolstoy against this charge, except to say that perhaps Akhmatova did not mean it very seriously.[6] Though he loved gossip, issues of sexual morality never engaged Berlin's interest as a philosopher of ethics, and he likewise had little to say about all those late works of Tolstoy in which that issue is so central: "The Kreutzer Sonata," "The Devil," "Father Sergius," and *Resurrection*.

War and Peace, however, is another matter. Berlin was not a literary critic, and it is unclear to me how much thought he ever gave to purely artistic questions concerning that novel, its structure and design, its methods of characterization, its style. In commenting on the philosophy of history articulated in *War and Peace*, Berlin notes that some critics, among them Ivan Turgenev, have deplored the very presence in the novel of all the philosophizing, considering it an excrescence, "deeply inartistic and thoroughly foreign to the purpose and structure of the work of art as a whole."[7] Berlin himself, however, expresses no opinion on this point. Although when working on "The Hedgehog and the Fox" he systematically read the writings on Tolstoy of the great formalist critics Boris Eikhenbaum and Viktor Shklovskii, Berlin uses them primarily in his capacity as intellectual historian, drawing on their researches into Tolstoy's sources.[8] In this

---

[5] "Meetings with Russian Writers" (1980), in Isaiah Berlin, *Personal Impressions*, ed. Henry Hardy (New York: Penguin Books, 1982), 196. The "truth," as Akhmatova evidently saw it, was a larger, more nuanced, "fox-like" view of human sexual relations than the narrow "hedgehog-like" doctrine Tolstoy forced on his novel; Akhmatova thus would seem to have anticipated the basic hedgehog/fox antithesis. I am indebted to Liza Knapp for this perception.

[6] *Ibid.*

[7] Isaiah Berlin, *Russian Thinkers* (New York: Pelican Books, 1979), 25.

[8] It might be observed that in the works on Tolstoy by Eikhenbaum and Shklovskii that Berlin consulted, namely Eikhenbaum's two volumes, *Lev Tolstoi: piatidesiatye gody* (1928) and *Lev Tolstoi: shestidesiatye gody* (1932) and Shklovskii's *Mater'ial i stil' v romane L'va Tolstogo "Voina i mir"* (1928), the once militant formalists had retreated from doctrinal orthodoxy and operated more traditionally as source analysts.

job of source-hunting, one of the aims of "The Hedgehog and the Fox" was to draw attention to a source Berlin believed his Russian colleagues had neglected (though Eikhenbaum did mention him), Joseph de Maistre, an ultra-conservative, misanthropic ideologue about whom Berlin later wrote an independent essay.[9] De Maistre is also discussed at length in "The Counter Enlightenment" (1973).[10]

Though he never undertook to analyze how its effects are achieved, War and Peace affected Berlin emotionally as well as intellectually, as it has so many others. For instance, he describes as "one of the most moving in literature" the scene where Kutuzov, allegedly "at Fili," gets the news that the French army has left Moscow and is retreating en masse.[11] Berlin is surely right. The scene indeed displays Tolstoy at his best, moving easily and omnisciently between Kutuzov's inner world of thoughts, hopes and fears and the outer one of real events, rendered as concretely and palpably as possible.

The great news reaches Kutuzov's headquarters at night. A staff officer, Colonel von Toll, enters Kutuzov's bedroom to inform him. Becoming insistently physical and concrete, Tolstoy describes how the old man sat up, putting one leg down from the bed and rolling his large belly over onto the other, bent leg. He insists on hearing the news directly from the messenger and at last believes it. Then

> suddenly his face was screwed up in wrinkles. Waving Toll aside, he turned in the opposite direction, toward the hut's blackened icon corner. "O Lord, my Creator, Thou hast heard our prayer," he said in a tremulous voice, folding his hands. "Russia is saved. I thank Thee, O Lord." And he wept.[12]

No wonder Berlin was moved. The scene makes me weep too.[13]

---

[9] Isaiah Berlin, *The Crooked Timber of Humanity* (London: John Murray, 1990).

[10] Reprinted in *The Proper Study of Mankind*.

[11] Isaiah Berlin, *Russian Thinkers* (New York: Pelican Books, 1979), 43. Incidentally, Berlin is mistaken in locating the event at Fili. Kutuzov was then at Letishovka in Kaluzhskaia guberniia. Fili was the site of the council of war after Borodino at which the decision was reached to retreat through Moscow without fighting another battle.

[12] Vol. 4, part 2, chapter 17. The usually excellent Maude translation spoils the Biblical effect by including the "And he wept" (*I on zaplakal*) in the previous sentence.

[13] Some of Tolstoy's contemporaries felt differently, disapproving especially of the humanizing physicality in the representation of Kutuzov. Petr Bartenev, for example, wrote: "Helping Count L. N. Tolstoy with the first edition of his *War and Peace*, we pointed out to him the inaccuracy (*neosnovatel'nost'*) in his representation of Kutuzov (who supposedly did nothing, read novels, and rolled his heavy old body from side to side)." Quoted in N. N. Gusev, ed., *L. N. Tolstoi: Letopisi Gosudarstvennogo literaturnogo muzeia*, 2 (Moscow, 1938), 38.

Berlin's emphasis on a linkage between Tolstoy and de Maistre was not simply a matter of pinpointing an influence that helped shape Tolstoy's ideas, though the writer's reading of de Maistre undoubtedly did serve that purpose. Though they differed in important respects—Tolstoy in no way shared de Maistre's misanthropic and ultramontane Catholic views—Berlin perceived a deep parallelism in their mentalities. Both had immense "negative capability," a powerful capacity for seeing the weaknesses, evasions, non sequiturs, and absurdities in others' ideas. Each, according to Berlin, notably lacked a corresponding capacity for creating a positive system of his own.

To demonstrate this perception in the case of Tolstoy Berlin focuses on the philosophical issues treated at such length (for many readers, tedious length) in *War and Peace*, the question of historical determinism. (Berlin's essay was originally entitled "Lev Tolstoy's Historical Scepticism"[14].) This was a question that had engaged Berlin for many years, perhaps dating back to his life of Marx (1939), if not earlier, and would engage him for a long time to come. Adapting Hegel, Marx had perceived history as a convulsive process, a series of violent displacements of one ruling class by another, but a process governed by rigorous laws, under which individual wills and purposes count for nothing in the face of the "dialectic." This doctrine ran counter to what became one of Berlin's deepest beliefs, his conviction that human history has no predetermined destiny or prescribed course, that it consists mainly of a series of improvised efforts to cope with particular problems under particular circumstances. Within this chaotic sequence of *ad hoc* solutions, Berlin found most congenial in history those societies that offered individuals a high degree of what he called "negative" liberty, i.e., relative freedom to pursue their own goals and interests without constraint from society or the state—in other words, to do what they want.

Perhaps looking back on earlier readings or current rereadings of *War and Peace*, Berlin perceived in that novel a striking contradiction. In the novelistic or "peace" sections, readers follow the private destinies of characters who pretty much "do what they want," within the limits of the constraints imposed upon them by external circumstances, such as wealth or lack of it, and by the conflicting wills of other people. There is no sense that in their private lives the characters are puppets following a predetermined script. They strive and suffer, stumble and fall, pick themselves up and press onward. By the end of the novel four of the

---

[14] *Oxford Slavonic Papers*, 2 (1951). I had the good fortune to be present when this paper was delivered orally, at Berlin's usual breakneck speed, in Phillips Brooks House at Harvard, I believe sometime in 1951. It left a powerful impression, but I cannot say that at the time I fully grasped the ideas expounded so eloquently.

major characters, Pierre and Natasha, Nikolai and Mar'ia, after countless vicissitudes and false moves, have at last prevailed in the difficult mating game and formed biologically fruitful marriages to the right partners. On the way they may have lacked wisdom, their impulses may have been in conflict, and their success certainly depended partly on luck. But within the many limitations of circumstance and chance, their personal fates were the product of their own wills, their free choices.

But when we turn to public affairs, the picture Tolstoy draws is very different. Perhaps under the influence of Marx's mentor Hegel,[15] perhaps independently, Tolstoy concludes in *War and Peace* that the course of history is determined by supernatural forces beyond human ken, which he calls Providence (*Providenie*), perhaps to be identified with what Hegel called the "world spirit" (*Weltgeist*), whose ultimate aims and purposes are unknowable. Most human beings spend their lives pursuing their own private ends without thought of their place in history, but in so doing they unwittingly advance the historical process. Moreover, according to Tolstoy, the less they think about the larger meaning of their acts, the more effective they are as historical agents. As for leaders, most of them almost by definition are incapable of "free," independent acts performed with conscious historical purpose "The king is the slave of history" is Tolstoy's aphorism[16]. Vainglorious leaders, such as Napoleon, usually *think* that their decisions govern the course of history, but they are deluded.

Such leaders issue hundreds of "decisions," most of which cannot be carried out as impossible or irrelevant. The only decisions that are remembered—and duly recorded by equally deluded historians—are those that happen to coincide with what occurred, and would have occurred, anyway. Tolstoy assures us that if Napoleon had issued an order calling off the battle of Borodino, his soldiers would have killed him: the battle had to take place. A very few leaders, such as Kutuzov, sometimes

---

[15] The question of possible influence of Hegel on Tolstoy, despite the latter's many disparaging remarks about the German philosopher, is discerningly examined in A. Skaftymov, "Obraz Kutuzova i filosofiia istorii v romane L. Tolstogo 'Voina i mir'," *Russkaia literatura*, 2 (1959), 72–94. The possibility of Hegelian influence had been suggested earlier in M. Rubinshtein, "Filosofiia istorii v romane L. N. Tolstogo 'Voina i mir'," *Russkaia mysl'* (July, 1911), 94 ff. Isaiah Berlin speaks disparagingly of the Rubinshtein article: "[I]n the end [it] seems to me to establish nothing at all" (*Russian Thinkers*, 27). Berlin does, however, acknowledge that Tolstoy was affected in his youth by the Hegelian historicism then so prevalent in Russia, "but the metaphysical content he rejected instinctively" (*ibid.*, 30).

[16] "*Tsar'—est' rab istorii*," vol. 3, part 1, chapter 1. This aphorism is juxtaposed with Proverbs 21:1, "The king's heart is in the hand of the Lord" (*Serdtse tsarevo v rutse Bozh'ei*), and it suggests that the word *tsar'* in Tolstoy's sentence should be translated in Biblical style as a generic 'king' instead of the specifically Russian 'tsar.' The Maudes have it right.

intuitively sense the larger meaning of events and are able consciously to shape their decisions in accordance with the will of Providence. This may seem a distinction without a difference, since what must happen will happen, whatever leaders do. But such wise ones as Kutuzov are at least vouchsafed some awareness of where history is going and are thus less likely to issue inapposite orders.

As has often been noted, battles in *War and Peace* serve as microcosms of history at large. Battles are chaotic and unmanageable affairs, a series of on-the-spot reactions and improvisations by individual soldiers and officers. Pompous, self-important generals like Napoleon imagine that their decisions determine the strategy and tactics of battles, but in fact their orders can seldom be executed and are generally irrelevant; circumstances are too fluid. Only wise old Kutuzov understands that the function of a general is not to manage battles, but to serve as a symbol of the unity of the army and insofar as he can, to promote its fighting spirit. (Despite his conviction that the outcome of battles is predetermined, Tolstoy does stress the importance of morale.)

Many critics, however, have overstated the degree of Kutuzov's passivity and drawn unwarranted conclusions from it.[17] Kutuzov's sleeping, for example, at the nocturnal council of war before the battle of Austerlitz has been taken as a sign of his contempt for such councils of war in general and in particular for the elaborate dispositions expounded in such tedious detail, in German, by the Austrian general Franz von Weyrother ("Die erste Kolonne marschiert; die zweite Kolonne marschiert . . . "). But in fact, Kutuzov's somnolence at that council has a more specific explanation. Kutuzov had advised against fighting a battle at Austerlitz at all and had foreseen that the battle would be lost. His advice had been rejected, however, by a power from which there was no appeal, the young autocrat himself, Alexander I, who was with the army and full of martial enthusiasm, confident of victory. Kutuzov had the ingrained habits of a lifetime soldier: when you are overruled by higher authority, you shut down your mind, assume an air of compliance, and "go to sleep." The pre-Austerlitz council of war is markedly contrasted with the one at Fili, after Borodino. There Kutuzov has no thought of sleeping. He listens patiently to all the arguments, the displays of super-patriotism (and vanity and desire to promote their own careers at Kutuzov's expense) by other generals, mostly of German origin, arguing that to abandon Moscow without another

---

[17] I myself was guilty of this oversimplification in the oral version of this paper presented at the AATSEEL convention in December, 1998. This erroneous view was in my opinion decisively refuted in the above cited article by Skaftymov, who chides some Russian scholars who had made the same mistake.

fight would be disgraceful and unthinkable. But this time the tsar is far away in St. Petersburg. Kutuzov as commander-in-chief is the supreme authority and can act in accordance with what he regards as ultimately in the best interests of the nation. Though he knows that the decision will shock the Emperor and perhaps lead to his dismissal, at this critical moment he assumes the historic responsibility:

> "Eh bien, messieurs! Je vois que c'est moi qui payerai les pots cassés," he said. And, slowly rising, he went up to the table. "Gentlemen, I have heard your opinions. Some will not agree with me. But I (he stopped) by the authority entrusted to me by my Sovereign and the Fatherland, I—order a retreat." (Vol. 3, part 3, chapter 4)

Of course, in Tolstoy's view Kutuzov, though actively assuming responsibility, was only ordering what had to happen anyway. Kutuzov even senses that the decision had, as it were, been taken without his knowing it:

> Dismissing the guards, Kutuzov sat for a long time, leaning on the table with his elbows and kept turning over in his mind the terrible question: "When, when was it decided at last to abandon Moscow? What was done that decided the question, and who is to blame for it?" [*Ibid.*]

But at least his will had coincided with the will of Providence, and even in Tolstoy's telling it sounds very much like a decision that not only had real results, but was made, pronounced, and received with the conviction that it would have this effect. As has often been observed, Tolstoy the artist was not always in full harmony with Tolstoy the philosopher.

Pitiless in his unmasking of the Napoleons of this world, Tolstoy is equally savage in his treatment of historians who claim to know the "whys" of history. He mocks the way historians write of the "causes" of the French Revolution and its aftermath:

> Louis XIV was a very proud and self-assured man; he had such-and-such mistresses and such-and-such ministers, and he ruled France badly. Louis's successors were also weak men and also ruled France badly. They too had such-and-such favorites and such-and-such mistresses. Moreover, certain people at that time wrote books [*knizhki*, in this case a contemptuous diminutive]. At the end of the eighteenth century a couple of dozen people gathered in Paris and began to say that all men are equal and free. Because of this all over France people began to knife and drown one another. These people killed the king and a great many more. At that time in France there was a man of very great genius, Napoleon. He conquered everyone everywhere; that is, he killed many people, because his genius was very great... [Etc.] (Epilogue, part 2, chapter 1)

Such "explanations" are obviously silly and trivial, yet this is essentially all historians have to offer. In theory, Tolstoy admits, it might be possible to explain historical occurrences, but only if we had the capacity to know the wills and motives of every actor in them, including every soldier. Tolstoy refuses to acknowledge any hierarchy of wills. Napoleon's will and the will of the corporal who decides to reenlist weigh equally on the scales of history. Since total knowledge of all participants' wills and motives is impossible, we should admit that it is impossible to explain history at all. This is the essence of Lev Tolstoy's historical scepticism.

In his famous essay, as in other reflections on thinkers of the past, Berlin tries to follow the method he believed Vissarion Belinsky had applied so successfully in *his* essays on various writers, namely, to identify imaginatively with one's subject, no matter how deeply one may disagree with him, and identify so closely that one can follow with full understanding each stage of his thought. Belinsky

> himself said that no one could understand a poet or thinker who did not for a time become wholly immersed in his world, letting himself be dominated by his outlook, identified with his emotions; who did not, in short, try to live through the writer's experiences, beliefs, and convictions.[18]

Berlin himself followed this prescription perhaps even better, at any rate far more dispassionately, than Belinsky ever did—so much so that some critics wondered whether the chameleon Berlin had any core of belief, any ultimate commitment of his own.

Certainly Berlin tried hard to apply the Belinsky method to Tolstoy, at least the Tolstoy of *War and Peace*, Tolstoy the thinker about history. Berlin especially admires the boldness and sweep of Tolstoy's mind, its unrelenting pursuit of truth, its ruthless power to see through fallacious reasoning and to annihilate false claims. Perhaps his fundamental insight into Tolstoy's mentality was his perception of the "immense superiority of Tolstoy's offensive over his defensive weapons," in other words, the superiority of his critical intellect over his ability to formulate synthesizing ideas, to arrive at solutions.[19] Here, of course, is where the famous antithesis comes in, between the hedgehog, who "knows one big thing," and the fox, who "knows many things."

This celebrated contrast began its life as a sort of parlor game, suggested to Berlin by Lord Oxford, then a student of classics at Oxford,

---

[18] *Russian Thinkers*, 162.
[19] *Ibid.*, 49.

who had discovered the fable in the writings of Archilochus, a Greek poet of the seventh century B.C., and passed it on to Berlin. Berlin seized it eagerly and immediately set about classifying thinkers of the past as hedgehogs or foxes.[20] The hedgehog-fox distinction proved especially rewarding in its application to Tolstoy. As an artist, Tolstoy was so clearly the classic fox:

> [H]e saw the manifold objects and situations on earth in their full multiplicity; he grasped their individual essences, and what divided them from what they were not, with a clarity to which there is no parallel.[21]

But Tolstoy was not happy with his foxiness. He longed for an overarching theory, one that would "collect, relate, synthesise, . . . a universal explanatory principle."[22] Yet the more he sought for unity, the more "merciless and ingenious" were the "executions of more and more false claimants to the truth."[23]

With regard to the problem of historical determinism in *War and Peace*, the only unifying theory Tolstoy finally arrived at, as noted above, was to identify, as the true cause of historical events, the inscrutable will of "Providence," which seems to be another word for God. God thus "caused" the battle of Borodino, which is an example, Tolstoy says, of "that terrible business [of war] that takes place not by the will of men, but by the will of Him Who governs men and worlds" (vol. 3, part 2, chapter 39).[24] On earth, however, the will of Providence is accomplished by human beings, the wills, words, and acts of *all* the participants in a particular event. Berlin plays down the Providential aspect of Tolstoy's theory, but concentrates on the "theory of minute particles," according to which in events like the Napoleonic wars the number of causes—the individual wills of all the participants—is so large that there is no hope of ever encompassing them, and we cannot therefore reasonably speak of the war's causes at all. But as an overarching theory, Berlin notes, this one has seemed to most people paltry, inadequate, and unsatisfying, a prime example of the weakness of Tolstoy's positive, synthesizing side as compared with the enormous power of his critical, destructive, and analytical faculties.

---

[20] Pursuing Archilochus a little further, I was pleased to find in him an example of the immense power of the word. He fell in love with one Neobule, daughter of Lycambes, but her father forbade the marriage. Archilochus then avenged himself with such biting satires that father and daughter both hanged themselves!

[21] *Ibid.*, 48.

[22] *Ibid.*

[23] *Ibid.*, 49.

[24] " . . . po vole Togo, Kto rukovodit liud'mi i mirami." Soviet editions, such as *SS* 6 (1962): 298, demote the *Togo* and *Kto* to the lower case. The Jubilee Edition, however, preserves Tolstoy's capitalization. *PSS* 11:261.

Much later in his life Tolstoy claimed to have found a much broader unifying principle or set of principles to govern human life, a rationalized and purified version of Christianity which bears his name, "Tolstoyism" (*tolstovstvo*). Despite his own exceptional empathetic powers, Berlin could not effectively follow him there; Tolstoyism just did not appeal. Berlin resisted not so much as a Jew, though this allegiance did play its part, but as an atheist—not a militant one, but a skeptic who acknowledged in a letter, "I have never known the meaning of the word God."[25]

Berlin did, however, understand very well the problems facing a fox who longed to be a hedgehog: it was his own dilemma. As Ignatieff puts it,

> This was also a fissure within himself. Most of his friends saw him as an arch-fox—nimble, cunning, quick-witted, darting from subject to subject, eluding pursuit. Yet he was also the type of fox who longs to be a hedgehog—to know one thing, to feel one thing more truly than anything else. It would take him more than a decade to discover what that was.[26]

The overarching theory that Berlin-as-hedgehog eventually discovered was essentially a canonization of foxiness. He gave it the name of "pluralism." Pluralism is

> the conception that there are many different ends that men[27] may seek and still be fully rational, fully men, capable of understanding each other and sympathising and deriving light from each other ... Ends, moral principles are many. But not infinitely many: they must be within the human horizon.[28]

Both liberty and equality are values, but they are at least partly incompatible. As Berlin puts it, "total liberty for the wolves is death to the lambs."[29] There is not and never will be a perfect world where all contradictions will be solved. All efforts to coerce mankind into a final solution are morally wrong because they cause present suffering in the name of abstract and probably unattainable happiness in the future. The answer, therefore, is compromise,

> a precarious equilibrium that will prevent the occurrence of desperate situations, of intolerable choices—that is the first requirement of

---

[25] Ignatieff, 41.
[26] *Ibid.*, 173.
[27] No doubt Berlin did not mean this term to be gender-exclusive; had he written a decade or so later, he would surely have used the more politically correct "human beings."
[28] *The Proper Study of Mankind*, 9–10.
[29] *Ibid.*, 10.

a decent society . . . So we must engage in what are called trade-offs—rules, values, principles must yield to each other in varying degrees in specific situations.[30]

This solution may seem "flat," "a little dull," as Berlin readily admits. But he was contented with it, and it seems to have made him happy: the fissure was closed. The fox had become a hedgehog by turning foxiness itself into "one big thing." After a lifetime of seeking, he had arrived at a moral philosophy that satisfied him as the best and most humane solution that mankind is likely to reach.

Of course, personal happiness, even for the most committed intellectuals, depends on other factors than the resolution of philosophical dilemmas. Though the Ignatieff biography perhaps overstates it, Berlin did have a surprisingly happy life, despite having lived through the cataclysmic events of the twentieth century—both world wars, the Russian Revolution, exile, assimilation into a new and not especially welcoming society. To be sure, he suffered many vicissitudes, disappointments, and sorrows. He had a withered arm, a fact which no doubt caused him much psychological pain, especially in his youth, and perhaps contributed to his belief, which lasted until quite late in his life, that he could never be attractive to women. He also had to come to terms with his own conviction, painfully arrived at, that as a philosopher he would never be the equal of his Oxford colleagues A. J. Ayer and J. L. Austin. "I knew I wasn't first rate," Ignatieff quotes him as saying.[31] Several of his close relations perished in the Holocaust, and he both grieved for them and perhaps suffered survivor's guilt. Nevertheless, Berlin's exuberance and seemingly limitless vitality prevailed. He was blessed with economic security, loving parents, countless friends, and—though only rather late in his life—a close and fulfilling marriage that contributed much to the serenity of his later years. Though he may perhaps not have been a first-rate technical philosopher, his writings as an intellectual historian, thinker, and commentator on human affairs won him not only a knighthood, but international admiration and recognition.[32] As twentieth-century lives go, his was surely a good one.

The contrast with Tolstoy is striking. Tolstoy too had for a time enjoyed a notably happy marriage, biologically fruitful as Berlin's never was. In the early 1870s he had reached a Berlin-like equilibrium, and he congratulates himself on the quiescence of his critical faculty:

---

[30] *Ibid.*, 15.
[31] Ignatieff, 86.
[32] I am grateful to Nicholas Riasanovsky for pointing out to me the weakness in Ignatieff's presentation of Berlin as a "happy warrior."

> From my youth I have prematurely undertaken to analyze and mercilessly destroy everything. I was often afraid: nothing will be left. But now as I grow older, I find that I have preserved more things unshaken than others have . . . love for one woman, [our] children and my whole relationship to them, learning, art.[33]

But a few years later the fearsome engine of destruction resumed its course, and all these cherished values were crushed by it.[34]

After completing *Anna Karenina*, Tolstoy recommenced the search for an overarching set of principles that would provide an answer to all human contradictions and show mankind the way to a world of peace, love, and unity. He found it, of course, in the rationalized and demythicized Christianity we call Tolstoyism. It preached love for all mankind, especially love for one's enemies. But it seemed there was not much primitive, biological, pre-Christian—or even Christian—love left for *izhe po ploti*, the members of his family. He would admit no pluralism for them. Those close to him, including his wife, must accept his doctrines or lose his love. Tolstoy's capacity to inflict misery on himself and his family was enormous.

> Very painful in the family. It is painful that I cannot sympathize with them. All their joys, examinations, success in society, music, furniture, purchases—all that I consider a misfortune and an evil and I cannot tell them that. But I can and I do tell them, but my words do not affect anyone. They seem to know not the meaning of my words, but the fact that I have the bad habit of uttering them. In my weak moments—this is such a moment—I am amazed at their heartlessness. How can they help seeing that it is not just that I am suffering, but I have been deprived of life for three years now. They assign me the role of a grumpy old man.[35]

But he could not bring himself to abandon them altogether, choosing to regard family life as the cross that God had assigned him to bear. So he stayed and for thirty years made himself, and them, miserable, until the final *ukhod*, the "going away," at the age of eighty-two.

---

[33] SS 19:275. Diary entry for 6 November 1873.
[34] Martin Malia has written an interesting article on the phenomenon of maturation, with Tolstoy as the Russian case. Tolstoy is said to have reached—and to represent—full maturity in the two great novels, *War and Peace* and *Anna Karenina*, with their pictures of men and women forming, and in the best instances sustaining, biologically fruitful unions. After the "crisis," however, Tolstoy's maturity went awry, an effect Malia attributes partly to something like "male menopause," though he does not use this term, fading sexual potency paralleling weakening artistic powers. Martin E. Malia, "Adulthood Refracted: Russia and Leo Tolstoy," *Daedalus*, vol. 105 (1976), 169–83.
[35] SS 19:316. Diary entry for 4 April 1884.

Perhaps more tragic still was the fact that the overarching solution, the body of doctrine he worked so hard to assemble and then propagate, was never fully secure in his mind. The hedgehog never completely overpowered the fox. An enormous amount of energy and vast numbers of words—diaries, letters, treatises—were generated in the effort to construct and maintain the edifice of Tolstoyism. But occasionally there were glimpses of an older, unregenerate Tolstoy, a Tolstoy who took a richer, more varied, more inclusive view of human life than the one preached so insistently in such treatises as *The Kingdom of God Is Within You*, a Tolstoy who was perhaps bored by all the piety. It was this Tolstoy who would sneak away, as late as the age of seventy-seven, to work on *Khadji Murat*, a work that seems to celebrate a set of archaic, pre-Christian values—tribalism, blood vengeance, *macho* aggressiveness, courage under fire—which the official Tolstoy had repudiated. *This* Tolstoy was surely wearied by the pedantic smallness of even his beloved disciple-in-chief, Vladimir Chertkov, who once priggishly reproved the master for swatting a mosquito on his, Chertkov's, bald head.[36]

It was the image of this Tolstoy, a Tolstoy torn by terrible inner conflicts, that Berlin perceived so penetratingly and invoked so powerfully at the end of his essay, a self-blinded Tolstoy, but self-blinded not like Oedipus, in remorse for having committed terrible crimes, incest and patricide, without knowing it, but self-blinded in an intense, decades-long, but ultimately futile effort to stifle the rich, varied, *pluralistic* talent he was born with.

> At once insanely proud and filled with self-hatred, omniscient and doubting everything, cold and violently passionate, contemptuous and self-abasing, tormented and detached, surrounded by an adoring family, by devoted followers, by the admiration of the entire civilised world, and yet almost wholly isolated, he is the most tragic of the great writers, a desperate old man, beyond human aid, wandering self-blinded at Colonus.[37]

---

[36] A. N. Wilson, *Tolstoy* (London: Hamish Hamilton, 1988), 485.
[37] *Russian Thinkers*, 81.

Works Cited

Most quotations from Tolstoy are taken either from the Jubilee Edition, *Полное собрание сочинений*, ed. V. G. Chertkov et al., 90 vols. (Moscow, Leningrad: Gosudarstvennoe izdatel'stvo khudozhestvennoi literatury, 1928–1964), identified in the text as *PSS*, with volume and page no., or from *Собрание сочинений*, ed. N. N. Akopova et al., 20 vols. (Moscow: Gosudarstvennoe izdatel'stvo khudozhestvennoi literatury, 1960–1963), identified in the text as *SS*, with volume and page no. All translations from these editions are mine. A few other quotations from Tolstoy, taken from sources other than the above, are listed separately below under the name Толстой, Л. Н. or Tolstoi, Lev Nikolaevich.

Абросимова, В. Н. "Л. Н. Толстой в антологии Е. Хемингуэя 'Люди на войне'," in *Литературные связи и проблема взаимовлияния*, под ред. И. В. Киреева. Gor'kii, 1983, 14–23.

Алпатов, Михаил. *Александр Иванов*. Moscow: Molodaia gvardiia, 1959.

Allgemeines Lexicon der bildenden Künstler. Leipzig: E. A. Seemann, 1921.

Антонович, М. А. "Теория происхождения видов в царстве животных," *Sovremennik*, 3 (1864), 63–107.

Atkinson, Dorothy et al., eds. *Women in Russia*. Stanford: Stanford University Press, 1977.

Baker, Carlos. *Hemingway: The Writer as Artist*. 4th. ed. Princeton: Princeton University Press, 1972.

_____, ed. *Ernest Hemingway: Selected Letters*. New York: Charles Scribner's Sons, 1981.

Benson, Ruth Crego. *Women in Tolstoy: The Ideal and the Erotic*. Urbana, Chicago and London: University of Illinois Press, 1973.

Berlin, Sir Isaiah. *Personal Impressions*, ed. Henry Hardy. New York: Penguin Books, 1982.

_____, *The Crooked Timber of Humanity*. London: John Murray, 1990.

_____,*The Hedgehog and the Fox: An Essay on Tolstoy's View of History*. New York: Simon & Schuster, 1953. Original title, "Lev Tolstoy's Historical Skepticism," *Oxford Slavonic Papers*, 2 (1951).

_____, *Karl Marx: His Life and Environment*. London: T. Butterworth, Ltd., 1939.

_____, *The Proper Study of Mankind: An Anthology of Essays*, ed. Henry Hardy and Roger Hausheer. New York: Farrar, Straus & Giroux, 1980.

_____, *Russian Thinkers*. New York: Pelican Books, 1979.

Biriukov, Pavel. *Tolstoi und der Orient: Briefe und sonstige Zeugnisse über Tolstois Beziehungen zu den Vertretern orientalischen Religionen*. Zurich: Rotappel-Verlag, 1925.

Бирман, Ю. "О характере времени в 'Войне и мире'." *Russkaia literatura*, 3 (1966).

Boyer, Paul Jean Marie. *Chez Tolstoi: Entretiens à Iasnaia Poliana*. Paris: Institut d'Études slaves de l'Université de Paris, 1950.

Бродский, Н. Л., ред. *В. П. Боткин и И. С. Тургенев. Неизданная переписка, 1851–1869*. Moscow-Leningrad: Academia, 1930.

Bruccoli, Matthew J., ed. *The Only Thing That Counts: The Ernest Hemingway/Maxwell Perkins Correspondence, 1925–1947*. New York: Scribner, 1996.

Бурлака, Д. К., ред. *Максим Горький: pro et contra; личность и творчество Максима Горького в оценке русских мыслителей и исследователей, 1890–1910; антология*. St. Petersburg: Izdatel'stvo russkogo khristianskogo gumanitarnogo instituta, 1997.

Caro, E. "La démocratie devant la morale de l'avenir," *Revue des deux mondes* (November 1, 1885), 5–36.

Чернышевский, Н. Г. (Старый трансформист). "Происхождение теории благотворности борьбы за жизнь," *Russkaia mysl'*, 9 (1888), 79–114. Rpt. Чернышевский, *Полное собрание сочинений*, под ред. В. Я. Кирпотина и др. Moscow: Gosizdat Khudozhestvennoi literatury, 1951. 10:737–772.

Чехов, А. П. *Переписка А. П. Чехова в двух томах*. Moscow: Khudozhestvennaia literatura, 1984.

Christian, R. F. *Tolstoy: A Critical Introduction*. Cambridge: Cambridge University Press, 1969.

Чуковский, Корней. *Две души Максима Горького*. Leningrad: A. F. Marks, 1924.

_____, *Люди и книги*, 2nd. ed., expanded. Moscow: Khudozhestvennaia literatura, 1960.

Cruise, Edwina. "The Ideal Woman in Tolstoi: *Resurrection*," *Canadian-American Slavic Studies*, 11, no. 2 (Summer, 1977), 281–86.

Darwin, Charles. *The Correspondence of Charles Darwin*. Cambridge: Cambridge University Press, 1997.

_____, *The Origin of Species by Means of Natural Selection; The Descent of Man and Selection in Relation to Sex.* Chicago: Encyclopedia Britannica, 1952.

_____, *Происхождение человека и подбор по отношению к полу*, под ред. И. М. Сеченова. St. Petersburg, 1871.

Данилевский, Н. Я. *Дарвинизм: Критическое исследование.* St. Petersburg: Izd. Merkuriia Eleazarovicha Komarova, 1885.

_____, *Россия и Европа. Взгляд на культурные и политические отношения славянского мира к германо-романскому.* St. Petersburg: Tovarishchestvo "Obshchestvennaia Pol'za", 1871.

Demars, Aline. *Clémence Royer l'intrépide: la plus savante des savants.* Paris: L'Harmattan, 2005.

Донсков, А. А., ред. *Л. Н. Толстой и Н. Н. Страхов. Полное собрание переписки.* Ottawa: Slavic Research Group at the University of Ottawa and State L. N. Tolstoy Museum, Moscow, 2003. 2 vols.

Dorothée, Michèle. *La philosophie et l'anthropologie de Clémence Royer: Un exemple de circulation des idées philosophiques et scientifiques en France et en Europe dans la seconde moitié du XIXème siècle.* Paris: Presses Universitaires de Septentrion, 1998.

Достоевский, Ф. М. *Письма*, под ред. А. С. Долинина. Moscow: Gosizdat, 1928–1959. 4 vols.

_____, *Полное собрание сочинений в тридцати томах.* Том 28: *Письма, 1832–1859.* Leningrad: Nauka, 1985.

(Дружинин). *Письма к А. В. Дружинину.* Moscow: Gosudarstvennyi literaturnyi muzei, 1948.

Эйхенбаум, Б. М. *Лев Толстой*: кн. 1: *пятидесятые годы.* Leningrad: Priboi, 1928. кн. 2: *шестидесятые годы*, 1931.

_____, *Лев Толстой в семидесятые годы.* Leningrad: Sovetskii pisatel', 1960.

Фаминцын, А. С. "Н. Я. Данилевский и дарвинизм," *Vestnik Evropy* (Fevral', 1889), 616–43.

Георгиевский, А. Б. "Особенности развития эволюционной теории в России," in *Развитие эволюционной теории в СССР (1917–1970-ые годы)*, под ред. С. П. Микулинского и Ю. И. Полянского. Leningrad: Nauka, 1983, 43–61.

Горький, М. *О русском крестьянстве.* Berlin: Izdatel'stvo I. P. Ladyzhnikova, 1924.

_____, *Собрание сочинений в тридцати томах.* Moscow: Izdatel'stvo Khudozhestvennoi literatury, 1951–1954. Referred to in the text as *GSS*.

_____, *Untimely Thoughts: Essays on Revolution, Culture and the Bolsheviks, 1917–1918*, tr. Herman Ermolaev. New York: Paul S. Erikson, 1968.

Григорович, А. В. *Литературные воспоминания.* Moscow: Khudozhestvennaia literatura, 1987.

Grimsley, Ronald. *Rousseau and the Religious Quest*. Oxford: Clarendon Press, 1968.

Гусев, Н. Н. *Л. Н. Толстой. Летописи Государственного литературного музея*, 2. Moscow, 1938.

―――, *Летопись жизни и творчества Льва Николаевича Толстого, 1828–1890*. Moscow: Khudozhestvennaia literatura, 1958.

―――, *Лев Николаевич Толстой: Материалы к биографии с 1855 по 1869 год*. Moscow: Akademiia Nauk SSSR, 1957.

―――, *Лев Николаевич Толстой: Материалы к биографии с 1881 по 1885 год*. Moscow: Izdatel'stvo "Nauka", 1970.

Gustafson, Richard F. *Leo Tolstoy: Resident and Stranger*. Princeton: Princeton University Press, 1986.

Gutkin, Irina. "The Dichotomy between Flesh and Spirit: Plato's *Symposium* in *Anna Karenina*," in *In the Shade of the Giant*, ed. Hugh McLean. Berkeley, Los Angeles, London: University of California Press, 1989, 84–99.

Heldt, Barbara. *Terrible Perfection: Women in Russian Literature*. Bloomington: Indiana University Press, 1987.

Hemingway, Ernest. *Death in the Afternoon*. New York, London: Charles Scribner's Sons, 1932.

―――, *Green Hills of Africa*. New York: Charles Scribner's Sons, 1935.

―――, ed., *Men at War*. New York: Crown Publishers, 1942.

―――, *A Moveable Feast*. New York: Simon & Schuster, 1992.

Huxley, Thomas H. *Evolution and Ethics*. London: Macmillan, 1893. Rpt. *Evolution & Ethics: T. H. Huxley's* Evolution and Ethics *with New Essays on Its Victorian and Sociobiological Context*, ed. James Paradis and George C. Williams. Princeton: Princeton University Press, 1989.

Ignatieff, Michael. *Isaiah Berlin: A Life*. New York: Henry Holt, 1998.

Ивакин, И. М. "Записки И. М. Ивакина," *Литературное наследство*, 69: *Лев Толстой*, 2. Moscow: Akademiia Nauk SSSR, 1961, 21–124.

Измайлов, Н. В. и др., ред. *Тургенев и круг "Современника"*. Moscow-Leningrad: Academia, 1930.

Jacquet, Christian. *La pensée religieuse de Jean-Jacques Rousseau*. Louvain: Bibliothèque de l'Université; Leiden, E. J. Brill, 1975.

Jahn, Gary R. "A Structural Analysis of Leo Tolstoy's 'God Sees the Truth but Waits'," *Studies in Short Fiction*, 12 (1975), 261–70.

Josephs, F. Allen. "Hemingway's Poor Spanish: Chauvinism and Loss of Credibility in *For Whom the Bell Tolls*," in Donald R. Noble, ed., *Hemingway: A Revaluation*. Troy, N.Y.: Whitson Publishing Co., 1983, 205–224.

Kennan, George. "A Visit to Count Tolstoy," *The Century Illustrated Monthly Magazine*, vol. 34, no. 2 (1887).

Kenworthy, John Coleman. *Tolstoy: His Life and Works.* London and Newcastle-on-Tyre: The Walter Scott Publishing Co., 1902.

Ходасевич, Владислав. "Горький," in *Некрополь: Воспоминания; литература и власть.* Moscow: SS, 1996.

Kline, George. "Darwinism and the Russian Orthodox Church," in E. J. Simmons, ed., *Continuity and Change in Russian and Soviet Thought.* Cambridge: Harvard University Press, 1955, 307–328.

———, *Religious and Anti-Religious Thought in Russia.* Chicago: University of Chicago Press, 1968.

Knapp, Liza, and Amy Mandelker. *Approaches to Teaching Tolstoy's* Anna Karenina. New York: Modern Language Association of America, 2003.

Лесскис, Г. *Лев Толстой (1852–1869).* Moscow: O.G.I., 2000.

Lewis, Robert W. *Hemingway on Love.* Austin and London: University of Texas Press, 1965.

Ломунов, Константин. *Драматургия Л. Н. Толстого.* Moscow: Iskusstvo, 1956.

———, *Над страницами "Воскресения".* Moscow: Sovremennik, 1979.

Lynn, Kenneth. *Hemingway.* New York: Simon & Schuster, 1987.

Macmaster, Robert E. *Danilevsky: A Russian Totalitarian Philosopher.* Cambridge: Harvard University Press, 1967.

Маянц, Зильма. *Человек один не может... Эрнест Хемингуэй, жизнь и творчество.* Moscow: Prosveshchenie, 1966.

Makovický, D. P. (Маковицкий). *У Толстого, 1904–1910. Яснополянские записки = Литературное наследство,* 90.

Malia, Martin E. "Adulthood Refracted: Russia and Leo Tolstoy," *Daedalus,* 105 (1976), 169–83.

Mandelker, Amy. *Framing* Anna Karenina. Columbus: Ohio State University Press, 1993.

Markovitch, Milan I. *Jean-Jacques Rousseau et Tolstoi.* Paris: Librarie Ancienne Honoré Champion, 1928.

McLean, Hugh. "Tolstoy Made Whole," *Russian Review* 46 (1987), 321–28.

Melzer, Arthur M. "The Origin of the Counter-Enlightenment: Rousseau and the New Religion of Sincerity," *American Political Science Review* 90 (1996): 344–60.

———, "Rousseau and the Modern Cult of Sincerity," in *The Legacy of Rousseau,* eds. Clifford Orwin and Nathan Tarcov. Chicago and London: University of Chicago Press, 1997.

Miller, D. A. *Narrative and Its Discontents.* Princeton: Princeton University Press, 1981.

Модзалевский, Б. Л., ред. *Переписка Л. Н. Толстого с гр. А. А. Толстой, 1857–1903.* St. Petersburg, 1911.

Morson, Gary Saul. *Hidden in Plain View: Narrative and Creative Potentials in War and Peace.* Stanford: Stanford University Press, 1987.

Moser, Charles A. *Antinihilism in the Russian Novel of the 1860s.* The Hague: Mouton & Co., 1964.

Mossman, Carol A. *Stendhal's Narrative Matrix:* Le rouge et le noir. Lexington: French Forum, 1984.

Nabokov, Vladimir. *Lectures on Russian Literature*, ed. Fredson Bowers. San Diego, New York, London: Bruccoli, Clark, Layman, 1981.

Опульская, Л. Д. *Лев Николаевич Толстой. Материалы к биографии с 1892 по 1899 год.* Moscow: Rossiiskaia Akademiia nauk, 1998.

Orwin, Donna Tussing. *Tolstoy's Art and Thought, 1847–1880.* Princeton: Princeton University Press, 1993.

———, "The Riddle of Prince Nexljudov," *Slavic and East European Journal,* 30, no. 4 (1986), 473–86.

Paperno, Irina. *Chernyshevsky and the Age of Realism: A Study in the Semiotics of Behavior.* Stanford: Stanford University Press, 1988.

Pavlov, P. "Tolstoy's Novel *Family Happiness,*" *Slavonic Review,* 7 (January, 1929), 492–510.

Пирожкова, Т. Ф., ред. *Б. Н. Чичерин. Москва 40-ых годов.* Moscow: Izdatel'stvo Moskovskogo universiteta, 1997.

Писарев, Д. И. "Прогресс в мире животных и растений," *Russkoe slovo,* nos. 4, 5, 6, 7, and 9 (1864). Rpt. Писарев, *Полное собрание сочинений и писем в двенадцати томах,* под ред. Ф. Ф. Кузнецова и др. Moscow: Nauka, 2003. 6:7–175.

———, "Промахи незрелой мысли," *Russkoe slovo,* no. 12 (1864), 1–56. Rpt. Писарев, *Полное,* 3:428–73.

———, "'Три смерти'. Рассказ графа Л. Н. Толстого." *Rassvet,* no. 12 (1859). Rpt. Писарев, *Собрание сочинений в четырех томах.* Moscow: Gosizdat Khudozhestvennoi literatury, 1955. 1:34–44.

Poggioli, Renato. *The Oaken Flute: Essays on Pastoral Poetry and the Pastoral Ideal.* Cambridge: Harvard University Press, 1975.

Pomorska, Krystyna. "Tolstoy—Contra Semiosis," *International Journal of Slavic Linguistics and Poetics,* 25/26 (1982).

Рачинский, С. А. "Цветы и насекомые," *Русский Вестник,* № 1 (1863), 347–396.

Renan, Ernest. *L'Abesse de Jouarre.* Paris, n.d.

———, *L'Avenir de la science.* Paris: Calmann-Lévy, 1890.

———, *Marc-Aurèle et la fin du monde antique.* Paris: Calmann-Lévy, 1894.

———, *Vie de Jésus.* Paris: Calmann-Lévy, 1863.

Reynolds, Michael S. *Hemingway's Reading, 1910–1940: An Inventory.* Princeton: Princeton University Press, 1981.

Rischin, Ruth. "*Allegro Tumultuosissimente:* Beethoven in Tolstoy's Fiction," in *In the Shade of the Giant: Essays on Tolstoy*, ed. Hugh McLean. Berkeley, Los Angeles, London: University of California Press, 1989, 12–60.

Rolland, Roman. *Vie de Tolstoi*, 3d. ed. Paris: Hachette, 1911.

Rousseau, Jean-Jacques. *Religious Writings*, ed. Ronald Grimsley. Oxford: Clarendon Press, 1970.

———, *The Confessions of Jean-Jacques Rousseau*, trans. J. M. Cohen. Baltimore: Penguin Books, 1954.

———, *Oeuvres complètes*. Paris: Bibliothèque de la Pléiade, 1959.

Rogers, James Allen. "Charles Darwin and Russian Scientists," *Russian Review*, 19 (1960), 371–83.

———, "The Reception of Darwin's *Origin of Species* by Russian Scientists," *ISIS*, 64 (1973), 484–503.

———, "The Russian Populists' Response to Darwin," *Slavic Review*, 22, no. 3 (1963), 456–68.

Royer, Clémence. *Théorie de l'impot ou la dîme sociale*. Paris: Guillaime et cie., 1862.

Рубинштейн, М. "Философия истории в романе Л. Толстого 'Война и мир'," *Russkaia Mysl'*, no. 7 (July, 1911).

Saylor, Ian. "*Anna Karenina* and *Don Giovanni:* The Vengeance Motif in Oblonsky's Dream," *Tolstoy Studies Journal*, VIII (1995–96), 112–16.

Scherr, Barry P. "Notes on Literary Life in Petrograd, 1918–1922: A Tale of Two Houses," *Slavic Review*, 36, no. 3 (1977), 256–67.

Semon, Marie. "Le rôle de la mémoire dans *Résurrection*," in *À propos de* Résurrection, ed. Marie Semon. Paris: Institut d'Études Slaves, 1996, 15–25.

Sesterhenn, Raimund. *Das Bogostroitel'stvo bei Gorkij und Lunačarskij bis 1909: zur ideologischen und literarischen Vorgeschichte der Parteischule von Capri*. Munich, 1982.

Sheldon, Richard. "Problems in the English Translations of *Anna Karenina*," in Lenore A. Grenoble and John M. Kopper, eds., *Essays in the Art and Theory of Translation*. Lewiston, N.Y.: The Edwin Mellon Press, 1997, 231–264.

Шифман, Александр. Лев Толстой и Восток. Moscow: Izdatel'stvo Vostochnoi literatury, 1960.

Шкловский, В. Б. *Матерьял и стиль в романе Льва Толстого "Война и мир."* Moscow: Federatsiia, 1928.

Siegel, George. "The Fallen Woman in Nineteenth-Century Russian Literature," *Harvard Slavic Studies*, ed. Horace G. Lunt et al., V (1970), 81–108.

Скафтымов, А. "Образ Кутузова и философия истории в романе Л. Н. Толстого 'Война и мир'," *Russkaia literatura*, no. 2 (1959), 72–94.

Sokolov, Jayme A. and Priscilla Roosevelt. *Leo Tolstoy's Christian Pacifism: The American Contribution*. Pittsburgh: Center for Russian and East European Studies, 1987 = Carl Beck Papers. No. 604.

Срезневский, В., ред. "Переписка Л. Н. Толстого с В. П. Боткиным," in *Толстой: Памятники творчества и жизни*, 4, Moscow, 1923.

Stites, Richard. *The Women's Liberation Movement in Russia: Feminism, Nihilism and Bolshevism, 1860–1930.* Princeton: Princeton University Press, 1978.

Страхов, Н. Н., "Дурные признаки," *Vremia*, no. 11 (1862). Rpt., Страхов, *Критические статьи*, под ред. И. П. Матченко. Kiev, 1902, 2:379–96.

———, *Мир как целое.* St. Petersburg, 1872.

———, *О методе естественных наук и значение их в общем образовании.* St. Petersburg, 1865.

———, "О развитии организмов. Попытка точно поставить вопрос," *Priroda*, no. 1 (1874),

———, "Переворот в науке," rpt. Страхов, *Борьба с Западом*, 2:250–70.

———, "Полное опровержение дарвинизма," *Russkii Vestnik*, no. 1 (Ianvar', 1887); rpt. *Борьба с Западом*, 2:281–342.

———, "Спор из-за книг Н. Я. Данилевского," *Russkii Vestnik* (Dekabr', 1889); rpt. *Борьба с Западом*, 2:445–65.

———, "Суждение А. С. Фаминцына о *Дарвинизме* Н. Я. Данилевского," *Russkii Vestnik* (Aprel', 1889); rpt. *Борьба с Западом в русской литературе*, 3ье изд., под ред. И. П. Матченко. Kiev, 1897, 2:421–44.

———, "Всегдашняя ошибка дарвинистов," *Russkii Vestnik* (Noiabr'-Dekabr', 1887); rpt. *Борьба с Западом*, 2:343–420.

Тимирязев, К. А. "Книга Дарвина, ее критики и комментаторы," *Otechestvennye zapiski*, № 8 (1864), 880–912 и № 12, 859–882.

———, *Краткий очерк теории Дарвина.* St. Petersburg, 1865 et seq.

———, "Отвергнут ли дарвинизм?" *Russkaia mysl'* (Mai-Iiun', 1887).

———, "Странный образчик научной критики," *Russkaia mysl'* (Mart, 1889), 90–102.

Тишкин, Г. А. ред. *Феминизм и российская культура; сборник статей.* St. Petersburg: Sankt-Peterburgskaia gosudarstvennaia akademiia kul'tury, 1995.

———, *Женский вопрос в России в 50–60 гг. XIX в.* Leningrad: Izdatel'stvo Leningradskogo Universiteta, 1984.

Todes, Daniel P. *Darwin without Malthus: The Struggle for Existence in Russian Evolutionary Thought.* New York, Oxford: Oxford University Press, 1989.

Tolstoi, Lev Nikolaevich, 1885. *Christ's Christianity.* London: Hegan Paul, French & Co.

———, 1913. *The Novels and Other Works of Lyof N. Tolstoy*, ed. Nathan Haskell Dole. New York: Charles Scribner's Sons, Vol. 11: *The Cossacks, Sevastopol.*

———, 1928. *Twenty-three Tales*, tr. Mr. and Mrs. Aylmer Maude. London: Humphrey Milford, Oxford University Press.

_____ 1942. *War and Peace*, tr. Louise and Aylmer Maude. New York: Simon & Schuster.

_____, 1960. *Anna Karenina*, tr. Joel Carmichael. Bantam Books.

_____, 1961. *Anna Karenina*, tr. David Magarshack. Signet Classics.

_____, 1965. *Anna Karenina*, tr. Constance Garnett, revised by Leonard J. Kent and Nina Berberova. New York: The Modern Library.

_____, 1978. *Anna Karenina*, tr. Rosemary Edmonds, revised ed. Penguin Books.

_____, 1995. *Anna Karenina*, tr. Louise and Aylmer Maude, revised by George Gibian, 2nd. ed. New York: W. W. Norton.

_____, 2001. *Anna Karenina*, tr. Richard Pevear and Larissa Volokhonsky. New York: Viking.

Толстой и зарубежный мир, кн. 1 = *Литературное наследство*, 75 (Moscow, 1965).

Толстой, Л. Н. *Первая завершенная редакция романа "Война и мир"* = *Литературное наследство*, 94 (Moscow, 1983).

Толстой, Н. Н. "Охота на Кавказе," *Современник*, № 2 (1857).

Толстой, Сергей Л. *Мать и дед Л. Н. Толстого*. Moscow: Federatsiia, 1928.

_____, *Очерки былого*, 3ье изд. Tula, 1968.

Troyat, Henri. *Tolstoy*. New York: Doubleday & Co., 1967.

Тургенев, И. С. *Собрание сочинений*. Moscow: Khudozhestvennaia literatura, 1958.

Вацуро, В. Е. *Л. Н. Толстой в воспоминаниях современников*. Moscow: Izdatel'stvo Khudozhestvennoi literatury, 1978. 2 vols.

Vucinich, Alexander. "Russia: Biological Sciences," in Thomas F. Glick, ed., *The Comparative Reception of Darwinism*. Austin and London: University of Texas Press, 1972:227–55.

_____, *Darwin in Russian Thought*. Berkeley and Los Angeles: University of California Press, 1988.

Weisbein, Nicolas. *L'Évolution religieuse de Tolstoi*. Paris: Librarie des Cinq Continents, 1960.

White, William, ed. *By-Line: Ernest Hemingway: Selected Articles and Dispatches of Four Decades*. New York: Charles Scribner's Sons, 1967.

Wilkinson, Myler. *Hemingway and Turgenev: The Nature of Literary Influence*. Ann Arbor: UMI Research Press, 1986.

Wilson, A. N. *Tolstoy*. London: Hamish Hamilton, 1988.

Wolfe, Bertram D. *The Bridge and the Abyss: The Troubled Friendship of Maxim Gorky and V. I. Lenin*. New York: Praeger, 1967.

Yedlin, Tovah. *Maxim Gorky: A Political Biography.* Westport, CT and London: Praeger, 1999.

Zbožilek, Vladimir. "Tolstoy and Rousseau: A Study in Literary Relationship." Ph. D. diss., University of California, Berkeley, 1969.

Жданов, Владимир. *Любовь в жизни Льва Толстого.* Moscow: Izdatel'stvo M. i S. Sabashnikovykh, 1928; rpt. Moscow: Planeta, 1993.

———, *Творческая история романа Л. Н. Толстого "Воскресение."* Moscow: Sovetskii pisatel', 1960.

Журов, П. А. "Л. Н. Толстой и В. В. Арсеньева (Автобиографические отражения в повести 'Семейное счастье'," *Ясно-полянский сборник 1976.* Tula, 1976.

Index of Tolstoy's Works

Albert (Альберт) 18n
Anna Karenina (Анна Каренина) 9, 10, 15, 20, 28n, 30–52, 53–69, 74, 76–79, 117, 120, 122, 124n, 127n, 170, 184n, 186, 199, 208–209, 211, 214–215, 225n
Bethink Yourselves (Одумайтесь) 184
Boyhood (Отрочество) 75
Confession (Исповедь) 36–37, 77, 147, 152
A Conversation on Science (Разговор о науке) 163, 170n
The Cossacks (Казаки) 77, 160, 200, 201
A Critique of Dogmatic Theology (Критика догматического богословия) 120
The Death of Ivan Ilyich (Смерть Ивана Ильича) 184n, 209
The Devil (Дьявол) 16, 72, 210, 215
Family Happiness (Семейное счастье) 3–20
Father Sergius (Отец Сергий) 72, 210, 215
God Sees the Truth but Waits (Бог правду видит, да не скоро скажет) 87–102
Hadji (Khadzhi) Murat (Хаджи Мурат) 142, 203, 226
The Kingdom of God Is Within You (Царство Божие внуртри Вас) 121, 146, 182n, 184n, 186n, 226
The Kreutzer Sonata (Крейцерова соната) 72, 122, 183n, 210, 215
A Landlord's Morning (Утро помещика) 39, 75
Lucerne (Люцерн) 75
Notes of a Billiard Marker (Записки маркера) 75
Kill Not (Не убий) 184
On Socialism (О социализме) 193
On the Social Movement in Russia (Об общественном движении в России) 187
Primer (Азбука) 87
A Prisoner of the Caucasus (Кавказский пленник) 98–99
Reminiscences (Воспоминания) 36–46
Resurrection (Воскресение) 15, 39. 71–86, 119, 147, 152, 184n, 186, 187n, 215
Sevastopol in May (Севастополь в мае) 118, 161
Sevastopol Sketches (Севастопольские рассказы) 200, 201
A Short Synopsis of the Gospel (Краткое изложение Евангелия) 123, 182, 183
A Snowstorm (Метель) 45

Third Russian Book for Reading (Третья русская книга для чтенья) 91
Three Deaths (Три смерти) 165n, 20
War and Peace (Война и мир) 4, 9, 10, 18, 21–30, 87–89, 120, 152, 160, 173, 193, 199, 201, 202–209, 214
What Is Art (Что такое искусство) 144n
What Shall We Do? (Что нам делать?) 185
What Then Must We Do? (Так что же нам делать?) 185n

Yasnaya Polyana (journal) (Ясная Поляна) 126
Youth (Юность) 36n, 75

Index of Names

A

Abrosimova, V. N. 202n
Akhmatova, Anna A. 215
Aksakov, Sergei
    A Family Chronicle 161n
Aleksandrov, N. A. 126
Aleksandrov, V. A. 202n
Alexander I 219
Alexander II 85
Alexander III 83
Anaxagoras 173
Anet, Claude 188n
Antonovich, M. A.
    "A Theory of the Origin of Species in the Animal Kingdom" 165
Archilochus 222
Arsen'eva, Olga V. (Engalycheva) 10
Arsen'eva, Valeriya V. (Talyzina, Volkova) 10–17, 19
Austen, Jane
    Emma 29
Austin, J. L. 224
Avenarius, Richard 180
Ayer, A. J. 224

B

Babaev, E. G. 55
Bach, J. S. 144, 159
Baker, Carlos 197n, 198n, 200n, 206n
Ballou, Adin 182n
Barsenev, Petr 216n
Bazykina, Aksiniya 16
Beach, Sylvia 199
Beethoven, Ludwig van 144, 159, 160
Belinsky, Vissarion 221
Benningsen, Count L. L. 205
Benson, Ruth Crego 105n
Berberova, Nina 54–70 *passim*
Berlin, Sir Isaiah 141, 182, 214–226
Bers, Andrei Evstafievich (father-in-law) 41n
Bers, Lyubov' A., née Islavina (mother-in-law) 41n
Biriukov, Pavel 72, 92n, 150n
Birman, Iu. 28n
Bogdanov, A. A. 190
Botkin, Vasily 3, 4, 6–7, 8–9, 15
Bouvier, Bernard 144n
Boyer, Paul 144
Brady, Mathew B. 201
Braque, Georges 212
Bronte, Charlotte, Emily, Anne 5
Bruccoli, Matthew J. 197n, 202n
Buckle, Henry Thomas 164
    A History of Civilization in England 160n
Bulgakov, M. A. 154, 189n
Burlaka, D. K. 190
Bychkov, S. P. 6
Byron, George Gordon, Lord 150

C

Carmichael, Joel 53n, 54–70 *passim*
Carpenter, Edward
    "Modern Science" 163
Caro, Elme-Marie
    "Democracy before the Morality of the Future" 171–172
Cervantes, Miguel de 198, 208n
Chekhov, Anton P. 76, 86, 164, 200n
Chernyshevsky, N. G. 110, 114,
    What Is To Be Done? 107, 115n, 116
    "The Origin of the Theory of a Beneficent Struggle for Life" 175
Chertkov, V. G. 91, 92–94, 184n, 189
Chicherin, B. N. 161n, 162
Christian, R. F. 5–6, 7n, 9, 18, 19
Chukovsky, Kornei 19, 190n
Cooke, Brett 171n
Crane, Stephen
    The Red Badge of Courage 201
Cruise, Edwina 57, 61–65, 77n
Cuvier, Baron G. L. C. F. Dagobert 175

D

Dallin, Alexander 106n
Danilevsky, Nikolai Ia.
    Russia and Europe 169, 173
    Darwinism: A Critical Investigation 169, 172–174
Dante Alighieri 141, 144, 159, 160, 199
Darwin, Charles 159–180 *passim*
    The Origin of Species 160, 165, 171
    The Descent of Man 160n, 168
Demars, Aline 166n
Diderot, Denis 145
Dokhturov, Fedor 42
Dolinin, A. S. 3n, 4, 16, 17, 110n, 157
Donskov, Andrew 170n, 177n
Dorothée, Michèle 167n
Dos Passos, John 213
Dostoevsky, Fedor M. 76, 84, 118, 132, 155m 166, 178, 188, 209
    The Karamazov Brothers 199n
Druzhinin, A. V. 3n, 4, 16, 17, 110n, 157

E

Edmonds, Rosemary 54–70 *passim*
Eikhenbaum, B. M. 5, 18, 116n, 215, 216
Engels, Friedrich 193

Epicurus 173
Ergol'skaya, Tat'iana ("auntie") 11, 13, 14, 48

F

Famintsyn, Andrei 173, 174
Fanger, Donald 54
Faulkner, William 213
Fet, A. A. 4n, 17, 49–50, 155
Fitzgerald, F. Scott 213
Fonvizina, N. D. 118n
Ford, Ford Madox 212
Fourier, F. M. C. 193

G

Garnett, Constance 54–70 *passim*
Garshin, Vsevolod 76
Ge, Nikolai 127–129, 211
George, Henry 82, 184
Georgievsky, A. B. 165n
Gibian, George 54, 69, 70
Gizycki, Georg von 177
Goethe, Johann Wolfgang von 141, 144
Gogol, N. V. 39, 40, 54, 76, 83, 200n
Goncharov, Ivan A. 107
Gorky, Maxim (A. M. Peshkov) 141, 117, 118, 155, 181–194
Grenier, François 211
Grenoble, Lenore 53n
Grigor'ev, Apollon A. 7
Grigorovich, D. V. 107, 110n
Gray, Asa 167n
Grimsky, Ronald 145n
Gudzy, N. K. 41n
Gusev, N. N. 3n, 7n, 11n, 18, 47n, 109n, 110n, 114n, 147n, 163n, 172n, 216n
Gustafson, Richard 141n, 149n
Gutkin, Irina 78

H

Haeckel, Ernst Heinrich 180
Hardy, Henry 214n
Hausheer, Roger 214n
Hegel, G. W. F. 159, 217, 218
Heldt, Barbara 105n
Helvétius, Claude Adrien 145
Heim, Michael Henry 54
Heine, Heinrich 55
Hemingway, Ernest 197–213
    Across the River and Into the Trees 209

INDEX OF NAMES

Death in the Afternoon 209
Farewell to Arms 199
For Whom the Bell Tolls 203, 206, 209
In Our Time 202
Islands in the Stream 204, 212
Men at War 202–205
"Monologue to the Maestro: A High Seas Letter" 197n, 199n
A Moveable Feast 200n
The Old Man and the Sea 209
"An Old Newsman Writes: A Letter from Cuba" 206
"Remembering Shooting-Flying: A Key West Letter" 199n
The Snows of Kilimanjaro 209
To Have and Have Not 209
Herzen, A. I. 21
Holbach, Baron Paul Henri d' 145
Homer 28n, 208n
Horowitz, Brian 53n, 105n
Hruska, Anne 53n
Hughes, Robert P. 53n, 87n, 105n, 214n
Huxley, Thomas
    Evolution and Ethics 176–178

I
Ibsen, Henrik 159
Ignatieff, Michael 214, 223
Islavin, Konstantin A. 41, 46
Islenev, A. M. 41n
Ivakin, I. M. 123n, 174
Ivanov, Aleksandr 120, 124–128

J
Jacquet, Christian 145n, 154n
Jahn, Gary 87–102
James, Henry 198
Jones, W. Gareth 54
Josephs, F. Allen 212n
Josephus Flavius 123, 124
Joyce, James 212

K
Kamenev, L. B. 190n
Karlinsky, Simon 53n
Kashkin, I. A. 205n
Keller, Gustav 163
Kent, Leonard J. 54–70 *passim*
Kenworthy, John Coleman 122, 140–141

Khodasevich, V. F. 192n
Kline, George 165n
Klobsky, Ivan M. 189
Knapp, Liza 53n, 143n, 214n, 215n
Kolbasin, Elisei 18n
Koni, Anatoly 71–73
Kopper, John 37, 53n
Korolenko, V. G. 188n, 194
Korsh, Evgeny 161n
Kozlovskaya, Princess Sofya Petrovna, née Countess Zavadovskaya 41n
Kramskoy, Ivan 127
Kropotkin, Prince Petr 161
Kutuzov, Prince M. I. 141n, 205, 216, 218, 219, 220

L
Lamarck, Jean Baptiste, Chevalier de 159
La Mettrie, Julien Offroy de 145
Lakshin, V, Ia. 6
Lapidus, Gail Warshavsky 106n
Lenin, V. I. 82, 84, 115n, 187n, 190, 191n
Lermontov, M. Iu. 27
Lewes, George Henry 126
Lewis, Robert W. 210n
Littré, Paul Émile 120
Lomunov, Konstantin 75n, 109n, 114n
Loseff, Lev 17n
Louis XIV 220
Louis XVI 220
Lunacharsky, A. V. 190
Lynn, Kenneth, 198n

M
MacLeish, Archibald 198, 200n
MacMaster, R. E. 169n
Magarshack, David 54, 55–70 *passim*
Maiants, Zil'ma 200n
Maistre, Joseph de 216, 217
Makhary, Metropolitan 120
Malia, Martin 225n
Malthus, Thomas Robert 167, 175, 176
Maltsov, S. I. 165n
Mandelker, Amy 53n, 105n
Mansfield, Katherine 200n
Markovitch, Milan I. 152n
Martov, L. O. 190n
Marx, Karl 180, 193, 217
Maude, Louise 53–70, *passim*, 93
Maude, Aylmer 53–70, *passim*, 92

Maupassant, Guy de 198
Melzer, Arthur M. 146n
Mendel'son, N. M. 163n
Michelangelo, 144a, 211
Michelet, Jules 5
Mikulinsky, S. R. 165n
Mill, John Stuart 120
    The Subjection of Women 120n
Miller, Robin Feuer 143n
Milton, John 144n, 199
Miró, Juan 212
Mishin, V. S. 177n
Morson, Gary Saul 28, 29, 204n
Moser, Charles A. 114n
Mossman, Carol A. 27n
Mozart, Wolfgang Amadeus 55, 93

N
Nabokov, V. V. 55, 208n
Napoleon I 26n. 28, 204–205, 207, 218, 219, 220, 221
Nekrasov, N. A. 18n, 76, 107, 110n
Nicholas II 189n
Nietzsche, Friedrich Wilhelm 179

O
Oni, Rozalia 71–72, 79
Opul'skaya, L. D. 177n
Orwin, Donna Tussing 76n, 105n, 143n, 145n, 148n, 181n
Ostrovsky, A. N. 107, 109n, 115
Owen, Robert 193

P
Panaev, Ivan 107–108, 161
Panaeva, Avdotya 107
Paperno, Irina 110n
Paradis, James 177n
Pascin, Jules 212
Paul, Saint 118, 130, 150, 183, 184n
Pavlov, P. 11n
Perkins, Maxwell 197n, 199, 202, 206
Peshkova, E. P. 188n
Pevear, Richard 54–70, *passim*
Picasso, Pablo 212
Pisarev, D. I.
    "Progress in the World of Animals and Plants" 165
Plato 77
Plekhanov, G. V. 188n

Pobedonostsev, K. P. 83
Poggioli, Renato 8, 14
Poliansky, Iu. I. 165n
Pomorska, Krystyna 27n, 28
Pontius Pilate 22
Pound, Ezra 212
Proudhon, Pierre Joseph 5
Pushkin, A. S. 27, 127, 170, 194

R
Rachinskaya, Varvara 161
Rachinsky, Konstantin 161
Rachinsky, Sergei 160–162, 165
Racine, Jean 7
Raevsky-Hughes, Olga 87n, 90n
Raphael 144, 159, 160, 211
Renan, Ernest 119–124, 126
Reynolds, Michael S. 199, 200n
Riasanovsky, N. V. 214n, 224n
Rice, James L. 17n, 53n, 105n
Rischin, Ruth 144n
Rogers, James Allen 165n
Rolland, Rolland 7, 190n
Ross, Lillian 198n
Rousseau, Jean-Jacques 143–158
Royer, Clémence 166, 168, 171, 176
Rubinshtein, M. 218n

S
Saint-Simon, Comte C. H. de 193
Salieri, Antonio 93
Sand, George 107–108, 116
Savodnik, V. F. 109n, 163n
Saylor, Ian 55n
Scherr, Barry 192n
Schopenhauer, Arthur 116n, 160
Scribner, Charles 197n
Sechenov, Ivan M. 160
Semon, Marie 80n
Sesterhenn, Raimund 190
Shakespeare, William 141, 144, 159, 160, 198, 199
Sheldon, Richard 53n
Shifman, A. I. 150
Shklovsky, Viktor 215
Siegel, George 76n
Sigalov, Pavel 127n
Skaftymov, A. P. 218n, 219n
Slezkine, Yuri 7n, 17n
Snow, C. P. 162

INDEX OF NAMES

Solovyov (Solov'ev), Vladimir   173
Spencer, Herbert   80, 159, 171, 172
Spiridonov, V. S.   89n, 92, 97
Stalin, I. V.   191, 194
Stasov, V. V.   129
Stendhal (Marie Henri Beyle)   198, 212
   La chartreuse de Parme, 202
   Le rouge et le noir, 27n
Stites, Richard   106n, 115n
Strakhov, N. N.   56, 116, 121n, 166–170, 172–177
Strauss, David Friedrich   119, 122–124, 126, 127n
Strauss, Johann   55n
Sukhotina, T. L. (née Countess Tolstaya, daughter), 180
Suvorin, A. S.   164n
Sytin, D. I.   97

T
Talyzin, A. A.   13n
Tasso, Torquato   144n, 199
Timiriazev, K.   166, 171, 173, 174, 175
Tishkin, G. A.   106n
Todes, Daniel   161n, 165n, 171n, 176n
Toll, Count Karl F. T. von   216
Tolstaya, Countess Aleksandra Andreevna   3, 4, 45, 46, 49, 109n, 118
Tolstaya, Countess Aleksandra L'vovna (daughter)   180n
Tolstaya, Countess Marya Nikolaevna, née Princess Volkonskaya (mother)   24, 48
Tolstaya, Countess Marya Nikolaevna (sister)   72, 114
Tolstaya, Countess Sofya Andreevna (née Bers, wife)   15, 52, 56, 59, 72, 80, 109, 155, 156, 165n, 189
Tolstoy, Count Dmitry Nikolaevich (brother)   30, 36–47, 50, 51, 52, 76, 77
Tolstoy, Count Nikolai Nikolaevich (brother)   38, 47–50, 107, 155, 158
Tolstoy, Count Sergei L'vovich (son)   163n, 180
Tolstoy, Count Sergei Nikolaevich (brother)   13, 38, 42, 43, 48, 49, 163n
Tretiakov, Pavel   126, 127, 128, 129

Trotsky, L. D.   190n
Troyat, Henri   6
Tsiavlovsky, M. A.   41n
Turgenev, Ivan S.   4n, 17, 18, 19, 27, 45, 107, 110, 198, 200n, 210, 215
   Asya   18
   Faust   18
   A Hunter's Notes   199n
   A Nest of Gentlefolk   19
Turner, C. J. G.   53n, 55, 56

V
Veresaev, V. V.   163n
Vergani, Genni   10
Vogt, Karl   120
Volkonskaya, Princess E. D., née Princess Trubetskaya (grandmother)   24
Volkonsky, Prince Nikolai S. (grandfather)   24
Volokhonsky, Larissa   54–70 *passim*
Voltaire (François Marie Arouet)   144n, 145, 147n, 151n
Vucinich, Alexander   165n, 172n

W
Wagner, Richard   144n, 159, 168, 185, 211
Weisbein, Nicolas   144n
Weyrother, Franz von   219
White, William   197n, 199n, 206n
Wilkinson, Myler   198n
Williams, George C.   177n
Wilson, A. N.   144n, 226n
Wolfe, Bertram D.   190n
Wundt, Wilhelm Max   160

Y
Yedlin, Tovah   188
Yushkova, Pelageya I'linichna (aunt)   41, 45, 72

Z
Zaidenshnur, Evelina   56
Zbožilek, Vladimir   144n
Zhdanov, Vladimir A.   11n, 16, 56, 75
Zhurov, P. A.   11n
Zweers, Alexander F.   94

www.ingramcontent.com/pod-product-compliance
Lightning Source LLC
Chambersburg PA
CBHW060600230426
43670CB00011B/1902